Excel® VBA Programming

FOR

DUMMIES®

2ND EDITION

by John Walkenbach

WILEY

John Wiley & Sons, Inc.

Excel® VBA Programming For Dummies®, 2nd Edition

Published by
John Wiley & Sons, Inc.
111 River Street
Hoboken, NJ 07030-5774

www.wiley.com

For general information on our other products and services, please contact our Customer Care Department within the U.S. at 877-762-2974, outside the U.S. at 317-572-3993, or fax 317-572-4002.

For technical support, please visit www.wiley.com/techsupport.

Wiley publishes in a variety of print and electronic formats and by print-on-demand. Some material included with standard print versions of this book may not be included in e-books or in print-on-demand. If this book refers to media such as a CD or DVD that is not included in the version you purchased, you may download this material at http://booksupport.wiley.com. For more information about Wiley products, visit www.wiley.com.

Library of Congress Control Number: 2010925699

ISBN 978-0-470-50369-0 (pbk); ISBN 978-0-470-63275-8 (ebk); ISBN 978-0-470-63276-5 (ebk); ISBN 978-0-470-63277-2 (ebk)

Manufactured in the United States of America

10 9 8 7 6

WILEY

About the Author

John Walkenbach is the bestselling author of more than 50 spreadsheet books and lives in southern Arizona. When he's not using Excel, he's probably playing clawhammer banjo.

Dedication

This book is dedicated to Toad and Mrs. Toad because I'm running out of people for book dedications.

Author's Acknowledgments

I'm grateful to all the talented people at Wiley Publishing for giving me the opportunity to write Excel books. Special thanks to Colleen Totz Diamond (project editor) and Jan Karel Pieterse (technical editor). They certainly made my job easier.

Publisher's Acknowledgments

We're proud of this book; please send us your comments at http://dummies.custhelp.com. For other comments, please contact our Customer Care Department within the U.S. at 877-762-2974, outside the U.S. at 317-572-3993, or fax 317-572-4002.

Some of the people who helped bring this book to market include the following:

Acquisitions, Editorial, and Vertical Websites

Project Editor: Colleen Totz Diamond

Acquisitions Editor: Katie Mohr

Copy Editor: Melba Hopper

Technical Editor: Jan Karel Pieterse

Editorial Manager: Jodi Jensen

Vertical Websites Assistant Project Manager: Jenny Swisher

Vertical Websites Associate Producer: Josh Frank

Editorial Assistant: Amanda Graham

Sr. Editorial Assistant: Cherie Case

Cartoons: Rich Tennant (www.the5thwave.com)

Composition Services

Project Coordinator: Kristie Rees

Layout and Graphics: Ashley Chamberlain, Samantha K. Cherolis

Proofreaders: Laura L. Bowman, Jessica Kramer

Indexer: Rebecca Salerno

Publishing and Editorial for Technology Dummies

Richard Swadley, Vice President and Executive Group Publisher

Andy Cummings, Vice President and Publisher

Mary Bednarek, Executive Acquisitions Director

Mary C. Corder, Editorial Director

Publishing for Consumer Dummies

Kathleen Nebenhaus, Vice President and Executive Publisher

Composition Services

Debbie Stailey, Director of Composition Services

Contents at a Glance

Table of Contents

Introduction

● ●

*G*reetings, prospective Excel programmer . . .

Thanks for buying my book. I think you'll find that it offers a fast, enjoyable way to discover the ins and outs of Microsoft Excel programming. Even if you don't have the foggiest idea of what programming is all about, this book can help you make Excel jump through hoops in no time (well, it will take *some* time).

Unlike most programming books, this one is written in plain English, and even normal people can understand it. Even better, it's filled with information of the "just the facts, ma'am" variety — and not the drivel you might need once every third lifetime.

Is This the Right Book?

Go to any large bookstore and you'll find many Excel books (far too many, as far as I'm concerned). A quick overview can help you decide whether this book is really right for you. This book

- ✔ Is designed for intermediate to advanced Excel users who want to get up to speed with Visual Basic for Applications (VBA) programming.
- ✔ Requires no previous programming experience.
- ✔ Covers the most commonly used commands.
- ✔ Is appropriate for Excel 2007 or Excel 2010.
- ✔ Just might make you crack a smile occasionally — it even has cartoons.

If you are using Excel 2000, XP, or 2003, this book is not for you. Excel 2007 and Excel 2010 are very different from previous versions. If you're still using a pre-2007 version of Excel, locate a book that is specific to that version.

Oh yeah, this is *not* an introductory Excel book. If you're looking for a general-purpose Excel book, check out any of the following books, which are all published by Wiley:

- ✔ *Excel 2010 For Dummies,* by Greg Harvey
- ✔ *Excel 2010 Bible,* by John Walkenbach (yep, that's me)
- ✔ *Excel 2010 For Dummies Quick Reference,* by John Walkenbach (me again) and Colin Banfield

These books are also available in Excel 2007 editions.

Notice that the title of this book isn't *The Complete Guide to Excel VBA Programming For Dummies.* I don't cover all aspects of Excel programming — but then again, you probably don't want to know *everything* about this topic. In the unlikely event that you want a more comprehensive Excel programming book, you might try *Microsoft Excel 2010 Power Programming with VBA,* by John Walkenbach (is this guy prolific, or what?), also published by Wiley. And, yes, an edition for Excel 2007 is also available.

So You Want to Be a Programmer . . .

Besides earning money to pay my bills, my main goal in writing this book is to show Excel users how to use the VBA language — a tool that helps you significantly enhance the power of the world's most popular spreadsheet. Using VBA, however, involves programming. (Yikes! The *p* word.)

If you're like most computer users, the word *programmer* conjures up an image of someone who looks and behaves nothing like you. Perhaps words such as *nerd, geek,* and *dweeb* come to mind.

Times have changed. Computer programming has become much easier, and even so-called normal people now engage in this activity — and even admit it to friends and family. *Programming* simply means developing instructions that the computer automatically carries out. *Excel programming* refers to the fact that you can instruct Excel to automatically do things that you normally do manually — saving you lots of time and (you hope) reducing errors. I could go on, but I need to save some good stuff for Chapter 1.

If you've read this far, it's a safe bet that you need to become an Excel programmer. This could be something you came up with yourself or (more likely) something your boss decided. In this book, I tell you enough about Excel programming so that you won't feel like an idiot the next time you're trapped in a conference room with a group of Excel aficionados. And by the time you finish this book, you can honestly say, "Yeah, I do some Excel programming."

Why Bother?

Most Excel users never bother to explore VBA programming. Your interest in this topic definitely places you among an elite group. Welcome to the fold! If you're still not convinced that mastering Excel programming is a good idea, I've come up with a few good reasons why you might want to take the time to learn VBA programming:

- ✔ **It will make you more marketable.** Like it or not, Microsoft's applications are extremely popular. You may already know that all applications in Microsoft Office support VBA. The more you know about VBA, the better your chances for advancement in your job.

- ✔ **It lets you get the most out of your software investment** (or, more likely, your *employer's* software investment). Using Excel without knowing VBA is sort of like buying a TV set and watching only the odd-numbered channels.

- ✔ **It will improve your productivity (eventually).** Mastering VBA definitely takes some time, but you'll more than make up for this in the amount of time you ultimately save because you're more productive. Sort of like what they told you about going to college.

- ✔ **It's fun (well, sometimes).** Some people really enjoy making Excel do things that are otherwise impossible. By the time you finish this book, you just might be one of those people.

Now are you convinced?

What I Assume about You

People who write books usually have a target reader in mind. For this book, my target reader is a conglomerate of dozens of Excel users I've met over the years (either in person or out in cyberspace). The following points more or less describe my hypothetical target reader:

- ✔ You have access to a PC at work — and probably at home.

- ✔ You're running Excel 2007 or Excel 2010.

- ✔ You've been using computers for several years.

- ✔ You use Excel frequently in your work, and you consider yourself to be more knowledgeable about Excel than the average bear.

- ✔ You need to make Excel do some things that you currently can't make it do.

- ✔ You have little or no programming experience.

✔ You understand that the Help system in Excel can actually be useful. Face it, this book doesn't cover everything. If you get on good speaking terms with the Help system, you'll be able to fill in some of the missing pieces.

✔ You need to accomplish some work, and you have a low tolerance for thick, boring computer books.

Obligatory Typographical Conventions Section

All computer books have a section like this. (I think some federal law requires it.) Read it or skip it.

Sometimes, I refer to key combinations — which means you hold down one key while you press another. For example, Ctrl+Z means you hold down the Ctrl key while you press Z.

For menu commands, I use a distinctive character to separate menu items. For example, you use the following command to open a workbook file:

File➪Open

Note that in Excel 2007, there is no such thing as a "File" menu visible on your screen. In Excel 2007, the File menu was replaced with the Office Button, a little round contraption that shows up on the top-left side of any Office 2007 application that has implemented what is called the Ribbon. At some point, Microsoft decided that the Office Button wasn't such a great idea, and Excel 2010 dumped that round Office Button and replaced it with a Ribbon tab named File. In this book, I call it "File," so if you're using Excel 2007, just remember that "File" means "little round contraption on the top-left side."

Any text you need to enter appears in **bold**. For example, I might say, enter **=SUM(B:B)** in cell A1.

Excel programming involves developing *code* — that is, the instructions Excel follows. All code in this book appears in a monospace font, like this:

```
Range("A1:A12").Select
```

Some long lines of code don't fit between the margins in this book. In such cases, I use the standard VBA line continuation character sequence: a space followed by an underscore character. Here's an example:

```
Selection.PasteSpecial Paste:=xlValues, _
    Operation:=xlNone, SkipBlanks:=False, _
    Transpose:=False
```

When you enter this code, you can type it as written or place it on a single line (omitting the spaces and the underscore characters).

Check Your Security Settings

It's a cruel world out there. It seems that some scam artist is always trying to take advantage of you or cause some type of problem. The world of computing is equally cruel. You probably know about computer viruses, which can cause some nasty things to happen to your system. But did you know that computer viruses can also reside in an Excel file? It's true. In fact, it's relatively easy to write a computer virus by using VBA. An unknowing user can open an Excel file and spread the virus to other Excel workbooks, and to other systems.

Over the years, Microsoft has become increasingly concerned about security issues. This is a good thing, but it also means that Excel users need to understand how things work. You can check Excel's security settings by using the File➪Options➪Trust Center➪Trust Center Settings command. There is a plethora of options in there, and people have been known to open that dialog box and never be heard from again.

If you click the Macro Settings tab (on the left side of the Trust Center dialog box), your options are as follows:

- **Disable all macros without notification:** Macros will not work, regardless of what you do.

- **Disable all macros with notification:** When you open a workbook with macros, you will either see the Message Bar open with an option you can click to enable macros, or (if the VBE is open) you'll get a message asking if you want to enable macros.

- **Disable all macros except digitally signed macros:** Only macros with a digital signature are allowed to run (but even for those signatures you haven't marked as trusted, you still get the security warning).

- **Enable all macros (not recommended; potentially dangerous code can run).**

Consider this scenario: You spend a week writing a killer VBA program that will revolutionize your company. You test it thoroughly and then send it to your boss. He calls you into his office and claims that your macro doesn't do anything at all. What's going on? Chances are, your boss's security setting does not allow macros to run. Or maybe he chose to go along with Microsoft's default suggestion and disable the macros when he opened the file.

Bottom line? Just because an Excel workbook contains a macro, it is no guarantee that the macro will ever be executed. It all depends on the security setting and whether the user chooses to enable or disable macros for that file.

In order to work with this book, you will need to enable macros for the files you work with. My advice is to use the second security level. Then when you open a file that you've created, you can simply enable the macros. If you open a file from someone you don't know, you should disable the macros and check the VBA code to ensure that it doesn't contain anything destructive or malicious. Usually, it's pretty easy to identify suspicious VBA code.

How This Book Is Organized

I divided this book into six major parts, each of which contains several chapters. Although I arranged the chapters in a fairly logical sequence, you can read them in any order you choose. Here's a quick preview of what's in store for you.

Part I: Introducing VBA

Part I has but two chapters. I introduce the VBA language in the first chapter. In Chapter 2, I let you get your feet wet right away by taking you on a hands-on guided tour.

Part II: How VBA Works with Excel

In writing this book, I assume that you already know how to use Excel. The four chapters in Part II give you a better grasp on how VBA is implemented in Excel. These chapters are all important, so I don't recommend skipping them, okay?

Part III: Programming Concepts

The eight chapters in Part III get you into the nitty-gritty of what programming is all about. You may not need to know all this stuff, but you'll be glad it's there if you ever do need it.

Part IV: Communicating with Your Users

One of the coolest parts of programming in Excel is designing custom dialog boxes (well, at least *I* like it). The five chapters in Part IV show you how to create dialog boxes that look like they came straight from the software lab at Microsoft.

Part V: Putting It All Together

The two chapters in Part V pull together information from the preceding chapters. You discover how to include your own custom buttons in the Excel user interface, and you find out how to develop custom worksheet functions, create add-ins, design user-oriented applications, and even work with other Office applications.

Part VI: The Part of Tens

Traditionally, books in the *For Dummies* series contain a final part that consists of short chapters with helpful or informative lists. Because I'm a sucker for tradition, this book has two such chapters that you can peruse at your convenience. (If you're like most readers, you'll turn to this part first.)

But Wait, There's More!

I got carried away, and I wrote two more chapters that wouldn't fit in this book because I ran out of pages. So I put them on this book's Web site, along with the sample files (see "Getting the Sample Files," later in this Introduction). The two extra chapters are "Working With Colors" and "Ten VBA Do's and Don'ts."

Icons Used in This Book

Somewhere along the line, a market research company must have shown that publishers can sell more copies of their computer books if they add icons to the margins of those books. *Icons* are those little pictures that supposedly draw your attention to various features or help you decide whether something is worth reading.

I don't know if this research is valid, but I'm not taking any chances. So here are the icons you encounter in your travels from front cover to back cover:

When you see this icon, the code being discussed is available on the Web. Download it to eliminate lots of typing. See "Getting the Sample Files" for more information.

This icon flags material that you might consider technical. You may find it interesting, but you can safely skip it if you're in a hurry.

Don't skip information marked with this icon. It identifies a shortcut that can save you lots of time (and maybe even allow you to leave the office at a reasonable hour).

This icon tells you when you need to store information in the deep recesses of your brain for later use.

Read anything marked with this icon. Otherwise, you may lose your data, blow up your computer, cause a nuclear meltdown — or maybe even ruin your whole day.

Getting the Sample Files

This book has its very own Web site where you can download the example files and view the Bonus Chapters. To get these files, point your Web browser to www.dummies.com/go/excelvbaprogrammingfd2e.

Having the sample files will save you a lot of typing. Better yet, you can play around with them and experiment with various changes. In fact, I highly recommend playing around with these files. Experimentation is the best way to master VBA.

Now What?

Reading this introduction was your first step. Now, it's time to move on and become a programmer (there's that *p* word again!).

If you're a programming virgin, I strongly suggest that you start with Chapter 1 and progress through the book until you've discovered enough to do what you want to do. Chapter 2 gives you some immediate hands-on experience, so you have the illusion that you're making quick progress.

But it's a free country (at least it was when I wrote these words); I won't sic the Computer Book Police on you if you opt to thumb through randomly and read whatever strikes your fancy.

I hope you have as much fun reading this book as I did writing it.

Part I
Introducing VBA

The 5th Wave By Rich Tennant

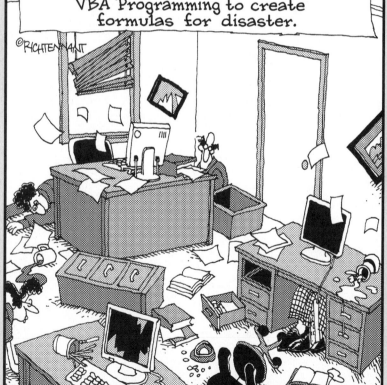

At FEMA, employees often use Excel VBA Programming to create formulas for disaster.

In this part . . .

Every book must start somewhere. This one starts by introducing you to Visual Basic for Applications (and I'm sure you two will become very good friends over the course of a few dozen chapters). After the introductions are made, Chapter 2 walks you through a real-live Excel programming session.

Chapter 1

What Is VBA?

*I*f you're anxious to jump into VBA programming, hold your horses. This chapter is completely devoid of any hands-on training material. It does, however, contain some essential background information that assists you in becoming an Excel programmer. In other words, this chapter paves the way for everything else that follows and gives you a feel for how Excel programming fits into the overall scheme of the universe. It's not as boring as you might think.

Okay, So What Is VBA?

VBA, which stands for *Visual Basic for Applications,* is a programming language developed by Microsoft — you know, the company that tries to get you to buy a new version of Windows every few years. Excel, along with the other members of Microsoft Office, includes the VBA language (at no extra charge). In a nutshell, VBA is the tool that people like you and me use to develop programs that control Excel.

Imagine an intelligent robot that knows all about Excel. This robot can read instructions, and it can also operate Excel very fast and accurately. When you want the robot to do something in Excel, you write up a set of robot instructions by using special codes. Tell the robot to follow your instructions, while you sit back and drink a glass of lemonade. That's kind of what VBA is all about — a code language for robots. Note, however, that Excel does not come with a robot or lemonade.

A few words about terminology

Excel programming terminology can be a bit confusing. For example, VBA is a programming language, but it also serves as a macro language. What do you call something written in VBA and executed in Excel? Is it a *macro,* or is it a *program?* Excel's Help system often refers to VBA procedures as *macros,* so I use that terminology. But I also call this stuff a *program.*

I use the term *automate* throughout this book. This term means that a series of steps are completed automatically. For example, if you write a macro that adds color to some cells, prints the worksheet, and then removes the color, you have *automated* those three steps.

By the way, *macro* does not stand for **M**essy **A**nd **C**onfusing **R**epeated **O**peration. Rather, it comes from the Greek *makros,* which means large — which also describes your paycheck after you become an expert macro programmer.

What Can You Do with VBA?

You're probably aware that people use Excel for thousands of different tasks. Here are just a few examples:

- ✔ Analyzing scientific data
- ✔ Budgeting and forecasting
- ✔ Creating invoices and other forms
- ✔ Developing charts from data
- ✔ Keeping lists of things such as customers' names, students' grades, or holiday gift ideas (a nice fruitcake would be lovely)
- ✔ Yadda, yadda, yadda

The list could go on and on, but I think you get the idea. My point is simply that Excel is used for a wide variety of things, and everyone reading this book has different needs and expectations regarding Excel. One thing virtually every reader has in common is the *need to automate some aspect of Excel.* That, dear reader, is what VBA is all about.

For example, you might create a VBA program to import some numbers, and then format and print your month-end sales report. After developing and testing the program, you can execute the macro with a single command, causing Excel to automatically perform many time-consuming procedures. Rather than struggle through a tedious sequence of commands, you can grab a cup of joe and let your computer do the work — which is how it's supposed to be, right?

In the following sections, I briefly describe some common uses for VBA macros. One or two of these may push your button.

Inserting a bunch of text

If you often need to enter your company name, address, and phone number in your worksheets, you can create a macro to do the typing for you. You can extend this concept as far as you like. For example, you might develop a macro that automatically types a list of all salespeople who work for your company.

Automating a task you perform frequently

Assume you're a sales manager and you need to prepare a month-end sales report to keep your boss happy. If the task is straightforward, you can develop a VBA program to do it for you. Your boss will be impressed by the consistently high quality of your reports, and you'll be promoted to a new job for which you are highly unqualified.

Automating repetitive operations

If you need to perform the same action on, say, 12 different Excel workbooks, you can record a macro while you perform the task on the first workbook and then let the macro repeat your action on the other workbooks. The nice thing about this is that Excel never complains about being bored. Excel's macro recorder is similar to recording live action on a video recorder. But it doesn't require a camera, and the battery never needs to be recharged.

Creating a custom command

Do you often issue the same sequence of Excel menu commands? If so, save yourself a few seconds by developing a macro that combines these commands into a single custom command, which you can execute with a single keystroke or button click. You probably won't save *that* much time, but you'll probably be more accurate. And the guy in the next cubicle will be really impressed.

Creating a custom button

You can customize your Quick Access toolbar with your own buttons that execute the macros you write. Office workers tend to be very impressed by buttons that perform magic.

If you're using Excel 2010, you can even add buttons to the Ribbon — something that's off-limits in Excel 2007.

Developing new worksheet functions

Although Excel includes numerous built-in functions (such as SUM and AVERAGE), you can create *custom* worksheet functions that can greatly simplify your formulas. I guarantee you'll be surprised by how easy this is. (I show you how to do this in Chapter 20.) Even better, the Insert Function dialog box displays your custom functions, making them appear built-in. Very snazzy stuff.

Creating complete, macro-driven applications

If you're willing to spend some time, you can use VBA to create large-scale applications complete with a custom Ribbon tab, dialog boxes, on-screen help, and lots of other accoutrements. This book doesn't go quite that far, but I'm just telling you this to impress you with how powerful VBA really is.

Creating custom add-ins for Excel

You're probably familiar with some of the add-ins that ship with Excel. For example, the Analysis ToolPak is a popular add-in. You can use VBA to develop your own special-purpose add-ins. I developed my Power Utility Pak add-in by using only VBA, and people all around the world pay me real money so they can use it.

Advantages and Disadvantages of VBA

In this section, I briefly describe the good things about VBA — and I also explore its darker side.

VBA advantages

You can automate almost anything you do in Excel. To do so, you write instructions that Excel carries out. Automating a task by using VBA offers several advantages:

- Excel always executes the task in exactly the same way. (In most cases, consistency is a good thing.)

- Excel performs the task much faster than you can do it manually (unless, of course, you're Clark Kent).

- If you're a good macro programmer, Excel always performs the task without errors (which probably can't be said about you or me).

- If you set things up properly, someone who doesn't know anything about Excel can perform the task.

- You can do things in Excel that are otherwise impossible — which can make you a very popular person around the office.

- For long, time-consuming tasks, you don't have to sit in front of your computer and get bored. Excel does the work, while you hang out at the water cooler.

VBA disadvantages

It's only fair that I give equal time to listing the disadvantages (or *potential* disadvantages) of VBA:

- You have to know how to write programs in VBA (but that's why you bought this book, right?). Fortunately, it's not as difficult as you might expect.

- Other people who need to use your VBA programs must have their own copies of Excel. It would be nice if you could press a button that transforms your Excel/VBA application into a stand-alone program, but that isn't possible (and probably never will be).

- Sometimes, things go wrong. In other words, you can't blindly assume that your VBA program will always work correctly under all circumstances. Welcome to the world of debugging and, if others are using your macros, technical support.

- VBA is a moving target. As you know, Microsoft is continually upgrading Excel. Even though Microsoft puts great effort into compatibility between versions, you may discover that VBA code you've written doesn't work properly with older versions or with a future version of Excel.

VBA in a Nutshell

Just to let you know what you're in for, I've prepared a quick and dirty summary of what VBA is all about. Of course, I describe all this stuff in semi-excruciating detail later in the book.

- ✔ **You perform actions in VBA by writing (or recording) code in a VBA module.** You view and edit VBA modules by using the Visual Basic Editor (VBE).

- ✔ **A VBA module consists of Sub procedures.** A Sub procedure has nothing to do with underwater vessels or tasty sandwiches. Rather, it's a chunk of computer code that performs some action on or with objects (discussed in a moment). The following example shows a simple Sub procedure called AddEmUp. This amazing program displays the result of 1 plus 1.

```
Sub AddEmUp()
    Sum = 1 + 1
    MsgBox "The answer is " & Sum
End Sub
```

 A Sub procedure that doesn't perform properly is said to be substandard.

- ✔ **A VBA module can also have Function procedures.** A Function procedure returns a single value. You can call it from another VBA procedure or even use it as a function in a worksheet formula. An example of a Function procedure (named AddTwo) follows. This Function accepts two numbers (called arguments) and returns the sum of those values.

```
Function AddTwo(arg1, arg2)
    AddTwo = arg1 + arg2
End Function
```

 A Function procedure that doesn't work correctly is said to be dysfunctional.

- ✔ **VBA manipulates objects.** Excel provides dozens and dozens of objects that you can manipulate. Examples of objects include a workbook, a worksheet, a cell range, a chart, and a shape. You have many more objects at your disposal, and you can manipulate them by using VBA code.

- ✔ **Objects are arranged in a hierarchy.** Objects can act as *containers* for other objects. At the top of the object hierarchy is Excel. Excel itself is an object called Application. The Application object contains other objects such as Workbook objects and Add-In objects. The Workbook object can contain other objects, such as Worksheet objects and Chart

objects. A Worksheet object can contain objects such as Range objects and PivotTable objects. The term *object model* refers to the arrangement of these objects. (Object model mavens can find out more in Chapter 4.)

✔ **Objects of the same type form a collection.** For example, the Worksheets collection consists of all the worksheets in a particular workbook. The Charts collection consists of all Chart objects in a workbook. Collections are themselves objects.

✔ **You refer to an object by specifying its position in the object hierarchy, using a dot (that is, a period) as a separator.** For example, you can refer to the workbook Book1.xlsx as

```
Application.Workbooks("Book1.xlsx")
```

This refers to the workbook Book1.xlsx in the Workbooks collection. The Workbooks collection is contained in the Application object (that is, Excel). Extending this to another level, you can refer to Sheet1 in Book1. xlsx as

```
Application.Workbooks("Book1.xlsx"). _
        Worksheets("Sheet1")
```

As shown in the following example, you can take this to still another level and refer to a specific cell (in this case, cell A1):

```
Application.Workbooks("Book1.xlsx").
        Worksheets("Sheet1").Range("A1")
```

✔ **If you omit specific references, Excel uses the *active* objects.** If Book1. xlsx is the active workbook, you can simplify the preceding reference as follows:

```
Worksheets("Sheet1").Range("A1")
```

If you know that Sheet1 is the active sheet, you can simplify the reference even more:

```
Range("A1")
```

✔ **Objects have properties.** You can think of a property as a *setting* for an object. For example, a Range object has such properties as Value and Address. A Chart object has such properties as HasTitle and Type. You can use VBA to determine object properties and also to change properties.

✔ **You refer to a property of an object by combining the object name with the property name, separated by a dot.** For example, you can refer to the Value property in cell A1 on Sheet1 as follows:

```
Worksheets("Sheet1").Range("A1").Value
```

✔ **You can assign values to variables.** A *variable* is a named element that stores information. You can use variables in your VBA code to store such things as values, text, or property settings. To assign the value in cell A1 on Sheet1 to a variable called *Interest,* use the following VBA statement:

```
Interest = Worksheets("Sheet1").Range("A1").Value
```

✔ **Objects have methods.** A *method* is an action Excel performs with an object. For example, one of the methods for a Range object is ClearContents. This aptly named method clears the contents of the range.

✔ **You specify a method by combining the object with the method, separated by a dot.** For example, the following statement clears the contents of cell A1:

```
Worksheets("Sheet1").Range("A1").ClearContents
```

✔ **VBA includes all the constructs of modern programming languages, including arrays and looping.** In other words, if you're willing to spend a little time mastering the ropes, you can write code that does some incredible things.

Believe it or not, the preceding list pretty much describes VBA in a nutshell. Now you just have to find out the details. That's why this book has more pages.

An Excursion into Versions

If you plan to develop VBA macros, you should have some understanding of Excel's history. I know you weren't expecting a history lesson when you picked up this book, but bear with me. This is important stuff that might make you a hit at the next nerd party.

Here are all the major Excel for Windows versions that have seen the light of day, along with a few words about how they handle macros:

✔ **Excel 2:** The original version of Excel for Windows was called Version 2 (rather than 1) so that it would correspond to the Macintosh version. Excel 2 first appeared in 1987, but nobody uses it anymore, so you can pretty much forget that it ever existed.

✔ **Excel 3:** Released in late 1990, this version features the XLM macro language. Nobody uses this version either.

- **Excel 4:** This version hit the streets in early 1992. It also uses the XLM macro language. A small number of people still use this version. (They subscribe to the philosophy *if it ain't broke, don't fix it.*)

- **Excel 5:** This one came out in early 1994. It was the first version to use VBA (but it also supports XLM). Excel 5 users are becoming increasingly rare.

- **Excel 95:** Technically known as Excel 7 (there is no Excel 6), this version began shipping in the summer of 1995. It's a 32-bit version and requires Windows 95 or Windows NT. It has a few VBA enhancements, and it supports the XLM language.

- **Excel 97:** This version (also known as Excel 8) was born in January, 1997. It has *many* enhancements and it features an entirely new interface for programming VBA macros. Excel 97 also uses a new file format (which previous Excel versions cannot open). Occasionally, I run into someone who still uses this version.

- **Excel 2000:** This version's numbering scheme jumped to four digits. Excel 2000 (also known as Excel 9) made its public debut in June 1999. It includes only a few enhancements from a programmer's perspective, with most enhancements being for users — particularly online users. With Excel 2000 came the option to digitally sign macros, thus enabling you to guarantee that the code delivered to your users is truly yours. Excel 2000 still has a modest number of users.

- **Excel 2002:** This version (also known as Excel 10 or Excel XP) appeared in late 2001. Perhaps this version's most significant feature is the ability to recover your work when Excel crashes. This is also the first version to use copy protection (known as *product activation*).

- **Excel 2003:** Of all the Excel upgrades I've ever seen (and I've seen them all), Excel 2003 has the fewest new features. In other words, most hardcore Excel users (including yours truly) were very disappointed with Excel 2003. Yet people still bought it. I think these were the folks moving up from a pre-Excel 2002 version. As I write this, Excel 2003 is probably the most commonly used version.

- **Excel 2007:** Excel 2007 signaled the beginning of a new era. Excel 2007 dumped the old menu and toolbar interface and introduced the Ribbon. It also allows much larger worksheets — more than a million rows.

- **Excel 2010:** The latest, and without a doubt, the greatest. Microsoft outdid its corporate self with this version. This version has some slick new features (such as sparkline graphics), and it also performs quite a bit better in some areas. And if you need really, really huge workbooks, you can install the 64-bit version.

This book is written for Excel 2007 and Excel 2010, so if you don't have one of those versions, you run the risk of getting confused in a few places.

So what's the point of this mini history lesson? If you plan to distribute your Excel/VBA files to other users, it's vitally important that you understand which version of Excel they use. People using an older version won't be able to take advantage of features introduced in later versions. For example, if you write VBA code that references cell XFD1048576 (the last cell in a workbook), those who use a version prior to Excel 2007 will get an error because those pre-Excel 2007 worksheets only had 65,536 rows and 255 columns (the last cell is IV65536).

Excel 2007 and Excel 2010 also have some new objects, methods, and properties. If you use these in your code, users with an older version of Excel will get an error when they run your macro — and you'll get the blame. However, Microsoft has made available an Office Compatibility Pack, which allows users of Excel 2003 and Excel XP to open and save workbooks in the new file format. This product (which is free, by the way) doesn't give these older versions the new features. It just lets them open and save files in the Excel 2007/2010 file format.

Chapter 2

Jumping Right In

I'm not much of a swimmer, but I have found that the best way to get into a cold body of water is to jump right in — no sense prolonging the agony. By wading through this chapter, you can get your feet wet immediately but avoid getting in over your head.

By the time you reach the end of this chapter, you may start feeling better about this Excel programming business, and you'll be glad you took the plunge. This chapter provides a step-by-step demonstration of how to develop a simple but useful VBA macro.

First Things First

Before you can call yourself an Excel programmer, you must go through the initiation rites. That means you need to make a small change so Excel will display a new tab at the top of the screen: Developer.

When you click the Developer tab, the Ribbon displays information that is of interest to programmers (that's you!). Figure 2-1 shows how the Ribbon looks when the Developer tab is selected.

The Developer tab is not visible when you first open Excel; you need to tell Excel to show it. Getting Excel to display the Developer tab is easy (and you only have to do it one time). The procedure varies, though, depending on which version of Excel you use.

Excel 2010 Users

Follow these steps:

1. **Right-click any part of the Ribbon, and choose Customize The Ribbon.**

2. **In the Customize Ribbon tab of the Excel Options dialog box, locate Developer in the second column.**

3. **Put a check mark next to Developer.**

4. **Click OK, and you're back to Excel with a brand-new tab: Developer.**

Excel 2007 Users

Follow these steps:

1. **Choose File⊃Excel Options.**

 Remember, in Excel 2007 the File command means clicking the round button in the upper left.

2. **In the Excel Options dialog box, select Popular.**

3. **Place a check mark next to Show Developer tab in the Ribbon.**

4. **Click OK to see the new Developer tab displayed in the Ribbon.**

What You'll Be Doing

In this section, I describe how to create your first macro. The macro that you're about to create will do this

 ✔ Type your name into a cell.

 ✔ Enter the current date and time into the cell below.

 ✔ Format both cells to display bold.

 ✔ Change the font size of both cells to 16 point.

This macro won't be winning any prizes in the Annual VBA Programmer's Competition, but everyone must start somewhere. The macro accomplishes all these steps in a single action. As I describe in the following sections, you start by recording your actions as you go through these steps. Then you test the macro to see whether it works. Finally, you edit the macro to add some finishing touches. Ready?

Taking the First Steps

This section describes the steps you take prior to recording the macro. In other words, you need to make a few preparations before the fun begins.

1. **Start Excel if it's not already running.**

2. **If necessary, create a new, empty workbook (Ctrl+N is my favorite way to do that).**

3. **Click the Developer tab, and take a look at the Use Relative References button in the Code group.**

 If the color of that button is different than the other buttons, then you're in good shape. If the Use Relative References button is the same color as the other buttons, then you need to click it.

I explain more about the Use Relative References button in Chapter 6. For now, just make sure that the option is turned on. When it's turned on, it will be a different color.

Recording the Macro

Here comes the hands-on part. Follow these instructions carefully:

1. **Select a cell — any cell will do.**

2. **Choose Developer⇨Code⇨Record Macro, or click the macro recording button on the status bar.**

 The Record Macro dialog box appears, as shown in Figure 2-2.

Figure 2-2:
The Record
Macro
dialog box
appears
when you're
about to
record a
macro.

3. **Enter a name for the macro.**

 Excel provides a default name, but it's better to use a more descriptive name. *NameAndTime* (with no spaces) is a good name for this macro.

4. **Click in the Shortcut Key box and enter Shift+N (for an uppercase N) as the shortcut key.**

 Specifying a shortcut key is optional. If you do specify one, then you can execute the macro by pressing a key combination — in this case, Ctrl+Shift+N.

5. **Make sure the Store Macro In setting is This Workbook.**

6. **You can enter some text in the Description box if you like. This is optional. Some people like to describe what the macro does (or is *supposed* to do).**

7. **Click OK.**

 The dialog box closes, and Excel's macro recorder is turned on. From this point, Excel monitors everything you do and converts it to VBA code.

8. **Type your name in the active cell.**

9. **Move the cell pointer to the cell below, and enter this formula:**

    ```
    =NOW()
    ```

 The formula displays the current date and time.

10. **Select the formula cell and press Ctrl+C to copy that cell to the Clipboard.**

11. **Choose Home⇨Clipboard⇨Paste⇨Values.**

 This command converts the formula to its value.

12. **With the date cell selected, press Shift+up arrow to select that cell and the one above it (which contains your name).**

13. **Use the controls in the Home⇨Font group to change the formatting to Bold, and make the font size 16 point.**

14. **Choose Developer⇨Code⇨Stop Recording.**

 The macro recorder is turned off.

Congratulations! You just created your first Excel VBA macro. You may want to phone your mother and tell her the good news.

Testing the Macro

Now you can try out this macro and see whether it works properly. To test your macro, move to an empty cell and press Ctrl+Shift+N.

In a flash, Excel executes the macro. Your name and the current date are displayed in large, bold letters.

Another way to execute the macro is to choose Developer⇨Code⇨Macros (or press Alt+F8) to display the Macros dialog box. Select the macro from the list (in this case, NameAndTime) and click Run. Make sure you select the cell that will hold your name before executing the macro.

Examining the Macro

So far, you've recorded a macro and you've tested it. If you're a curious type, you're probably wondering what this macro looks like. And you might even wonder where it's stored.

Remember when you started recording the macro? You indicated that Excel should store the macro in This Workbook. The macro is stored in the workbook, but you need to activate the Visual Basic Editor (VBE, for short) to see it.

Follow these steps to see the macro:

1. **Choose Developer⇨Code⇨Visual Basic (or press Alt+F11).**

 The Visual Basic Editor program window appears, as shown in Figure 2-3. This window is highly customizable, so your VBE window may look a bit different. The VBE program window contains several other windows and is probably very intimidating. Don't fret; you'll get used to it.

2. **In the VBE window, locate the window called Project.**

 The Project window (also known as the Project Explorer window) contains a list of all workbooks and add-ins that are currently open. Each project is arranged as a *tree* and can be expanded (to show more information) or contracted (to show less information).

Figure 2-3:
The Visual Basic Editor is where you view and edit VBA code.

The VBE uses quite a few different windows, any of which can be either open or closed. If a window isn't immediately visible in the VBE, you can choose an option from the View menu to display the window. For instance, if the Project window is not visible, you can choose View⇨Project Explorer (or press Ctrl+R) to display it. You can display any other VBE window in a similar manner. I explain more about the components of the Visual Basic Editor in Chapter 3.

3. **Select the project that corresponds to the workbook in which you recorded the macro.**

 If you haven't saved the workbook, the project is probably called VBAProject (Book1).

4. **Click the plus sign (+) to the left of the folder named Modules.**

The tree expands to show Module1, which is the only module in the project.

5. Double-click Module1.

The VBA code in that module is displayed in a Code window. Figure 2-4 shows how it looks on my screen. Your screen may not look exactly the same.

Figure 2-4:
The VBE displays the VBA code in Module1 of Book1.

At this point, the macro probably looks like Greek to you. Don't worry. Travel a few chapters down the road, and all will be as clear as the view from Olympus.

The NameAndTime macro (also known as a *Sub procedure*) consists of several statements. Excel executes the statements one by one, from top to bottom. A statement preceded by an apostrophe (') is a comment. Comments are included only for your information and are essentially ignored. In other words, Excel skips right over comments.

The first actual VBA statement (which begins with the word *Sub*) identifies the macro as a Sub procedure and gives its name — you provided this name before you started recording the macro. If you read through the code, you may be able to make sense of some of it. You see your name, the formula you entered, and lots of additional code that changes the font. The Sub procedure ends with the End Sub statement.

Hey, I didn't record that!

Earlier in this chapter, I mentioned that the macro recorder is like recording sound on a tape recorder. When you play back an audiotape and listen to your own voice, you invariably say, "I don't sound like that." And when you look at your recorded macro, you may see some actions that you didn't think you recorded.

When you recorded the NameAndTime example, you changed only the font size, yet the recorded code shows all sorts of font-changing statements (Strikethrough, Superscript, Shadow, and so on). Don't worry; it happens all the time. Excel often records lots of seemingly useless code. In later chapters, you find out how to remove the extra stuff from a recorded macro.

Modifying the Macro

As you might expect, not only can you view your macro in the VBE, you can also change it. If you look at the code, some of it will actually make sense. Even though you have no idea what you're doing at this point, I'll bet you can make these changes to the code:

- ✔ Change the name that's entered into the active cell. If you have a dog, use your dog's name.

- ✔ Change the font name or size.

- ✔ See if you can figure out the appropriate location for a new statement:

```
Selection.Font.Italic = True
```

Working in a VBA code module is much like working in a word-processing document (except there's no word wrap and you can't format the text). On second thought, I guess it's more like working in Windows Notepad. You can press Enter to start a new line, and the familiar editing keys work as expected.

After you've made your changes, jump back to Excel and try out the revised macro to see how it works. Just as you can press Alt+F11 in Excel to display the VBE, you can press Alt+F11 in the VBE to switch back to Excel.

Saving Workbooks That Contain Macros

If you store one or more macros in a workbook, the file must be saved with "macros enabled." In other words, the file must be saved with an XLSM extension rather than the normal XLSX extension.

For example, when you save the workbook that contains your NameAndTime macro, the file format in the Save As dialog box defaults to XLSX (a format that cannot contain macros!). Unless you change the file format to XLSM, Excel displays the warning shown in Figure 2-5. You need to click No, and then choose Excel Macro-Enabled Workbook (*.xlsm) from the Save As Type drop-down list.

Figure 2-5:
If your
workbook
contains
macros,
and you
attempt to
save it in a
non-macro
file format,
Excel
warns you.

Understanding Macro Security

Macro security is a key feature in Excel. The reason is that VBA is a powerful language — so powerful that even a simple macro can do serious damage to your computer. A macro can delete files, send information to other computers, and even destroy Windows so that you can't even start your system.

The macro security features in Excel 2007 and Excel 2010 were created to help prevent these types of problems.

Figure 2-6 shows the Macro Settings section of the Trust Center dialog box. To display this dialog box, choose Developer⇨Codem⇨Macro Security.

By default, Excel uses the Disable All Macros with Notification section. With this setting in effect, if you open a workbook that contains macros (and the file is not digitally "signed" or stored in a trusted location), Excel displays a warning like the one in Figure 2-7. If you are certain that the workbook comes from a trusted source, click Enable Macros, and the macros will be enabled.

You see the pop-up box in Figure 2-7 only if the VBE is open. Otherwise, Excel displays an eye-catching Security Warning above the Formula bar. You can click the button to enable the macros.

Figure 2-6:
The Macro
Settings
section of
the Trust
Center dia-
log box.

If you use Excel 2010, Excel will remember if you've designated a workbook
to be safe. So, the next time you open it, you won't see the Security Warning.
That's not the case with Excel 2007 though. You'll get the security warning
every time — unless you store that workbook in a trusted location.

Figure 2-7:
Excel's
warning that
the file to
be opened
contains
macros.

Perhaps the best way to handle macro security is to designate one or
more folders as *trusted locations.* All the workbooks in a trusted location
are opened without a macro warning. You designate trusted folders in the
Trusted Locations section of the Trust Center dialog box.

If you want to find out what the other macro security settings imply, press
F1 while the Macro Settings section of the Trust Center dialog box is in view.
The Help screen opens and the subject "Enable or disable macros in Office
documents" is shown in the Help window.

More about the NameAndTime Macro

By the time you finish this book, you'll completely understand how the NameAndTime macro works — and you'll be able to develop more-sophisticated macros. For now, I wrap up the example with a few additional points about the macro:

- ✔ For this macro to work, its workbook must be open. If you close the workbook, the macro doesn't work (and the Ctrl+Shift+N shortcut has no effect).

- ✔ As long as the workbook containing the macro is open, you can run the macro while any workbook is active. In other words, the macro's own workbook doesn't have to be active.

- ✔ The macro isn't "pro-quality" code. It will overwrite existing text with no warning — and its effects can't be undone.

- ✔ Before you started recording the macro, you assigned it a new shortcut key. This is just one of several ways to execute the macro.

- ✔ You can enter this macro manually rather than record it. To do so, you need a good understanding of VBA. (Be patient, you'll get there.)

- ✔ You can store this macro in your Personal Macro Workbook. If you do so, the macro is available automatically whenever you start Excel. See Chapter 6 for details about your Personal Macro Workbook.

- ✔ You can also convert the workbook to an add-in file. (More about this in Chapter 21.)

You've been initiated into the world of Excel programming. (Sorry, there's no secret handshake or decoder ring.) I hope this chapter helps you realize that Excel programming is something you can actually do — and even live to tell about. Keep reading. Subsequent chapters almost certainly answer any questions you have, and you'll soon understand exactly what you did in this hands-on session.

Part II
How VBA Works
with Excel

"Look - what if we just increase the size of the charts?"

In this part . . .

The next four chapters provide the necessary foundation for discovering the ins and outs of VBA. You find out about modules (the sheets that store your VBA code) and are introduced to the Excel object model (something you won't want to miss). You also discover the difference between subroutines and functions, and you get a crash course in the Excel macro recorder.

Chapter 3

Working In the Visual Basic Editor

· ·

In This Chapter

▶ Understanding the Visual Basic Editor

▶ Discovering the Visual Basic Editor parts

▶ Knowing what goes into a VBA module

▶ Understanding three ways to get VBA code into a module

▶ Customizing the VBA environment

· ·

As a more-experienced-than-average Excel user, you probably know a good deal about workbooks, formulas, charts, and other Excel goodies. Now it's time to expand your horizons and explore an entirely new aspect of Excel: the Visual Basic Editor. In this chapter, you find out how to work with the Visual Basic Editor, and you get down to the nitty-gritty of writing some VBA code.

What Is the Visual Basic Editor?

I'm going to save some wear and tear on my fingers, and refer to the Visual Basic Editor as the VBE. The VBE is a separate application where you write and edit your VBA macros. It works seamlessly with Excel. By *seamlessly,* I mean that Excel takes care of opening the VBE when you need it.

You can't run the VBE separately; Excel must be running in order for the VBE to run.

Activating the VBE

The quickest way to activate the VBE is to press Alt+F11 when Excel is active. To return to Excel, press Alt+F11 again.

You can also activate the VBE by using the Developer⇨Code⇨Visual Basic command. If you don't have a Developer tab at the top of your Excel window, flip back to Chapter 2 where I explain how to get that handy Developer tab to show up.

Understanding VBE components

Figure 3-1 shows the VBE program, with some of the key parts identified. Because so much is going on in the VBE, I like to maximize the window to see as much as possible.

Chances are your VBE program window won't look exactly like what you see in Figure 3-1. The VBE contains several windows, and it's highly customizable. You can hide windows, rearrange windows, dock windows, and so on.

Figure 3-1:
The VBE is your cus-
tomizable friend.

Toolbar — Menu bar — Code window

Project window — Immediate window — Properties window

Actually, the VBE has even more parts than are shown in Figure 3-1. I discuss these additional components throughout the book, when they become relevant.

Menu bar

The VBE menu bar works just like every other menu bar you've encountered. It contains commands that you use to do things with the various components in the VBE. You also find that many of the menu commands have shortcut keys associated with them.

The VBE also features shortcut menus. You can right-click virtually anything in the VBE and get a shortcut menu of common commands.

Toolbar

The Standard toolbar, which is directly under the menu bar by default (refer to Figure 3-1), is one of four VBE toolbars available. You can customize the toolbars, move them around, display other toolbars, and so on. If you're so inclined, use the View⇨Toolbars command to work with VBE toolbars. Most people (including me) just leave them as they are.

Project window

The Project window displays a tree diagram that shows every workbook currently open in Excel (including add-ins and hidden workbooks). Double-click items to expand or contract them. I discuss this window in more detail in the upcoming "Working with the Project Window" section.

If the Project window is not visible, press Ctrl+R or use the View⇨Project Explorer command. To hide the Project window, click the Close button in its title bar. Or right-click anywhere in the Project window and select Hide from the shortcut menu.

Code window

A Code window contains VBA code. Every object in a project has an associated Code window. To view an object's Code window, double-click the object in the Project window. For example, to view the Code window for the Sheet1 object, double-click Sheet1 in the Project window. Unless you've added some VBA code, the Code window will be empty.

You find out more about Code windows later in this chapter's "Working with a Code Window" section.

Immediate window

The Immediate window may or may not be visible. If it isn't visible, press Ctrl+G or use the View⇨Immediate Window command. To close the Immediate window, click the Close button in its title bar (or right-click anywhere in the Immediate window and select Hide from the shortcut menu).

The Immediate window is most useful for executing VBA statements directly and for debugging your code. If you're just starting out with VBA, this window won't be all that useful, so feel free to hide it and free up some screen space for other things.

In Chapter 13, I discuss the Immediate window in detail. It may just become your good friend!

What's new in the Visual Basic Editor?

Excel 2007 introduced a brand-new user interface. Menus and toolbars are gone, and the new "Ribbon" replaces them. If you've used the Visual Basic Editor in a previous version of Excel, you'll be in familiar territory. In Excel 2007, Microsoft left the VBE essentially untouched. And they continued the hands-off tradition in Excel 2010.

The VBA programming language has been updated to accommodate the new Excel features, but the VBE has no new features, and the old-style toolbars and menus work exactly like they always have. Maybe they'll eventually get around to updating the VBE, but I'm not holding my breath.

Working with the Project Window

When you're working in the VBE, each Excel workbook and add-in that's open is a project. You can think of a *project* as a collection of objects arranged as an outline. You can expand a project by clicking the plus sign (+) at the left of the project's name in the Project window. Contract a project by clicking the minus sign (–) to the left of a project's name. Or you can double-click the items to expand and contract them.

Figure 3-2 shows a Project window with three projects listed: an add-in named pup7.xlam, a workbook named investments.xlsm, and the Personal Macro Workbook (which is always named PERSONAL.XLSB).

Figure 3-2:
This Project window lists three projects. One of them is expanded to show its objects.

Every project expands to show at least one *node* called Microsoft Excel Objects. This node expands to show an item for each sheet in the workbook (each sheet is considered an object) and another object called ThisWorkbook (which represents the Workbook object). If the project has

any VBA modules, the project listing also shows a Modules node. And, as you see in Part IV, a project may also contain a node called Forms, which contains UserForm objects (which hold custom dialog boxes).

The concept of objects may be a bit fuzzy for you. However, I guarantee that things become much clearer in subsequent chapters. Don't be too concerned if you don't understand what's going on at this point.

Adding a new VBA module

Follow these steps to add a new VBA module to a project:

1. **Select the project's name in the Project window.**
2. **Choose Insert⇨Module.**

Or

1. **Right-click the project's name.**
2. **Choose Insert⇨Module from the shortcut menu.**

 When you record a macro, Excel automatically inserts a VBA module to hold the recorded code. Which workbook holds the module for the recorded macro depends on where you chose to store the recorded macro, just before you started recording.

Removing a VBA module

Need to remove a VBA module from a project?

1. **Select the module's name in the Project window.**
2. **Choose File⇨Remove xxx, where xxx is the module name.**

Or

1. **Right-click the module's name.**
2. **Choose Remove xxx from the shortcut menu.**

 Excel, always trying to keep you from doing something you'll regret, will ask if you want to export the code in the module before you delete it. Almost always, you don't. (If you *do* want to export the module, see the next section.)

You can remove VBA modules, but there is no way to remove the other code modules — those for the Sheet objects or ThisWorkbook.

Exporting and importing objects

Every object in a VBA project can be saved to a separate file. Saving an individual object in a project is known as *exporting*. It stands to reason that you can also *import* objects to a project. Exporting and importing objects might be useful if you want to use a particular object (such as a VBA module or a UserForm) in a different project.

Follow these steps to export an object:

1. **Select an object in the Project window.**

2. **Choose File⇨Export File or press Ctrl+E.**

 You get a dialog box that asks for a filename. Note that the object remains in the project; only a copy of it is exported.

Importing a file to a project goes like this:

1. **Select the project's name in the Explorer window.**

2. **Choose File⇨Import File or press Ctrl+M.**

 You get a dialog box that asks for a file. Locate the file and click Open. You should only import a file if the file was exported by using the File⇨Export File command.

Working with a Code Window

As you become proficient with VBA, you spend lots of time working in Code windows. Macros that you record are stored in a module, and you can type VBA code directly into a VBA module.

Minimizing and maximizing windows

If you have several projects open, the VBE may have lots of Code windows at any given time. Figure 3-3 shows an example of what I mean.

Figure 3-3:
Code
window
overload
isn't pretty.

Code windows are much like workbook windows in Excel. You can minimize them, maximize them, resize them, hide them, rearrange them, and so on. Most people find it much easier to maximize the Code window that they're working on. Doing so lets you see more code and keeps you from getting distracted.

To maximize a Code window, click the Maximize button in its title bar (right next to the X). Or just double-click its title bar to maximize it. To restore a Code window to its original size, click the Restore button. When a window is maximized, its title bar isn't visible, so you'll find the Restore button below the VBE title bar.

Sometimes, you may want to have two or more Code windows visible. For example, you may want to compare the code in two modules or copy code from one module to another. You can arrange the windows manually, or use the Window⇨Tile Horizontally or Window⇨Tile Vertically command to arrange them automatically.

You can quickly switch among code windows by pressing Ctrl+Tab. If you repeat that key combination, you keep cycling through all the open code windows. Pressing Ctrl+Shift+Tab cycles through the windows in reverse order.

Minimizing a Code window gets it out of the way. You can also click the window's Close button (which displays "X") in a Code window's title bar to close the window completely. (Closing a window just hides it; you won't lose anything.) To open it again, just double-click the appropriate object in the Project window. Working with these Code windows *sounds* more difficult than it really is.

Creating a module

In general, a VBA module can hold three types of code:

- ✔ **Declarations:** One or more information statements that you provide to VBA. For example, you can declare the data type for variables you plan to use, or set some other module-wide options.
- ✔ **Sub procedures:** A set of programming instructions that performs some action.
- ✔ **Function procedures:** A set of programming instructions that returns a single value (similar in concept to a worksheet function, such as SUM).

A single VBA module can store any number of Sub procedures, Function procedures, and declarations. Well, there is a limit — about 64,000 characters per module. By way of comparison, this particular chapter has about half that many characters. After more than 15 years of VBA programming, I haven't even come close to reaching that limit. And if I did, the solution is simple: Just insert a new module.

How you organize a VBA module is completely up to you. Some people prefer to keep all their VBA code for an application in a single VBA module; others like to split up the code into several different modules. It's a personal choice, just like arranging furniture.

Getting VBA code into a module

An empty VBA module is like the fake food you see in the windows of some Chinese restaurants; it looks good but it doesn't really do much for you. Before you can do anything meaningful, you must have some VBA code in the VBA module. You can get VBA code into a VBA module in three ways:

- ✔ Enter the code directly.
- ✔ Use the Excel macro recorder to record your actions and convert them to VBA code (see Chapter 6).
- ✔ Copy the code from one module and paste it into another.

Pause for a terminology break

I need to digress for a moment to discuss terminology. Throughout this book, I use the terms *Sub procedure, routine, procedure,* and *macro.* These terms are a bit confusing. Programming folks usually use the word *procedure* to describe an automated task. Technically, a procedure can be a Sub procedure or a Function procedure — both of which are sometimes called *routines.* I use all these terms interchangeably. As detailed in later chapters, however, there is an important difference between Sub and Function procedures. For now, don't worry about the terminology. Just try to understand the concepts.

Entering code directly

Sometimes, the best route is the most direct one. Entering code directly involves . . . well, entering the code directly. In other words, you type the code via your keyboard. Entering and editing text in a VBA module works as you might expect. You can select, copy, cut, paste, and do other things to the text.

Use the Tab key to indent some of the lines to make your code easier to read. This isn't necessary, but it's a good habit to acquire. As you study the code I present in this book, you'll understand why indenting code lines is helpful.

A single line of VBA code can be as long as you like. However, you may want to use the line-continuation character to break up lengthy lines of code. To continue a single line of code (also known as a *statement*) from one line to the next, end the first line with a space followed by an underscore (_). Then continue the statement on the next line. Here's an example of a single statement split into three lines:

```
Selection.Sort Key1:=Range("A1"), _
    Order1:=xlAscending, Header:=xlGuess, _
    Orientation:=xlTopToBottom
```

This statement would perform exactly the same way if it were entered in a single line (with no line-continuation characters). Notice that I indented the second and third lines of this statement. Indenting is optional, but it helps clarify the fact that these lines are not separate statements.

The white-coated engineers who designed the VBE realized that people like us would be making mistakes. Therefore, the VBE has multiple levels of undo and redo. If you deleted a statement that you shouldn't have, use the Undo button on the toolbar (or press Ctrl+Z) until the statement shows up again. After undoing, you can use the Redo button to perform the changes you've undone. This undo/redo business is more complicated to describe than it is to

use. I recommend playing around with this feature until you understand how it works.

Ready to enter some real-live code? Try the following steps:

1. **Create a new workbook in Excel.**

2. **Press Alt+F11 to activate the VBE.**

3. **Click the new workbook's name in the Project window.**

4. **Choose Insert⇨Module to insert a VBA module into the project.**

5. **Type the following code into the module:**

```
Sub GuessName()
    Msg = "Is your name " & Application.UserName & "?"
    Ans = MsgBox(Msg, vbYesNo)
    If Ans = vbNo Then MsgBox "Oh, never mind."
    If Ans = vbYes Then MsgBox "I must be
        psychic!"
End Sub
```

6. **Make sure the cursor is located anywhere within the text you typed, and press F5 to execute the procedure.**

 F5 is a shortcut for the Run⇨Run Sub/UserForm command. If you entered the code correctly, Excel executes the procedure, and you can respond to the simple dialog box shown in Figure 3-4. Unless your name happens to be the same as mine, the dialog box will be different from the one shown in the figure.

Figure 3-4:
The
GuessName
procedure
displays this
dialog box.

When you enter the code listed in Step 5, you might notice that the VBE makes some adjustments to the text you enter. For example, after you type the Sub statement, the VBE automatically inserts the End Sub statement. And if you omit the space before or after an equal sign, the VBE inserts the space for you. Also, the VBE changes the color and capitalization of some text. This is all perfectly normal. It's just the VBE's way of keeping things neat and readable.

If you followed the previous steps, you just wrote a VBA Sub procedure, also known as a *macro*. When you press F5, Excel executes the code and follows the instructions. In other words, Excel evaluates each statement and does

what you told it to do. (Don't let this newfound power go to your head.) You can execute this macro any number of times — although it tends to lose its appeal after a few dozen times.

For the record, this simple macro uses the following concepts, all of which are covered later in this book:

✔ Defining a Sub procedure (the first line)

✔ Assigning values to variables (Msg and Ans)

✔ *Concatenating* (joining) a string (using the & operator)

✔ Using a built-in VBA function (MsgBox)

✔ Using built-in VBA constants (vbYesNo, vbNo, and vbYes)

✔ Using an If-Then construct (twice)

✔ Ending a Sub procedure (the last line)

Not bad for a beginner, eh?

Using the macro recorder

Another way you can get code into a VBA module is by recording your actions, using the Excel macro recorder. If you worked through the hands-on exercise in Chapter 2, you already have some experience with this technique.

By the way, there is absolutely no way you can record the GuessName procedure shown in the preceding section. You can record only things that you can do directly in Excel. Displaying a message box is not in Excel's normal repertoire. (It's a VBA thing.) The macro recorder is useful, but in many cases, you'll probably need to enter at least some code manually.

Here's a step-by-step example that shows you how to record a macro that turns off the cell gridlines in a worksheet. If you want to try this example, start with a new, blank workbook and follow these steps:

1. **Activate a worksheet in the workbook.**

 Any worksheet will do. If the worksheet is not displaying gridlines, add a new worksheet that does. You need to start with a worksheet that has gridlines.

2. **Choose Developer⇨Code⇨Record Macro. Or you can click the icon with a small red dot in the left side of the status bar.**

 Excel displays its Record Macro dialog box.

3. **In the Record Macro dialog box, name the macro Gridlines, and use Ctrl+Shift+G for the shortcut key.**

4. **Click OK to start recording.**

 Excel automatically inserts a new VBA module into the project that cor-responds to the active workbook. From this point on, Excel converts your actions into VBA code. While recording, the icon in the status bar turns into a small blue square. This is a reminder that the macro recorder is running. You can also click that blue square to stop the macro recorder.

5. **Choose View⇨Show - Gridlines.**

 The gridlines in the worksheet disappear.

6. **Choose Developer⇨Code⇨Stop Recording. Or click the Stop Recording button in the status bar (the blue square).**

 Excel stops recording your actions.

To view this newly recorded macro, press Alt+F11 to activate the VBE. Locate the workbook's name in the Project window. You see that the project has a new module listed. The name of the module depends on whether you had any other modules in the workbook when you started recording the macro. If you didn't, the module will be named Module1. You can double-click the module to view the Code window for the module.

Here's the code generated by your actions:

```
Sub Gridlines()
'
' Gridlines Macro
'
' Keyboard Shortcut: Ctrl+Shift+G
'
    ActiveWindow.DisplayGridlines = False
End Sub
```

To try out this macro, activate a worksheet that has gridlines displayed and then press the shortcut key that you assigned in Step 3: Ctrl+Shift+G.

If you didn't assign a shortcut key to the macro, don't worry. Here's how to display a list of all macros available and run the one you want.

1. **Choose Developer⇨Code⇨Macros.**

 Keyboard fans can press Alt+F8. Either of these methods displays a dialog box that lists all the available macros.

2. **Select the macro in the list (in this case, Gridlines).**

3. **Click the Run button.**

 Excel executes the macro, and the gridlines magically disappear.

Of course, you can execute any number of commands and perform any number of actions while the macro recorder is running. Excel dutifully translates your mouse actions and keystrokes to VBA code. It works similarly to a tape recorder, but Excel never runs out of tape.

This recorded macro isn't really all that useful. After all, it's easy enough to turn off gridlines without a macro. It would be more useful if it would toggle gridlines on and off. To make this change, activate the module and change the statement to this:

```
ActiveWindow.DisplayGridlines = _
    Not ActiveWindow.DisplayGridlines
```

This modification makes the macro serve as a *toggle*. If gridlines are displayed, the macro turns them off. If gridlines are not displayed, the macro turns them on. Oops, I'm getting ahead of myself — sorry, but I couldn't resist that simple enhancement. By the way, this is another example of a macro that can't be recorded. You can record a macro to turn gridlines on or turn them off — but you can't record one that will toggle the gridlines.

Copying VBA code

The final method for getting code into a VBA module is to copy it from another module or from some other place (such as a Web site). For example, a Sub or Function procedure that you write for one project might also be useful in another project. Instead of wasting time reentering the code, you can activate the module and use the normal Clipboard copy-and-paste procedures (I'm rather fond of the keyboard shortcuts, Ctrl+C to copy and Ctrl+V to paste). After pasting it into a VBA module, you can modify the code if necessary.

You'll also find lots of VBA code examples on the Web. If you'd like to try them, select the code in your browser and press Ctrl+C to copy it. Then, activate a module and press Ctrl+V to paste it.

Customizing the VBA Environment

If you're serious about becoming an Excel programmer, you'll spend a lot of time with VBA modules on your screen. To help make things as comfortable as possible (no, please keep your shoes on), the VBE provides quite a few customization options.

When the VBE is active, choose Tools⇨Options. You'll see a dialog box with four tabs: Editor, Editor Format, General, and Docking. I discuss some of the most useful options in the sections that follow.

Using the Editor tab

Figure 3-5 shows the options accessed by clicking the Editor tab of the Options dialog box. Use the options in the Editor tab to control how certain things work in the VBE.

Figure 3-5: This is the Editor tab in the Options dialog box.

Auto Syntax Check option

The Auto Syntax Check setting determines whether the VBE pops up a dialog box if it discovers a syntax error while you're entering your VBA code. The dialog box tells roughly what the problem is. If you don't choose this setting, VBE flags syntax errors by displaying them in a different color from the rest of the code, and you don't have to deal with any dialog boxes popping up on your screen.

I usually keep this setting turned off because I find the dialog boxes annoying and I can usually figure out what's wrong with a statement. Before I was a VBA veteran, I found this assistance quite helpful.

Require Variable Declaration option

If the Require Variable Declaration option is set, VBE inserts the following statement at the beginning of each new VBA module you insert:

```
Option Explicit
```

Changing this setting affects only new modules, not existing modules. If this statement appears in your module, you must explicitly define each variable you use. In Chapter 7, I explain why you should develop this habit.

Auto List Members option

If the Auto List Members option is set, VBE provides some help when you're entering your VBA code. It displays a list that would logically complete the statement you're typing. This bit of magic is sometimes called "IntelliSense."

This is one of the best features of the VBE, and I always keep it turned on. Figure 3-6 shows an example (which will make lots more sense when you start writing VBA code).

Figure 3-6:
An example
of Auto List
members.

Auto Quick Info option

If the Auto Quick Info option is set, VBE displays information about functions and their arguments as you type. This can be very helpful. Figure 3-7 shows this feature in action, telling me about the arguments for the MsgBox function.

Auto Data Tips option

If the Auto Data Tips option is set, VBE displays the value of the variable over which your cursor is placed when you're debugging code. When you enter the wonderful world of debugging, as I describe in Chapter 13, you'll appreciate this option.

Figure 3-7:
Auto Quick
Info offers
help about
the MsgBox
function.

Auto Indent setting

The Auto Indent setting determines whether VBE automatically indents each new line of code the same as the previous line. I'm big on using indentations in my code, so I keep this option on.

Use the Tab key to indent your code, not the spacebar. Also, you can use Shift+Tab to "unindent" a line of code. If you want to indent more than just one line, select all the lines you want to indent. Then press the Tab key.

The VBE's Edit toolbar (which is hidden by default) contains two useful buttons: Indent and Outdent. These buttons let you quickly indent or "unindent" a block of code. Select the code and click one of these buttons to change the block's indenting.

Drag-and-Drop Text Editing option

The Drag-and-Drop Text Editing option, when enabled, lets you copy and move text by dragging and dropping with your mouse. I keep this option turned on, but I never use it. I prefer to copy and move by using the keyboard.

Default to Full Module View option

The Default to Full Module View option sets the default state for new modules. (It doesn't affect existing modules.) If set, procedures in the Code window appear as a single scrollable list. If this option is turned off, you can see only one procedure at a time. I keep this option turned on.

Procedure Separator option

When the Procedure Separator option is turned on, separator bars appear at the end of each procedure in a Code window. I like the idea of separator bars, so I keep this option turned on.

Using the Editor Format tab

Figure 3-8 shows the Editor Format tab of the Options dialog box. With this tab, you can customize the way the VBE looks.

Code Colors option

The Code Colors option lets you set the text color and background color displayed for various elements of VBA code. This is largely a matter of personal preference. Personally, I find the default colors to be just fine. But for a change of scenery, I occasionally play around with these settings.

Figure 3-8:
Change
the VBE's
looks with
the Editor
Format tab.

Font option

The Font option lets you select the font that's used in your VBA modules. For best results, stick with a fixed-width font such as Courier New. In a *fixed-width font,* all characters are exactly the same width. This makes your code more readable because the characters are nicely aligned vertically, and you can easily distinguish multiple spaces (which is sometimes useful).

Size setting

The Size setting specifies the point size of the font in the VBA modules. This setting is a matter of personal preference determined by your video display resolution and how many carrots you've been eating.

Margin Indicator Bar option

This option controls the display of the vertical margin indicator bar in your modules. You should keep this turned on; otherwise, you won't be able to see the helpful graphical indicators when you're debugging your code.

Using the General tab

Figure 3-9 shows the options available under the General tab in the Options dialog box. In almost every case, the default settings are just fine.

The most important setting is Error Trapping. I strongly suggest that you use the Break On Unhandled Errors setting (which is the default). If you use a different setting, your error-handling code won't work. You can read more about this in Chapter 12.

If you're really interested in these options, click the Help button for details.

Figure 3-9:
The General
tab of the
Options dia-
log box.

Using the Docking tab

Figure 3-10 shows the Docking tab. These options determine how the various windows in the VBE behave. When a window is *docked,* it is fixed in place along one of the edges of the VBE program window. This makes it much easier to identify and locate a particular window. If you turn off all docking, you have a big, confusing mess of windows. Generally, the default settings work fine.

Figure 3-10:
The Docking
tab of the
Options
dialog box.

Chapter 4

Introducing the Excel Object Model

*E*veryone is familiar with the word *object*. Well, folks, forget the definition you think you know. In the world of programming, the word *object* has a different meaning. You often see it used as part of the expression *object-oriented programming,* or *OOP* for short. OOP is based on the idea that software consists of distinct objects that have attributes (or properties) and can be manipulated. These objects are not material things. Rather, they exist in the form of bits and bytes.

In this chapter, I introduce you to the Excel object model, which is a hierarchy of objects contained in Excel. By the time you finish this chapter, you'll have a reasonably good understanding of what OOP is all about — and why you need to understand this concept to become a VBA programmer. After all, Excel programming really boils down to manipulating Excel objects. It's as simple as that.

The material in this chapter may be a bit overwhelming. But please take my advice and plow through it, even if you don't fully grasp it at first. The important concepts presented here will make a lot more sense as you progress through the book.

Excel Is an Object?

You've used Excel for quite a while, but you probably never thought of it as an object. The more you work with VBA, the more you view Excel in those terms. You'll understand that Excel is an object and that it contains other objects. Those objects, in turn, contain still more objects. In other words, VBA programming involves working with an object hierarchy.

At the top of this hierarchy is the Application object — in this case, Excel itself (the mother of all objects).

Climbing the Object Hierarchy

The Application object contains other objects. Following is a list of some of the more useful objects contained in the Excel Application:

- Addin
- Window
- Workbook
- WorksheetFunction

Each object contained in the Application object can contain other objects. For example, the following is a list of objects that can be contained in a Workbook object:

- Chart
- Name
- VBProject
- Window
- Worksheet

In turn, each of these objects can contain still other objects. Consider a Worksheet object, which is contained in a Workbook object, which is contained in the Application object. Some of the objects that can be contained in a Worksheet object are:

- Comment
- Hyperlink
- Name
- PageSetup

✔ PivotTable

✔ Range

Put another way, if you want to do something with a range on a particular worksheet, you may find it helpful to visualize that range in the following manner:

Range⇨contained in Worksheet⇨contained in Workbook⇨contained in Excel

Is this beginning to make sense?

Figure 4-1 shows part of Excel's Object Model Map. If you really want to be overwhelmed, display the VBA Help system and search for *object model map*. It's a huge diagram that lists all objects, and each one is clickable so you can read all about it.

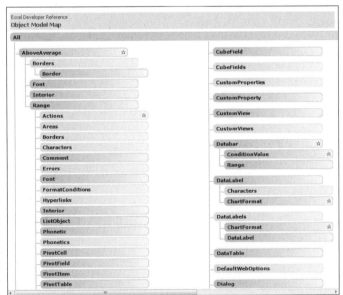

Figure 4-1:
Visualizing
a part of the
Excel object
model.

Yes folks, Excel has more objects than you can shake a stick at, even old-timers like me can get overwhelmed. The good news is that you'll never have to actually deal with most of these objects. When you're working on a problem, you can just focus on a few relevant objects — which you can often discover by recording a macro.

Wrapping Your Mind around Collections

Collections are another key concept in VBA programming. A *collection* is a group of objects of the same type. And to add to the confusion, a collection is itself an object.

Here are a few examples of commonly used collections:

- ✔ **Workbooks:** A collection of all currently open Workbook objects
- ✔ **Worksheets:** A collection of all Worksheet objects contained in a particular Workbook object
- ✔ **Charts:** A collection of all Chart objects (chart sheets) contained in a particular Workbook object
- ✔ **Sheets:** A collection of all sheets (regardless of their type) contained in a particular Workbook object

You may notice that collection names are all plural, which makes sense (at least I hope).

"What are collections for?" you may rightfully ask. Well, for example, they are very useful when you want to do stuff with not just one worksheet, but with a couple of them. As you'll see, your VBA code can loop through all members of a collection, and do something to each one.

Referring to Objects

I presented the information in the previous sections to prepare you for the next concept: referring to objects in your VBA code. Referring to an object is important because you must identify the object that you want to work with. After all, VBA can't read your mind — yet. I believe the mind-reading object will be introduced in Excel 2013.

You can work with an entire collection of objects in one fell swoop. More often, however, you need to work with a specific object in a collection (such as a particular worksheet in a workbook). To reference a single object from a collection, you put the object's name or index number in parentheses after the name of the collection, like this:

```
Worksheets("Sheet1")
```

Notice that the sheet's name is in quotation marks. If you omit the quotation marks, Excel won't be able to identify the object (Excel will think it's a variable name).

If Sheet1 is the first (or only) worksheet in the collection, you can also use the following reference:

```
Worksheets(1)
```

In this case, the number is *not* in quotation marks. Bottom line? If you refer to an object by using its name, use quotation marks. If you refer to an object by using its index number, use a plain number without quotation marks.

Another collection, called Sheets, contains all the sheets (worksheets and Chart sheets) in a workbook. If Sheet1 is the first sheet in the workbook, you can reference it as

```
Sheets(1)
```

Navigating through the hierarchy

If you want to work with the Application object, it's easy: You start by typing **Application**.

Every other object in Excel's object model is under the Application object. You get to these objects by moving down the hierarchy and connecting each object on your way with the dot (.) operator. To get to the Workbook object named "Book1.xlsx", start with the Application object and navigate down to the Workbooks collection object.

```
Application.Workbooks("Book1.xlsx")
```

To navigate farther to a specific worksheet, add a dot operator and access the Worksheets collection object.

```
Application.Workbooks("Book1.xlsx").Worksheets(1)
```

Not far enough yet? If you really want to get the value from cell A1 on the first Worksheet of the Workbook named Book1.xlsx, you need to navigate one more level to the Range object.

```
Application.Workbooks("Book1.xlsx"). _
        Worksheets(1).
    Range("A1").Value
```

When you refer to a Range object in this way, it's called a *fully qualified reference.* You've told Excel exactly which range you want, on which worksheet and in which workbook, and have left nothing to the imagination. Imagination is good in people, but not so good in computer programs.

By the way, workbook names also have a dot to separate the filename from the extension (for example Book1.xlsx). That's just a coincidence. The dot in a file name has nothing at all to do with the dot operator I referred to a few paragraphs ago.

Simplifying object references

If you were required to fully qualify every object reference you make, your code would get quite long, and it might be more difficult to read. Fortunately, Excel provides you with some shortcuts that can improve the readability (and save you some typing). For starters, the Application object is always assumed. There are only a few cases when it makes sense to type it. Omitting the Application object reference shortens the example from the previous section to

```
Workbooks("Book1.xlsx").Worksheets(1).Range("A1").Value
```

That's a pretty good improvement. But wait, there's more. If you're sure that Book1.xlsx is the active workbook, you can omit that reference, too. Now you're down to

```
Worksheets(1).Range("A1").Value
```

Now you're getting somewhere. Have you guessed the next shortcut? That's right, if you know the first worksheet is the currently active worksheet, then Excel will assume that reference and allow you to just type

```
Range("A1").Value
```

Contrary to what some people may think, Excel does not have a Cell object. A *cell* is simply a Range object that consists of just one element.

The shortcuts described here are great, but they can also be dangerous. What if you only *think* Book1.xlsx is the active workbook? You could get an error, or worse, you could get the wrong value and not even realize it's wrong. For that reason, it's often best to fully qualify your object references.

In Chapter 14, I discuss the With-End With structure, which helps you fully qualify your references but also helps to make the code more readable and cuts down on the typing. The best of both worlds!

Diving into Object Properties and Methods

Although knowing how to refer to objects is important, you can't do anything useful by simply referring to an object (as in the examples in the preceding sections). To accomplish anything meaningful, you must do one of two things:

- ✔ Read or modify an object's *properties*.
- ✔ Specify a *method* of action to be used with an object.

With literally thousands of properties and methods available, you can easily be overwhelmed. I've been working with this stuff for years, and I'm *still* overwhelmed. But as I've said before and I say again: You'll never need to use most of the available properties and methods.

Another slant on McObjects, McProperties, and McMethods

Here's an analogy that may help you understand the relationships among objects, properties, and methods in VBA. In this analogy, I compare Excel with a fast-food restaurant chain.

The basic unit of Excel is a Workbook object. In a fast-food chain, the basic unit is an individual restaurant. With Excel, you can add a workbook and close a workbook, and all the open workbooks are known as Workbooks (a collection of Workbook objects). Similarly, the management of a fast-food chain can add a restaurant and close a restaurant, and all the restaurants in the chain can be viewed as the Restaurants collection (a collection of Restaurant objects).

An Excel workbook is an object, but it also contains other objects such as worksheets, charts, VBA modules, and so on. Furthermore, each object in a workbook can contain its own objects. For example, a Worksheet object can contain Range objects, PivotTable objects, Shape objects, and so on.

Continuing with the analogy, a fast-food restaurant (like a workbook) contains objects such as the Kitchen, DiningArea, and Tables (a collection). Furthermore, management can add or remove objects from the Restaurant object. For example, management may add more tables to the Tables collection. Each of these objects can contain other objects. For example, the Kitchen object has a Stove object, VentilationFan object, Chef object, Sink object, and so on.

So far, so good. This analogy seems to work. Let me see if I can take it further.

Excel's objects have properties. For example, a Range object has properties such as Value and Name, and a Shape object has properties such as Width, Height, and so on. Not surprisingly, objects in a fast-food restaurant also have properties. The Stove object, for example, has properties such as Temperature and NumberofBurners. The VentilationFan has its own set of properties (TurnedOn, RPM, and so on).

Besides properties, Excel's objects also have methods, which perform an operation on an object. For example, the ClearContents method erases the contents of a Range object. An object in a fast-food restaurant also has methods. You can easily envision a ChangeThermostat method for a Stove object or a SwitchOn method for a VentilationFan object.

In Excel, methods sometimes change an object's properties. The ClearContents method for a Range changes the Range's Value property. Similarly, the ChangeThermostat method on a Stove object affects its Temperature property. With VBA, you can write procedures to manipulate Excel's objects. In a fast-food restaurant, the management can give orders to manipulate the objects in the restaurants. ("Turn the stove on and switch the ventilation fan to high.")

The next time you visit your favorite fast-food joint, just say, "I'll have a Burger object with the Onion property set to False."

Object properties

Every object has properties. You can think of *properties* as attributes that describe the object. An object's properties determine how it looks, how it behaves, and even whether it is visible. Using VBA, you can do two things with an object's properties:

✔ Examine the current setting for a property.

✔ Change the property's setting.

For example, a single-cell Range object has a property called Value. The Value property stores the value contained in the cell. You can write VBA code to display the Value property, or you may write VBA code to set the Value property to a specific value. The following macro uses the VBA built-in MsgBox function to bring up a box that displays the value in cell A1 on Sheet1 of the active workbook. See Figure 4-2.

```
Sub ShowValue()
    Contents = Worksheets("Sheet1").Range("A1").Value
    MsgBox Contents
End Sub
```

Figure 4-2: This message box displays a Range object's Value property.

By the way, MsgBox is a very useful function. You can use it to display results while Excel executes your VBA code. I tell you more about this function in Chapter 15, so be patient (or just skip and read all about it).

The code in the preceding example displays the current setting of a cell's Value property. What if you want to change the setting for that property? The following macro changes the value in cell A1 by changing the cell's Value property:

```
Sub ChangeValue()
    Worksheets("Sheet1").Range("A1").Value = 994.92
End Sub
```

After Excel executes this procedure, cell A1 on Sheet1 of the active workbook contains the value 994.92. If the active workbook does not have a sheet named Sheet1, executing that macro will display an error message. VBA just follows instructions, and it can't work with a sheet that doesn't exist.

Each object has its own set of properties, although some properties are common to many objects. For example, many (but not all) objects have a Visible property. Most objects also have a Name property.

Some object properties are read-only, which means that you can see the property's value, but you can't change it.

As I mention earlier in this chapter, a collection is also an object. This means that a collection also has properties. For example, you can determine how many workbooks are open by accessing the Count property of the Workbooks collection. The following VBA procedure displays a message box that tells you how many workbooks are open:

```
Sub CountBooks()
    MsgBox Workbooks.Count
End Sub
```

Object methods

In addition to properties, objects have methods. A *method* is an action you perform with an object. A method can change an object's properties or make the object do something.

This simple example uses the ClearContents method on a Range object to erase the contents of cell A1 on the active sheet:

```
Sub ClearRange()
    Range("A1").ClearContents
End Sub
```

Some methods take one or more arguments. An *argument* is a value that further specifies the action to perform. You place the arguments for a method after the method, separated by a space. Multiple arguments are separated by a comma.

The following example activates Sheet1 (in the active workbook) and then copies the contents of cell A1 to cell B1 by using the Range object's Copy method. In this example, the Copy method has one argument — the destination range for the copy operation:

```
Sub CopyOne()
    Worksheets("Sheet1").Activate
    Range("A1").Copy Range("B1")
End Sub
```

Notice that I omit the worksheet reference when I refer to the Range objects. I can do this safely because I used a statement to activate Sheet1 (using the Activate method).

Because a collection is also an object, collections have methods. The following macro uses the Add method for the Workbooks collection:

```
Sub AddAWorkbook()
    Workbooks.Add
End Sub
```

As you may expect, this statement creates a new workbook. In other words, it adds a new workbook to the Workbooks collection. After you execute this macro, a fresh workbook will be the active workbook.

Object events

In this section, I briefly touch on one more topic that you need to know about: events. Objects respond to various *events* that occur. For example, when you're working in Excel and you activate a different workbook, an Activate event occurs. You could, for example, have a VBA macro that is designed to execute whenever an Activate event occurs for a particular Workbook object.

Excel supports many events, but not all objects can respond to all events. And some objects don't respond to any events. The only events you can use are those made available by the programmers of Microsoft Excel. The concept of an event becomes clear in Chapter 11 and also in Part IV.

Finding Out More

Consider yourself initiated into the wonderful world of objects, properties, methods, and events. You find out more about these concepts in the chapters that follow this one. If you just can't get enough, you may also be interested in three other excellent tools:

- ✔ VBA's Help system
- ✔ The Object Browser
- ✔ Auto List Members

Using VBA's Help system

The VBA Help system describes every object, property, and method available to you. This is an excellent resource for finding out about VBA, and it is more comprehensive than any book on the market.

If you're working in a VBA module and want information about a particular object, method, or property, move the cursor to the word you're interested in and press F1. In a few seconds, you see the appropriate help topic, complete with cross-references and perhaps even an example or two.

Figure 4-3 shows a screen from the VBA Help system — in this case, for a Worksheet object.

✔ Click Properties to get a complete list of this object's properties.

✔ Click Methods to get a listing of its methods.

✔ Click Events to get a listing of the events it responds to.

Figure 4-3: An example from VBA's Help system.

Using the Object Browser

The VBE includes another tool known as the Object Browser. As the name implies, this tool lets you browse through the objects available to you. To access the Object Browser, press F2 when the VBE is active (or choose View➪Object Browser). You see a window like the one shown in Figure 4-4.

Figure 4-4:
Browsing
for objects
with the
Object
Browser.

The drop-down list at the top contains a list of all currently available object libraries. Figure 4-4 shows All Libraries. If you want to browse through Excel's objects, select Excel from the drop-down list.

The second drop-down list is where you enter a search string. For example, if you want to look at all Excel objects that deal with comments, type **comment** into the second field and click the Search button. (It has a pair of binoculars on it.) The Search Results window displays everything in the object library that contains the text *comment.* If you see something that looks like it may be of interest, select it and press F1 for more information.

Automatically listing properties and methods

In Chapter 3, I noted a handy feature called Auto List Members (AKA, "IntelliSense"). This feature provides a list of properties and methods as you type. Figure 4-5 shows an example for the Workbooks collection.

Figure 4-5:
The
Auto List
Members
feature
helps you
identify
properties
and meth-
ods for an
object.

After I typed the dot after *workbooks,* the VBE volunteered to help by display-
ing a list of properties and methods for that collection. After I typed the *c*
the list was narrowed to items that began with that letter. Highlight the item
you need, press Tab, and voilà! You've eliminated some typing — and also
ensured that the property or method was spelled correctly.

Chapter 5

VBA Sub and Function Procedures

In This Chapter

▶ Understanding the difference between Sub procedures and Function procedures

▶ Executing Sub procedures (many ways)

▶ Executing Function procedures (two ways)

S everal times in preceding chapters, I mention *Sub procedures* and allude
to the fact that *Function procedures* also play a role in VBA. In this chap-
ter, I clear up confusion about these concepts.

Subs versus Functions

The VBA code that you write in the Visual Basic Editor is known as a *proce-
dure.* The two most common types of procedures are Sub and Function.

✔ A Sub procedure is a group of VBA statements that performs an action
 (or actions) with Excel.

✔ A Function procedure is a group of VBA statements that performs a cal-
 culation and returns a single value.

Most of the macros you write in VBA are Sub procedures. You can think of
a Sub procedure as being like a command: Execute the Sub procedure and
something happens. (Of course, exactly *what* happens depends on the Sub
procedure's VBA code.)

A Function is also a procedure, but it's quite different from a Sub. You're
already familiar with the concept of a function. Excel includes many work-
sheet functions that you use every day (well, at least every weekday).
Examples include SUM, PMT, and VLOOKUP. You use these worksheet func-
tions in formulas. Each function takes one or more arguments (although a
few functions don't use any arguments). The function does some behind-the-
scenes calculations using those arguments, and then it returns a single value.
The same goes for Function procedures that you develop with VBA.

Looking at Sub procedures

Every Sub procedure starts with the keyword Sub and ends with an End Sub statement. Here's an example:

```
Sub ShowMessage()
    MsgBox "That's all folks!"
End Sub
```

This example shows a procedure named ShowMessage. A set of parentheses follows the procedure's name. In most cases, these parentheses are empty. However, you may pass arguments to Sub procedures from other procedures. If your Sub uses arguments, list them between the parentheses.

When you record a macro with the Excel macro recorder, the result is always a Sub procedure.

As you see later in this chapter, Excel provides quite a few ways to execute a VBA Sub procedure.

Looking at Function procedures

Every Function procedure starts with the keyword Function and ends with an End Function statement. Here's a simple example:

```
Function CubeRoot(number)
    CubeRoot = number ^ (1 / 3)
End Function
```

This function, named CubeRoot, takes one argument (named *number*), which is enclosed in parentheses. Functions can have any number of arguments or none at all. When you execute the function, it returns a single value — the cube root of the argument passed to the function.

VBA allows you to specify what type of information (also known as data type) is returned by a Function procedure. Chapter 7 contains more information on specifying data types.

You can execute a Function procedure in only two ways. You can execute it from another procedure (a Sub or another Function procedure) or use it in a worksheet formula.

No matter how hard you try, you can't use the Excel macro recorder to record a Function procedure. You must manually enter every Function procedure that you create.

Naming Subs and Functions

Like humans, pets, and hurricanes, every Sub and Function procedure must have a name. Although it is perfectly acceptable to name your dog Hairball Harris, it's usually not a good idea to use such a freewheeling attitude when naming procedures. When naming procedures, you must follow a few rules:

- ✔ You can use letters, numbers, and some punctuation characters, but the first character must be a letter.

- ✔ You can't use any spaces or periods in the name.

- ✔ VBA does not distinguish between uppercase and lowercase letters.

- ✔ You can't embed any of the following characters in a procedure name: #, $, %, &, @, ^, *, or !.

- ✔ If you write a Function procedure for use in a formula, don't use a name that looks like a cell address (for example, AK47). Actually, Excel allows such function names, but why make things more confusing than they are already?

- ✔ Procedure names can be no longer than 255 characters. (Of course, you would never make a procedure name this long.)

Ideally, a procedure's name describes the routine's purpose. A good practice is to create a name by combining a verb and a noun — for example, ProcessData, PrintReport, Sort_Array, or CheckFilename.

Some programmers prefer using sentence-like names that provide a complete description of the procedure. Some examples include WriteReportToTextFile and Get_Print_Options_and_Print_Report. The use of such lengthy names has pros and cons. On the one hand, such names are descriptive and usually unambiguous. On the other hand, they take longer to type. Everyone develops a naming style, but the main objectives are to make the names descriptive and to avoid meaningless names such as DoIt, Update, Fix, and Macro1.

Executing Sub procedures

Although you may not know much about developing Sub procedures at this point, I'm going to jump ahead a bit and discuss how to execute these procedures. This is important because a Sub procedure is worthless unless you know how to execute it.

By the way, *executing* a Sub procedure means the same thing as *running* or *calling* a Sub procedure. You can use whatever terminology you like.

How do I run you? Let me count the ways. You can execute a VBA Sub in many ways — that's one reason you can do so many useful things with Sub procedures. Here's an exhaustive list of the ways (well, at least all the ways I could think of) to execute a Sub procedure:

- ✔ With the Run⇨Run Sub/UserForm command (in the VBE). Excel executes the Sub procedure in which the cursor is located. This menu command has two alternatives: the F5 key and the Run Sub/UserForm button on the Standard toolbar in the VBE. These methods don't work if the procedure requires one or more arguments.

- ✔ From Excel's Macro dialog box. You open this box by choosing Developer⇨Code⇨Macros or by choosing View⇨Macros⇨Macros. Or bypass the Ribbon and just press the Alt+F8 shortcut key. When the Macro dialog box appears, select the Sub procedure you want and click Run. This dialog box lists only the procedures that don't require an argument.

- ✔ Using the Ctrl+key shortcut assigned to the Sub procedure (assuming you assigned one).

- ✔ Clicking a button or a shape on a worksheet. The button or shape must have a Sub procedure assigned to it.

- ✔ From another Sub procedure that you write.

- ✔ From a button that you've added to the Quick Access toolbar. (See Chapter 19.)

- ✔ From a custom item on the ribbon you develop. (See Chapter 19.)

- ✔ Automatically, when you open or close a workbook. (See Chapter 11.)

- ✔ When an event occurs. As I explain in Chapter 11, these events include saving the workbook, making a change to a cell, activating a sheet, and other things.

- ✔ From the Immediate window in the VBE. Just type the name of the Sub procedure and press Enter.

I demonstrate some of these techniques in the following sections. Before I can do that, you need to enter a Sub procedure into a VBA module.

1. **Start with a new workbook.**

2. **Press Alt+F11 to activate the VBE.**

3. **Select the workbook in the Project window.**

4. **Choose Insert⇨Module to insert a new module.**

5. **Enter the following into the module:**

```
Sub CubeRoot()
    Num = InputBox("Enter a positive number")
    MsgBox Num ^ (1/3) & " is the cube root."
End Sub
```

This procedure asks the user for a number and then displays that number's cube root in a message box. Figures 5-1 and 5-2 show what happens when you execute this procedure.

Figure 5-1:
Using the built-in VBA InputBox function to get a number.

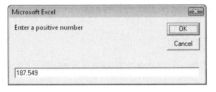

Figure 5-2:
Displaying the cube root of a number via the MsgBox function.

By the way, CubeRoot is not an example of a *good* macro. It doesn't check for errors, so it fails easily. To see what I mean, try clicking the Cancel button in the input box or entering a negative number.

Executing the Sub procedure directly

The quickest way to execute this procedure is by doing so directly from the VBA module in which you defined it. Follow these steps:

1. **Activate the VBE and select the VBA module that contains the procedure.**

2. **Move the cursor anywhere in the procedure's code.**

3. **Press F5 (or choose Run⇨Run Sub/UserForm).**

4. **Respond to the input box and click OK.**

 The procedure displays the cube root of the number you entered.

You can't use the Run⇨Run Sub/UserForm command to execute a Sub procedure that uses arguments, because you have no way to pass the arguments to the procedure. If the procedure contains one or more arguments, the only way to execute it is to call it from another procedure — which must supply the argument(s).

Executing the procedure from the Macro dialog box

Most of the time, you execute Sub procedures from Excel, not from the VBE. The following steps describe how to execute a macro by using Excel's Macro dialog box.

1. **Activate Excel.**

 Alt+F11 is the express route.

2. **Choose Developer⇨Code⇨Macros (or press Alt+F8).**

 Excel displays the dialog box shown in Figure 5-3.

3. **Select the macro.**

4. **Click Run (or double-click the macro's name in the list box).**

Figure 5-3:
The Macro
dialog box
lists all
available
Sub
procedures.

Executing a macro by using a shortcut key

Another way to execute a macro is to press its shortcut key. But before you can use this method, you must assign a shortcut key to the macro.

You have the opportunity to assign a shortcut key in the Record Macro dialog box when you begin recording a macro. If you create the procedure without using the macro recorder, you can assign a shortcut key (or change an existing shortcut key) by using the following procedure:

1. **Choose Developer⇨Code⇨Macros.**

2. **Select the Sub procedure name from the list box.**

 In this example, the procedure is named CubeRoot.

3. **Click the Options button.**

 Excel displays the dialog box shown in Figure 5-4.

4. **Click the Shortcut Key option and enter a letter in the box labeled Ctrl.**

 The letter you enter corresponds to the key combination you want to use for executing the macro. For example, if you enter the lowercase letter *c,* you can then execute the macro by pressing Ctrl+C. If you enter an uppercase letter, you need to add the Shift key to the key combination. For example, if you enter *C,* you can execute the macro by pressing Ctrl+Shift+C.

5. **Click OK or Cancel to close the Macro Options dialog box.**

Figure 5-4:
The Macro
Options
dialog box
lets you set
options
for your
macros.

After you've assigned a shortcut key, you can press that key combination to execute the macro.

The shortcut keys you assign to macros override Excel's built-in shortcut keys. For example, if you assign Ctrl+C to a macro, you can't use this shortcut key to copy data in your workbook. This is usually not a big deal because Excel always provides other ways to execute commands.

Executing the procedure from a button or shape

Sometimes, you might like the idea of assigning the macro to a button (or any other shape) on a worksheet. To assign the macro to a button, follow these steps:

1. **Activate a worksheet.**

2. **Add a button from the Form Controls group.**

 To display the Form Controls group, choose Developer➪Controls➪Insert (see Figure 5-5).

Figure 5-5:
The Ribbon, showing the controls available when you click Insert on the Developer tab.

3. **Click the Button tool in the Form Controls group.**

4. **Drag in the worksheet to create the button.**

 After you add the button to your worksheet, Excel jumps right in and displays the Assign Macro dialog box shown in Figure 5-6.

5. **Select the macro you want to assign to the button.**

6. **Click OK.**

Figure 5-6:
When you
add a but-
ton to a
worksheet,
Excel auto-
matically
displays
the Assign
Macro
dialog box.

After you've made the assignment, clicking the button will execute the macro — just like magic.

Note that the Assign Macro dialog box also gives you an opportunity to record a macro (by clicking the Record button). Or click the New button, and Excel will insert an empty Sub procedure with the name you specify. Most of the time, though, you'll assign an *existing* macro to a button.

When you add a button, note that the drop-down box shows two sets of controls: Form Controls and ActiveX Controls. These two groups of controls look similar, but they are actually very different. In practice, the Form Controls are easier to use.

You can also assign a macro to any other shape or object. For example, assume you'd like to execute a macro when the user clicks a Rectangle object.

1. **Add the Rectangle to the worksheet.**

 Insert a rectangle by using the Insert⇨Illustrations⇨Shapes command.

2. **Right-click the rectangle.**

3. **Choose Assign Macro from its shortcut menu.**

4. **Select the macro from the Assign Macro dialog box.**

5. **Click OK.**

After performing these steps, clicking the rectangle will execute the assigned macro.

Executing the procedure from another procedure

You can also execute a procedure from another procedure. Follow these steps if you want to give this a try:

1. **Activate the VBA module that holds the CubeRoot routine.**

2. **Enter this new procedure (either above or below CubeRoot code — it makes no difference):**

```
Sub NewSub()
    Call CubeRoot
End Sub
```

3. **Execute the NewSub macro.**

 The easiest way to do this is to move the cursor anywhere within the NewSub code and press F5. Notice that this NewSub procedure simply executes the CubeRoot procedure.

By the way, the keyword Call is optional. The statement can consist of only the Sub procedure's name. I find, however, that using the Call keyword makes it perfectly clear that a procedure is being called.

Executing Function procedures

Functions, unlike Sub procedures, can be executed in only two ways:

- ✔ By calling the function from another Sub procedure or Function procedure
- ✔ By using the function in a worksheet formula

Try this simple function. Enter it into a VBA module:

```
Function CubeRoot(number)
    CubeRoot = number ^ (1/3)
End Function
```

This function is pretty wimpy — it merely calculates the cube root of the number passed to it as its argument. It does, however, provide a starting point for understanding functions. It also illustrates an important concept about functions: how to return the value. (You do remember that a function returns a value, right?)

Notice that the single line of code that makes up this Function procedure performs a calculation. The result of the math (number to the power of ⅓) is assigned to the variable CubeRoot. Not coincidentally, CubeRoot is also the name of the function. To tell the function what value to return, you assign that value to the name of the function.

Calling the function from a Sub procedure

Because you can't execute a function directly, you must call it from another procedure. Enter the following simple procedure in the same VBA module that contains the CubeRoot function:

```
Sub CallerSub()
    Ans = CubeRoot(125)
    MsgBox Ans
End Sub
```

When you execute the CallerSub procedure (using any of the methods described earlier in this chapter), Excel displays a message box that contains the value of the Ans variable, which is 5.

Here's what's going on: The CubeRoot function is executed, and it receives an argument of 125. The calculation is performed by the function's code, and the function's returned value is assigned to the Ans variable. The MsgBox function then displays the value of the Ans variable.

Try changing the argument that's passed to the CubeRoot function and run the CallerSub macro again. It works just like it should — assuming that you give the function a valid argument (a positive number).

By the way, the CallerSub procedure could be simplified a bit. The Ans variable is not really required. You could use this single statement to obtain the same result:

```
    MsgBox CubeRoot(125)
```

Calling a function from a worksheet formula

Now it's time to call this VBA Function procedure from a worksheet formula. Activate a worksheet in the same workbook that holds the CubeRoot function definition. Then enter the following formula into any cell:

```
=CubeRoot(1728)
```

The cell displays 12, which is indeed the cube root of 1,728.

As you might expect, you can use a cell reference as the argument for the CubeRoot function. For example, if cell A1 contains a value, you can enter **=CubeRoot(A1)**. In this case, the function returns the number obtained by calculating the cube root of the value in A1.

You can use this function any number of times in the worksheet. As with Excel's built-in functions, your custom functions also appear in the Insert Function dialog box. Click the Insert Function toolbar button and choose the User Defined category. As shown in Figure 5-7, the Insert Function dialog box lists your very own function.

Figure 5-7: The CubeRoot function appears in the User Defined category of the Insert Function dialog box.

If you want the Insert Function dialog box to display a description of the function, follow these steps:

1. **Choose Developer➪Code➪Macros.**

 Excel displays the Macro dialog box, but CubeRoot doesn't appear in the list. (CubeRoot is a Function procedure, and this list shows only Sub procedures.) Don't fret.

2. **Type the word** CubeRoot **in the Macro Name box.**

3. **Click the Options button.**

4. **Enter a description of the function in the Description box.**

5. **Close the Macro Options dialog box.**

6. **Close the Macro dialog box by clicking the Cancel button.**

 This descriptive text now appears in the Insert Function dialog box.

By now, things may be starting to come together for you. (I wish I'd had this book when *I* was starting out.) You've found out lots about Sub and Function procedures. You start creating macros in Chapter 6, which discusses the ins and outs of developing macros by using the Excel macro recorder.

Chapter 6

Using the Excel Macro Recorder

In This Chapter

▶ Recording your actions by using the Excel built-in macro recorder

▶ Understanding the types of macros you can record

▶ Setting the appropriate options for macro recording

*Y*ou can use two methods to create an Excel macro:

✔ Record it by using the Excel macro recorder.

✔ Write it manually.

This chapter deals specifically with the ins and outs of using the Excel macro recorder. Recording a macro isn't always the best approach, and some macros simply can't be recorded, no matter how hard you try. You'll see, however, that the Excel macro recorder is very useful. Even if your recorded macro isn't quite what you want, the macro recorder can almost always lead you in the right direction.

Is It Live or Is It VBA?

In previous editions of this book, I compared recording a macro to using a tape recorder. However, it occurred to me that tape recorders are rapidly going the way of the dinosaurs. So I modernized this section, and it now compares macro recording to making a digital video. This analogy, like the previous one, goes only so far. Table 6-1 compares macro recording with making a video.

Table 6-1	Video Recording versus Macro Recording	
	Video Recorder	*Excel Macro Recorder*
What equipment is required?	A video camera.	A computer and a copy of Excel.
What is recorded?	Video and audio.	Actions taken in Excel.
Where is the recording stored?	On a flash memory card.	In a VBA module.
How do you play it back?	Locate the file and press Play.	Locate the macro in the Macros dialog box and click Run (or use other methods).
Can you edit the recording?	Yes, if you have the proper video-editing software.	Yes, if you know what you're doing.
Can you copy the recording?	Yes, just like copying any other file.	Yes (no additional equipment required).
Is the recording accurate?	Depends on the situation and the equipment quality.	Depends on how you set things up when you record the macro.
What if you make a mistake?	Rerecord the video (or edit it if possible).	Rerecord the macro (or edit it if possible).
Can you view the recording?	Yes, by opening the file with appropriate software.	Yes, by opening a module in the VBE.
Can you share it with the world?	Yes, YouTube is a good option.	Yes, post it at your Web site or blog.
Can you make money with the recording?	Yes, if it's really good (editing usually required).	Yes, but you need to do a lot of editing first.

Recording Basics

You take the following basic steps when recording a macro. I describe these steps in more detail later in this chapter.

1. **Determine what you want the macro to do.**

2. **Get things set up properly.**

 This step determines how well your macro works.

3. **Determine whether you want cell references in your macro to be relative or absolute.**

4. **Click the Record Macro button in the left side of the status bar (or choose Developer⇨Code⇨Record Macro).**

 Excel displays its Record Macro dialog box.

5. **Enter a name, shortcut key, macro location, and description.**

 Each of these items — with the exception of the name — is optional.

6. **Click OK in the Record Macro dialog box.**

 Excel automatically inserts a VBA module. From this point, Excel converts your actions into VBA code. It also displays a Stop Recording button on your status bar (a blue square).

7. **Perform the actions you want recorded by using the mouse or the keyboard.**

8. **After you're finished, click the Stop Recording button on the status bar (or choose Developer⇨Code⇨Stop Recording).**

 Excel stops recording your actions.

9. **Test the macro to make sure it works correctly.**

10. **As an option, you might want to clean up the code by removing extraneous statements.**

The macro recorder is best suited for simple, straightforward macros. For example, you might want a macro that applies formatting to a selected range of cells or that sets up row and column headings for a new worksheet.

The macro recorder is for Sub procedures only. You can't use the macro recorder to create Function procedures.

You may also find the macro recorder helpful for developing more complex macros. Often, I record some actions and then copy the recorded code into another, more complex macro. In most cases, you need to edit the recorded code and add some new VBA statements.

The macro recorder *cannot* generate code for any of the following tasks, which I describe later in the book:

✔ Performing any type of repetitive looping

✔ Performing any type of conditional actions (using an If-Then statement)

✔ Assigning values to variables

✔ Specifying data types

✔ Displaying pop-up messages

✔ Displaying custom dialog boxes

The macro recorder's limited capability certainly doesn't diminish its importance. I make the following point throughout the book: *Recording your actions is perhaps the best way to master VBA.* When in doubt, try recording. Although the result may not be exactly what you want, viewing the recorded code may steer you in the right direction.

Preparing to Record

Before you take the big step and turn on the macro recorder, spend a minute or two thinking about what you're going to do. You record a macro so that Excel can automatically repeat the actions you record.

Ultimately, the success of a recorded macro depends on five factors:

- ✔ How the workbook is set up while you record the macro
- ✔ What is selected when you start recording
- ✔ Whether you use absolute or relative recording mode
- ✔ The accuracy of your recorded actions
- ✔ The context in which you play back the recorded macro

The importance of these factors becomes crystal clear when I walk you through an example.

Relative or Absolute?

When recording your actions, Excel normally records absolute references to cells. (This is the default recording mode.) Very often, this is the *wrong* recording mode. If you use relative recording, Excel records relative references to cells. The distinction is explained in this section.

Recording in absolute mode

Follow these steps to record a simple macro in absolute mode. This macro simply enters three month names into a worksheet:

1. **Choose Developer⇨Code⇨Record Macro.**

2. **Type** Absolute **as the name for this macro.**

3. **Click OK to begin recording.**

4. **Activate cell B1 and type** Jan **in that cell.**

5. **Move to cell C1 and type** Feb.

6. **Move to cell D1 and type** Mar.

7. **Click cell B1 to activate it again.**

8. **Stop the macro recorder.**

9. **Press Alt+F11 to activate the VBE.**

10. **Examine the Module1 module.**

Excel generates the following code:

```
Sub Absolute()
'
' Absolute Macro
'
    Range("B1").Select
    ActiveCell.FormulaR1C1 = "Jan"
    Range("C1").Select
    ActiveCell.FormulaR1C1 = "Feb"
    Range("D1").Select
    ActiveCell.FormulaR1C1 = "Mar"
    Range("B1").Select
End Sub
```

When executed, this macro selects cell B1 and inserts the three month names in the range B1:D1. Then the macro reactivates cell B1.

These same actions occur regardless of which cell is active when you execute the macro. A macro recorded by using absolute references always produces the same results when it is executed. In this case, the macro always enters the names of the first three months into the range B1:D1.

Recording in relative mode

In some cases, you want your recorded macro to work with cell locations in a *relative* manner. You may want the macro to start entering the month names in the active cell. In such a case, you need to use relative recording.

You can change the manner in which Excel records your actions by clicking the Use Relative References button in the Code group in the Developer tab. This button is a toggle button. When the button appears in a different color, the recording mode is relative. When the button appears normally, you are recording in absolute mode.

You can change the recording method at any time, even in the middle of recording.

To see how relative mode recording works, erase the cells in B1:D1 and then perform the following steps:

1. **Activate cell B1.**

2. **Choose Developer⇨Code⇨Record Macro.**

3. **Name this macro** Relative.

4. **Click OK to begin recording.**

5. **Click the Use Relative References button to change the recording mode to relative.**

 When you click this button, it changes to a different color than the rest of the ribbon.

6. **Activate cell B1 and type** Jan **in that cell.**

7. **Move to cell C1 and type** Feb.

8. **Move to cell D1 and type** Mar.

9. **Select cell B1.**

10. **Stop the macro recorder.**

Notice that this procedure differs slightly from the previous example. In this example, you activate the beginning cell *before* you start recording. This is an important step when you record macros that use the active cell as a base.

This macro always starts entering text in the active cell. Try it. Move the cell pointer to any cell and then execute the Relative macro. The month names are always entered beginning at the active cell.

With the recording mode set to relative, the code that Excel generates is quite different from the code generated in absolute mode:

```
Sub Relative()
'
' Relative Macro
'
    ActiveCell.FormulaR1C1 = "Jan"
    ActiveCell.Offset(0, 1).Range("A1").Select
    ActiveCell.FormulaR1C1 = "Feb"
    ActiveCell.Offset(0, 1).Range("A1").Select
    ActiveCell.FormulaR1C1 = "Mar"
    ActiveCell.Offset(0, -2).Range("A1").Select
End Sub
```

To test this macro, activate any cell except B1. The month names are entered in three cells, beginning with the cell that you activated.

Notice that the code generated by the macro recorder refers to cell A1. This may seem strange because you never used cell A1 during the recording of the macro. This is simply a byproduct of the way the macro recorder works. (I discuss this in more detail in Chapter 8 where I talk about the Offset method.)

What Gets Recorded?

When you turn on the macro recorder, Excel converts your mouse and keyboard actions into valid VBA code. I could probably write several pages describing how Excel does this, but the best way to understand the process is by watching the macro recorder in action. (Figure 6-1 shows how my screen looked while I had the macro recorder turned on.)

Follow these steps:

1. **Start with a blank workbook.**

2. **Make sure that the Excel window is not maximized.**

3. **Press Alt+F11 to activate the VBE (and make sure that *this* program window is not maximized).**

4. **Resize and arrange the Excel window and the VBE window so that both are visible.**

 For best results, position the Excel window on top of the VBE window, and minimize any other applications that are running.

5. **Activate Excel and choose Developer⇨Code⇨Record Macro.**

6. **Click OK to start the macro recorder.**

 Excel inserts a new module (named Module1) and starts recording in that module.

7. **Activate the VBE program window.**

8. **In the Project Explorer window, double-click Module1 to display that module in the Code window.**

Jump back to Excel and play around for a while. Choose various Excel commands and watch the code being generated in the VBE window. Select cells, enter data, format cells, use the Ribbon commands, create a chart, change column widths, manipulate graphics objects, and so on — go crazy! I guarantee that you'll be enlightened as you watch Excel spit out the VBA code before your very eyes.

Figure 6-1: A convenient window arrangement for watching the macro recorder do its thing.

Recording Options

When recording your actions to create VBA code, you have several options. Recall that the Developer⊃Code⊃Record Macro command displays the Record Macro dialog box before recording begins, as shown in Figure 6-2.

The Record Macro dialog box, shown in Figure 6-2, lets you specify a few aspects of your macro. In the following sections, I describe these options.

Macro name

You can enter a name for the Sub procedure that you are recording. By default, Excel uses the names Macro1, Macro2, and so on for each macro you record. I usually just accept the default name. If the macro works correctly and I want to save it, I give it a more descriptive name later on. You, however, may prefer to name the macro upfront — the choice is yours.

Figure 6-2:
The Record
Macro
dialog box
provides
several
options.

Shortcut key

The Shortcut key option lets you execute the macro by pressing a shortcut key combination. For example, if you enter **w** (lowercase), you can execute the macro by pressing Ctrl+W. If you enter **W** (uppercase), the macro comes alive when you press Ctrl+Shift+W.

You can add or change a shortcut key at any time, so you don't have to set this option when recording a macro. See Chapter 5 for instructions on assigning a shortcut key to an existing macro.

Store Macro In

The Store Macro In option tells Excel where to store the macro that it is recording. By default, Excel puts the recorded macro in a module in the active workbook. If you prefer, you can record it in a new workbook (Excel opens a blank workbook) or in your Personal Macro Workbook.

Your Personal Macro Workbook is a hidden workbook that opens automatically when Excel starts. This is a good place to store macros that you'll use with multiple workbooks. The Personal Macro Workbook is named PERSONAL.XLSB. This file doesn't exist until you specify it as the location for a recorded macro. If you've made any changes to this file, Excel prompts you to save it when you exit.

Description

If you'd like to add some descriptive comments to your macro, use the Description box. You can put anything you like here or nothing at all. As far as I'm concerned, the Description option is a waste of time because it's just as easy to add comments to the recorded macro.

Is This Thing Efficient?

You might think that recording a macro would generate some award-winning VBA code — better than you could ever write manually. Think again. In many cases, the recorder spits out lots of extraneous garbage, and it often generates code that's less than efficient.

Don't get me wrong. I'm a staunch supporter of the macro recorder. It's a great tool for helping you master VBA. Other than simple macros, however, I've never used a recorded macro without fixing it up a bit (usually *quite* a bit).

To demonstrate just how inefficient the macro recorder's code can be, try this:

1. **Turn on the macro recorder.**

2. **Choose the Page Layout⇨Page Setup⇨Orientation⇨Landscape command.**

3. **Turn off the macro recorder.**

To take a look at the macro, activate the Module1 sheet. This single — and very simple — command generates the following code:

```
Sub Macro1()
    With ActiveSheet.PageSetup
        .PrintTitleRows = ""
        .PrintTitleColumns = ""
    End With
    ActiveSheet.PageSetup.PrintArea = ""
    With ActiveSheet.PageSetup
        .LeftHeader = ""
        .CenterHeader = ""
        .RightHeader = ""
        .LeftFooter = ""
        .CenterFooter = ""
        .RightFooter = ""
        .LeftMargin = Application.
            InchesToPoints(0.708661417322835)
        .RightMargin = Application.
            InchesToPoints(0.708661417322835)
        .TopMargin = Application.
            InchesToPoints(0.748031496062992)
        .BottomMargin = Application.
            InchesToPoints(0.748031496062992)
```

```
        .HeaderMargin = Application.
           InchesToPoints(0.31496062992126)
        .FooterMargin = Application.
           InchesToPoints(0.31496062992126)
        .PrintHeadings = False
        .PrintGridlines = False
        .PrintComments = xlPrintNoComments
        .PrintQuality = 300
        .CenterHorizontally = False
        .CenterVertically = False
        .Orientation = xlLandscape
        .Draft = False
        .PaperSize = xlPaperLetter
        .FirstPageNumber = xlAutomatic
        .Order = xlDownThenOver
        .BlackAndWhite = False
        .Zoom = 100
        .PrintErrors = xlPrintErrorsDisplayed
        .OddAndEvenPagesHeaderFooter = False
        .DifferentFirstPageHeaderFooter = False
        .ScaleWithDocHeaderFooter = True
        .AlignMarginsHeaderFooter = True
        .EvenPage.LeftHeader.Text = ""
        .EvenPage.CenterHeader.Text = ""
        .EvenPage.RightHeader.Text = ""
        .EvenPage.LeftFooter.Text = ""
        .EvenPage.CenterFooter.Text = ""
        .EvenPage.RightFooter.Text = ""
        .FirstPage.LeftHeader.Text = ""
        .FirstPage.CenterHeader.Text = ""
        .FirstPage.RightHeader.Text = ""
        .FirstPage.LeftFooter.Text = ""
        .FirstPage.CenterFooter.Text = ""
        .FirstPage.RightFooter.Text = ""
    End With
End Sub
```

You may be surprised by the amount of code generated by this single command. (I was the first time I tried something like this.) Although you changed only one print setting, Excel generated code that sets many other print-related properties.

This is a good example of macro-recording overkill. If you want a macro that just switches the page setup to landscape mode, you can simplify this macro considerably by deleting the extraneous code. This makes the macro faster and easier to read. Here's how the macro looks after I deleted the irrelevant lines:

```
Sub Macro1()
    With ActiveSheet.PageSetup
        .Orientation = xlLandscape
    End With
End Sub
```

I deleted all the code except the line that sets the Orientation property. Actually, you can simplify this macro even more because you don't really need the With.End With construct (I explain more about this construct in Chapter 14):

```
Sub Macro1()
    ActiveSheet.PageSetup.Orientation = xlLandscape
End Sub
```

In this case, the macro changes the Orientation property of the PageSetup object on the active sheet. All other properties are unchanged. By the way, xlLandscape is a built-in constant that makes your code easier to read. This constant has a value of 2, so the following statement works exactly the same (but isn't as easy to read):

```
ActiveSheet.PageSetup.Orientation = 2
```

Stay tuned. I discuss built-in constants in Chapter 7.

Rather than record this macro, you can enter it directly into a VBA module. To do so, you have to know which objects, properties, and methods to use. Although the recorded macro isn't all that great, by recording it, you realize that the PageSetup object has an Orientation property. Armed with this knowledge (and probably some experimentation), you can write the macro manually.

This chapter nearly sums it up when it comes to using the macro recorder. The only thing missing is experience. Eventually, you discover which recorded statements you can safely delete. Better yet, you discover how to modify a recorded macro to make it more useful.

Part III
Programming Concepts

The 5th Wave By Rich Tennant

©RICHTENNANT

"I started running 'what if' scenarios on my spreadsheet, like, 'What if I were sick of this dirtwad job and funneled some of the company's money into an off-shore account?'"

In this part . . .

This is the part of the book that you've been waiting for. In the next eight chapters, you find out about all the essential elements of Excel programming. And in the process, you see some illuminating examples that you can adapt to your own needs.

Chapter 7

Essential VBA Language Elements

· ·

In This Chapter

▶ Knowing when, why, and how to use comments in your code

▶ Using variables and constants

▶ Telling VBA what type of data you're using

▶ Knowing why you may need to use labels in your procedures

· ·

*B*ecause VBA is a real, live programming language, it uses many elements common to all programming languages. In this chapter, I introduce you to several of these elements: comments, variables, constants, data types, arrays, and a few other goodies. If you've programmed with other languages, some of this material will be familiar. If you're a programming newbie, it's time to roll up your sleeves and get busy.

Using Comments in Your VBA Code

A *comment* is the simplest type of VBA statement. Because VBA ignores these statements, they can consist of anything you want. You can insert a comment to remind yourself why you did something or to clarify some particularly elegant code you wrote. Use comments liberally and extensively to describe what the code does (which isn't always obvious by reading the code itself). Often, code that makes perfect sense today mystifies you tomorrow. Been there. Done that.

You begin a comment with an apostrophe ('). VBA ignores any text that follows an apostrophe in a line of code. You can use a complete line for your comment or insert your comment at the end of a line of code. The following example shows a VBA procedure with three comments, although they're not necessarily *good* comments:

```
Sub CommentsDemo()
'    This procedure does nothing of value
    x = 0    'x represents nothingness
    'Display the result
    MsgBox x
End Sub
```

The "apostrophe indicates a comment" rule has one exception: VBA doesn't interpret an apostrophe inside a set of quotation marks as a comment indicator. For example, the following statement doesn't contain a comment, even though it has an apostrophe:

```
Msg = "Can't continue"
```

When you're writing code, you may want to test a procedure by *excluding* a particular statement or group of statements. You *could* delete the statements and then retype them later. But that's a waste of time. A better solution is to simply turn those statements into comments by inserting apostrophes. VBA ignores statements beginning with apostrophes when executing a routine. To reactivate those "commented" statements, just remove the apostrophes.

Here's a quick way to convert a block of statements to comments. In the VBE, choose View➪Toolbars➪Edit to display the Edit toolbar. To convert a block of statements to comments, select the statements and click the Comment Block button. To remove the apostrophes, select the statements and click the Uncomment Block button.

Although comments can be helpful, not all comments are created equal. For example, the following procedure uses lots of comments, but they add nothing of value. In this case, the code is clear enough without the comments.

```
Sub BadComments()
'    Declare variables
    Dim x As Integer
    Dim y As Integer
    Dim z As Integer
'    Start the routine
    x = 100 ' Assign 100 to x
    y = 200 ' Assign 200 to y
'    Add x and y and store in z
    z = x + y
'    Show the result
    MsgBox z
End Sub
```

Everyone develops his or her own style of commenting. To be useful, however, comments should convey information that's not immediately obvious from reading the code. Otherwise, comments just chew up bytes and make files larger than necessary.

The following tips can help you make effective use of comments:

- ✔ Briefly describe the purpose of each Sub or Function procedure you write.

- ✔ Use comments to keep track of changes you make to a procedure.

- ✔ Use a comment to indicate that you're using a function or a construct in an unusual or nonstandard manner.

- ✔ Use comments to describe the variables you use, especially if you don't use meaningful variable names.

- ✔ Use a comment to describe any workarounds you develop to overcome bugs in Excel.

- ✔ Write comments as you develop code, instead of saving the task for a final step.

- ✔ Depending on your work environment, consider adding a joke or two as a comment. The person who takes over your job when you get promoted might appreciate the humor.

Using Variables, Constants, and Data Types

VBA's main purpose is to manipulate data. VBA stores the data in your computer's memory; it may or may not end up on disk. Some data, such as worksheet ranges, resides in objects. Other data is stored in variables that you create.

Understanding variables

A *variable* is simply a named storage location in your computer's memory. You have lots of flexibility in naming your variables, so make the variable names as descriptive as possible. You assign a value to a variable by using the equal sign operator. (More about this later in the "Using Assignment Statements" section.)

The variable names in these examples appear on both the left and right sides of the equal signs. Note that the last example uses two variables.

```
x = 1
InterestRate = 0.075
LoanPayoffAmount = 243089
DataEntered = False
x = x + 1
UserName = "Bob Johnson"
DateStarted = #3/14/2010#
MyNum = YourNum * 1.25
```

VBA enforces a few rules regarding variable names:

- ✔ You can use letters, numbers, and some punctuation characters, but the first character must be a letter.
- ✔ You cannot use any spaces or periods in a variable name.
- ✔ VBA does not distinguish between uppercase and lowercase letters.
- ✔ You cannot use the following characters in a variable name: #, $, %, &, or !.
- ✔ Variable names can be no longer than 255 characters. Of course, you're only asking for trouble if you use variable names 255 characters long.

To make variable names more readable, programmers often use mixed case (for example, InterestRate) or the underscore character (interest_rate).

VBA has many reserved words that you can't use for variable names or procedure names. These include words such as Sub, Dim, With, End, Next, and For. If you attempt to use one of these words as a variable, you may get a compile error (which means your code won't run). So, if an assignment statement produces an error message, double-check and make sure that the variable name isn't a reserved word.

VBA does allow you to create variables with names that match names in Excel's object model, such as Workbook and Range. But, obviously, using names like that just increases the possibility of getting confused. So resist the urge to use a variable named Workbook, and use something like MyWorkbook instead.

What are VBA's data types?

When I talk about *data type,* I'm referring to the manner in which a program stores data in memory — for example, as integers, real numbers, or strings. Although VBA can take care of these details automatically, it does so at a cost. (There's no free lunch.) Letting VBA handle your data typing results in slower execution and inefficient memory use. For small applications, this usually doesn't present much of a problem. But for large or complex applications, which may be slow or need to conserve every last byte of memory, you need to be on familiar terms with data types.

VBA automatically handles all the data details, which makes life easier for programmers. Not all programming languages provide this luxury. For example, some languages are *strictly typed,* which means the programmer must explicitly define the data type for every variable used.

VBA does not require that you declare the variables that you use, but it's definitely a good practice. You'll see why later in this chapter.

VBA has a variety of built-in data types. Table 7-1 lists the most common types of data that VBA can handle.

Table 7-1	VBA's Built-In Data Types	
Data Type	*Bytes Used*	*Range of Values*
Boolean	2	True or False
Integer	2	−32,768 to 32,767
Long	4	−2,147,483,648 to 2,147,483,647
Single	4	−3.402823E38 to 1.401298E45
Double (negative)	8	−1.79769313486232E308 to −4.94065645841247E-324
Double (positive)	8	4.94065645841247E−324 to 1.79769313486232E308
Currency	8	−922,337,203,685,477.5808 to 922,337,203,685,477.5807
Date	8	1/1/100 to 12/31/9999
String	1 per char	Varies
Object	4	Any defined object
Variant	Varies	Any data type
User defined	Varies	Varies

In general, choose the data type that uses the smallest number of bytes but can still handle all the data you want to store in the variable.

Loop counters are often declared as integers. If you use the counter in order to loop through rows in the worksheet, your program might just error out! Why? Integers cannot be larger than 32,767. Beginning with Excel 2007, worksheets have many more rows (1,048,576 to be exact). Instead, declare such loop counters as Long.

Declaring and scoping variables

If you read the previous sections, you now know a bit about variables and data types. In this section, you discover how to declare a variable as a certain data type.

If you don't declare the data type for a variable you use in a VBA routine, VBA uses the default data type: Variant. Data stored as a variant acts like a chameleon; it changes type depending on what you do with it. For example, if a variable is a Variant data type and contains a text string that looks like a number

(such as "143"), you can use this variable for string manipulations as well as numeric calculations. VBA automatically handles the conversion. Letting VBA handle data types may seem like an easy way out — but remember that you sacrifice speed and memory.

Before you use variables in a procedure, it's an excellent practice to *declare* your variables — that is, tell VBA each variable's data type. Declaring your variables makes your program run faster and use memory more efficiently. The default data type, Variant, causes VBA to repeatedly perform time-consuming checks and reserve more memory than necessary. If VBA knows a variable's data type, it doesn't have to investigate and can reserve just enough memory to store the data.

To force yourself to declare all the variables you use, include the following as the first statement in your VBA module:

```
Option Explicit
```

When this statement is present, you won't be able to run your code if it contains any undeclared variables.

You need to use Option Explicit only once: at the beginning of your module, prior to the declaration of any procedures in the module. Keep in mind that the Option Explicit statement applies only to the module in which it resides. If you have more than one VBA module in a project, you need an Option Explicit statement for each module.

Suppose that you use an undeclared variable (that is, a Variant) named CurrentRate. At some point in your routine, you insert the following statement:

```
CurentRate = .075
```

This misspelled variable, which is difficult to spot, will probably cause your routine to give incorrect results. If you use Option Explicit at the beginning of your module (forcing you to declare the CurrentRate variable), Excel generates an error if it encounters a misspelled variation of that variable.

To ensure that the Option Explicit statement is inserted automatically whenever you insert a new VBA module, turn on the Require Variable Definition option. You find it in the Editor tab of the Options dialog box (in the VBE, choose Tools⇨Options). I highly recommend doing so.

Declaring your variables also lets you take advantage of a shortcut that can save some typing. Just type the first two or three characters of the variable name, and then press Ctrl+Space. The VBE will either complete the entry for you or — if the choice is ambiguous — show you a list of matching words to select from. In fact, this slick trick works with reserved words and functions, too.

You now know the advantages of declaring variables, but *how* do you do this? The most common way is to use a Dim statement. Here are some examples of variables being declared:

```
Dim YourName As String
Dim AmountDue As Double
Dim RowNumber As Long
Dim X
```

The first three variables are declared as a specific data type. The last variable, X, is not declared as a specific data type, so it's treated as a Variant (it can be anything).

Besides Dim, VBA has three other keywords that are used to declare variables:

- ✔ Static
- ✔ Public
- ✔ Private

I explain more about the Dim, Static, Public, and Private keywords later on, but first I must cover two other topics that are relevant here: a variable's scope and a variable's life.

Recall that a workbook can have any number of VBA modules. And a VBA module can have any number of Sub and Function procedures. A variable's *scope* determines which modules and procedures can use the variable. Table 7-2 describes the scopes in detail.

Confused? Keep turning the pages and you'll see some examples that will make this stuff crystal clear.

Table 7-2	Variable's Scope
Scope	*How the Variable Is Declared*
Procedure only	By using a Dim or a Static statement in the procedure that uses the variable
Module only	By using a Dim or a Private statement before the first Sub or Function statement in the module
All procedures in all modules	By using a Public statement before the first Sub or Function statement in a module

Humorous declarations

Topic such as variables, data types, declarations, and scope can be pretty boring. So I put together some semi-humorous declaration statements for your amusement. These are all valid declarations.

```
Dim King As String, Kong As Long
Dim Mouthful as Byte
Dim Julian As Boolean
Dim Unmarried As Single
Dim Trouble As Double
Dim WindingRoad As Long
Dim Blind As Date
Public Nuisance
Private FirstClass
Static Cling, Electricity
Dim BaseballCards As New Collection
Dim DentalFloss As String
```

You can probably come up with some others.

Procedure-only variables

The lowest level of scope for a variable is at the procedure level. (A *procedure* is either a Sub or a Function procedure.) Variables declared with this scope can be used only in the procedure in which they are declared. When the procedure ends, the variable no longer exists (it goes to the great bit bucket in the sky), and Excel frees up its memory. If you execute the procedure again, the variable comes back to life, but its previous value is lost.

The most common way to declare a procedure-only variable is with a Dim statement. Dim doesn't refer to the mental capacity of the VBA designers. Rather, it's an old programming term that's short for *dimension,* which simply means you are setting aside memory for a particular variable. You usually place Dim statements immediately after the Sub or Function statement and before the procedure's code.

The following example shows some procedure-only variables declared by using Dim statements:

```
Sub MySub()
    Dim x As Integer
    Dim First As Long
    Dim InterestRate As Single
    Dim TodaysDate As Date
    Dim UserName As String
    Dim MyValue
'    ... [The procedure's code goes here] ...
End Sub
```

Notice that the last Dim statement in the preceding example doesn't declare a data type; it declares only the variable itself. The effect is that the variable MyValue is a Variant.

By the way, you can also declare several variables with a single Dim statement, as in the following example:

```
Dim x As Integer, y As Integer, z As Integer
Dim First As Long, Last As Double
```

Unlike some languages, VBA doesn't allow you to declare a group of variables to be a particular data type by separating the variables with commas. For example, though valid, the following statement does *not* declare all the variables as Integers:

```
Dim i, j, k As Integer
```

In this example, only k is declared to be an Integer; the other variables are declared to be Variants.

If you declare a variable with procedure-only scope, other procedures in the same module can use the same variable name, but each instance of the variable is unique to its own procedure. In general, variables declared at the procedure level are the most efficient because VBA frees up the memory they use when the procedure ends.

Module-only variables

Sometimes, you want a variable to be available to all procedures in a module. If so, just declare the variable (using Dim or Private) *before* the module's first Sub or Function statement — outside any procedures. This is done in the Declarations section, at the beginning of your module. (This is also where the Option Explicit statement is located.) Figure 7-1 shows how you know when you're working with the Declarations section.

Figure 7-1:
Each VBA module has a Declarations section, which appears before any Sub or Function procedures.

As an example, suppose that you want to declare the CurrentValue variable so that it's available to all the procedures in your module. All you need to do is use the Dim statement in the Declarations section:

```
Dim CurrentValue As Integer
```

With this declaration in place — and in the proper place — the CurrentValue variable can be used from any other procedure within the module, and it retains its value from one procedure to another.

Public variables

If you need to make a variable available to all the procedures in all your VBA modules in a workbook, declare the variable at the module level (in the Declarations section) by using the Public keyword. Here's an example:

```
Public CurrentRate As Long
```

The Public keyword makes the CurrentRate variable available to any procedure in the workbook — even those in other VBA modules. You must insert this statement before the first Sub or Function statement in a module.

If you would like a variable to be available to modules in other workbooks, you must declare the variable as Public and establish a reference to the workbook that contains the variable declaration. Set up a reference by using the Tools⇨References command in VBE. In practice, sharing a variable across workbooks is hardly ever done. In fact, I've never done it once in my entire VBA programming career. But I guess it's nice to know that it can be done, in case it ever comes up as a *Jeopardy!* question.

Static variables

Normally, when a procedure ends, all the procedure's variables are reset. *Static variables* are a special case because they retain their value even when the procedure ends. You declare a static variable at the procedure level. A static variable may be useful if you need to track the number of times you execute a procedure. You can declare a static variable and increment it each time you run the procedure.

As shown in the following example, you declare static variables by using the Static keyword:

```
Sub MySub()
    Static Counter As Integer
    Dim Msg As String
    Counter = Counter + 1
    Msg = "Number of executions: " & Counter
    MsgBox Msg
End Sub
```

The code keeps track of the number of times the procedure was executed. The value of the Counter variable is not reset when the procedure ends, but it is reset when you close and reopen the workbook.

Even though the value of a variable declared as Static is retained after a variable ends, that variable is unavailable to other procedures. In the preceding MySub procedure example, the Counter variable and its value are available only within the MySub procedure. In other words, it's a procedure-level variable.

Life of variables

Nothing lives forever, including variables. The scope of a variable not only determines where that variable may be used, it also affects under which circumstances the variable is removed from memory.

You can purge all variables from memory by using three methods:

- ✔ Click the Reset toolbar button (the little blue square button on the Standard toolbar in the VBE).
- ✔ Click "End" when a runtime error message dialog box shows up.
- ✔ Include an End statement anywhere in your code. This is not the same as an End Sub or End Function statement.

Otherwise, only procedure-level variables will be removed from memory when the macro code has completed running. Static variables, module level variables, and global (public) variables all retain their values in between runs of your code.

If you use module-level or global-level variables, make sure they have the value you expect them to have. You never know whether one of the situations I just mentioned may have caused your variables to lose their content!

Working with constants

A variable's value may (and usually does) change while your procedure is executing. That's why they call it a *variable*. Sometimes you need to refer to a value or string that never changes. In such a case, you need a *constant* — a named element whose value doesn't change.

As shown in the following examples, you declare constants by using the Const statement. The declaration statement also gives the constant its value:

```
Const NumQuarters As Integer = 4
Const Rate = .0725, Period = 12
Const ModName As String = "Budget Macros"
Public Const AppName As String = "Budget Application"
```

Using constants in place of hard-coded values or strings is an excellent programming practice. For example, if your procedure needs to refer to a specific value (such as an interest rate) several times, it's better to declare the value as a constant and refer to its name rather than the value. This makes your code more readable and easier to change. When the interest rate changes, you have to change only one statement rather than several.

Like variables, constants have a scope. Keep these points in mind:

- To make a constant available within only a single procedure, declare the constant after the procedure's Sub or Function statement.
- To make a constant available to all procedures in a module, declare the constant in the Declarations section for the module.
- To make a constant available to all modules in the workbook, use the Public keyword and declare the constant in the Declarations section of any module.

If you attempt to change the value of a constant in a VBA routine, you get an error. This isn't too surprising because a constant is constant. Unlike a variable, the value of a constant does not vary. If you need to change the value of a constant while your code is running, what you really need is a variable.

Pre-made constants

Excel and VBA contain many predefined constants, which you can use without the need to declare them yourself. The macro recorder usually uses constants rather than actual values. In general, you don't need to know the value of these constants to use them. The following simple procedure uses a built-in constant (xlCalculationManual) to change the Calculation property of the Application object. (In other words, this changes the Excel recalculation mode to manual.)

```
Sub CalcManual()
    Application.Calculation = xlCalculationManual
End Sub
```

I discovered the xlCalculationManual constant by recording a macro while I changed the calculation mode. I also could have looked in the Help system. Figure 7-2 shows the Help screen that lists the constants for the Calculation property.

The actual value of the built-in xlCalculationManual constant is –4135. Obviously, it's easier to use the constant's name than try to remember such an odd value. By the way, the constant for changing to automatic calculation mode is xlCalculationAutomatic; its value is –4105. As you can see, many of the built-in constants are just arbitrary numbers that have special meaning to VBA.

Figure 7-2:
Constants
that deter-
mine the
Calculation
mode.

To find the actual value of a built-in constant, use the Immediate window in the VBE, and execute a VBA statement such as the following:

```
? xlCalculationAutomatic
```

If the Immediate window isn't visible, press Ctrl+G. The question mark is a shortcut for typing **Print.**

Working with strings

Excel can work with both numbers and text, so it should come as no surprise that VBA has this same power. Text is often referred to as a *string*. You can work with two types of strings in VBA:

- **Fixed-length strings** are declared with a specified number of characters. The maximum length is 65,526 characters. That's a lot of characters! As a point of reference, this chapter contains about half that many characters.

- **Variable-length strings** theoretically can hold as many as two billion characters. If you type five characters per second, it would take you about 760 days to bang out two billion characters — assuming you don't take any breaks to eat or sleep.

When declaring a string variable with a Dim statement, you can specify the maximum length if you know it (it's a fixed-length string) or let VBA handle it dynamically (it's a variable-length string). The following example declares the MyString variable as a string with a maximum length of 50 characters. (Use an asterisk to specify the number of characters, up to the 65,526 character limit.) YourString is also declared as a string, but its length is unspecified:

```
Dim MyString As String * 50
Dim YourString As String
```

When declaring a fixed-length string, do not use a comma in the number that specifies the string size. In fact, never use commas when entering a numeric value in VBA. VBA doesn't like that.

Working with dates

Another data type you may find useful is Date. You can use a string variable to store dates, but then you can't perform date calculations. Using the Date data type gives your routines greater flexibility. For example, you might need to calculate the number of days between two dates. This would be impossible if you used strings to hold your dates.

A variable defined as a Date can hold dates ranging from January 1, 0100, to December 31, 9999. That's a span of nearly 10,000 years and more than enough for even the most aggressive financial forecast. You can also use the Date data type to work with time data (seeing as VBA lacks a time data type).

These examples declare variables and constants as a Date data type:

```
Dim Today As Date
Dim StartTime As Date
Const FirstDay As Date = #1/1/2010#
Const Noon = #12:00:00#
```

In VBA, place dates and times between two hash marks, as shown in the preceding examples.

Date variables display dates according to your system's short date format, and they display times according to your system's time format (either 12- or 24-hour formatting). The Windows Registry stores these settings, and you can modify them via the Regional and Language Options dialog box in the Windows Control Panel. Therefore, the VBA-displayed date or time format may vary, depending on the settings for the system on which the application is running.

When writing VBA code, however, you must use one of the U.S. date formats (such as mm/dd/yyyy). So the following statement assigns a day in October to the MyDate variable (even if your system is set to use dd/mm/yyyy for dates):

```
MyDate = #10/11/2009#
```

When you display the variable (with the MsgBox function, for example), VBA shows MyDate using your system settings. So if your system uses the dd/mm/yyyy date format, MyDate will be displayed as 11/10/2009.

Using Assignment Statements

An *assignment statement* is a VBA statement that assigns the result of an expression to a variable or an object. Excel's Help system defines the term *expression* as

> . . . a combination of keywords, operators, variables, and constants that yields a string, number, or object. An expression can be used to perform a calculation, manipulate characters, or test data.

I couldn't have said it better myself, so I won't even try.

Much of your work in VBA involves developing (and debugging) expressions. If you know how to create formulas in Excel, you'll have no trouble creating expressions. With a worksheet formula, Excel displays the result in a cell. A VBA expression, on the other hand, can be assigned to a variable.

Assignment statement examples

In the assignment statement examples that follow, the expressions are to the right of the equal sign:

```
x = 1
x = x + 1
x = (y * 2) / (z * 2)
HouseCost = 375000
FileOpen = True
Range("TheYear").Value = 2012
```

Expressions can be as complex as you need them to be; use the line continuation character (a space followed by an underscore) to make lengthy expressions easier to read.

Often, expressions use functions: VBA's built-in functions, Excel's worksheet functions, or functions that you develop with VBA. I discuss functions in Chapter 9.

About that equal sign

As you can see in the preceding example, VBA uses the equal sign as its assignment operator. You're probably accustomed to using an equal sign as

a mathematical symbol for equality. Therefore, an assignment statement like the following may cause you to raise your eyebrows:

```
z = z + 1
```

How can the variable z be equal to itself plus 1? Answer: It can't. In this case, the assignment statement is increasing the value of z by 1. Just remember that an assignment uses the equal sign as an operator, not a symbol of equality.

Smooth operators

Operators play a major role in VBA. Besides the equal sign operator (discussed in the previous section), VBA provides several other operators. Table 7-3 lists these operators, with which you are familiar from your worksheet formulas experience.

Table 7-3	VBA's Operators
Function	*Operator Symbol*
Addition	+
Multiplication	*
Division	/
Subtraction	-
Exponentiation	^
String concatenation	&
Integer division (the result is always an integer)	\
Modulo arithmetic (returns the remainder of a division operation)	Mod

The term *concatenation* is programmer speak for "join together." Thus, if you concatenate strings, you are combining strings to make a new and improved string.

As shown in Table 7-4, VBA also provides a full set of logical operators. Consult the Help system for complete details.

Table 7-4	VBA's Logical Operators
Operator	*What It Does*
Not	Performs a logical negation on an expression.
And	Performs a logical conjunction on two expressions.
Or	Performs a logical disjunction on two expressions.
XoR	Performs a logical exclusion on two expressions.
Eqv	Performs a logical equivalence on two expressions.
Imp	Performs a logical implication on two expressions.

The precedence order for operators in VBA is exactly the same as in Excel formulas. Exponentiation has the highest precedence. Multiplication and division come next, followed by addition and subtraction. You can use parentheses to change the natural precedence order, making whatever's sandwiched in parentheses come before any operator. Take a look at this code:

```
x = 3
y = 2
z = x + 5 * y
```

When this code is executed, what's the value of z? If you answered 13, you get a gold star that proves you understand the concept of operator precedence. If you answered 16, read this: The multiplication operation (5 * y) is performed first, and that result is added to x. If you answered something other than 13 or 16, I have no comment.

By the way, I can never remember how operator precedence works, so I tend to use parentheses even when they aren't required. For example, in real life I would write that last assignment statement like this:

```
z = x + (5 * y)
```

Don't be shy about using parentheses even if they aren't required — especially if doing so makes your code easier to understand. VBA doesn't care if you use extra parentheses.

Working with Arrays

Most programming languages support arrays. An *array* is a group of variables that share a common name. You refer to a specific variable in the array by using the array name and an index number in parentheses. For example, you can define an array of 12 string variables to hold the names of the months of the year. If you name the array *MonthNames*, you can refer to the first element of the array as MonthNames (1), the second element as MonthNames (2), and so on.

Declaring arrays

Before you can use an array, you *must* declare it. No exceptions. Unlike normal variables, VBA is very strict about this rule. You declare an array with a Dim or Public statement, just as you declare a regular variable. However, you also need to specify the number of elements in the array. You do this by specifying the first index number, the keyword To, and the last index number — all inside parentheses. The following example shows how to declare an array of 100 integers:

```
Dim MyArray(1 To 100) As Integer
```

When you declare an array, you can choose to specify only the upper index. VBA assumes that 0 is the lower index. Therefore, both of the following statements declare the same 101-element array:

```
Dim MyArray (0 To 100) As Integer
```

```
Dim MyArray (100) As Integer
```

If you want VBA to assume that 1 (rather than 0) is the lower index for your arrays, include the following statement in the Declarations section of your module:

```
Option Base 1
```

This statement forces VBA to use 1 as the first index number for arrays that declare only the upper index. If this statement is present, the following statements are identical, both declaring a 100-element array:

```
Dim MyArray (1 To 100) As Integer
```

```
Dim MyArray (100) As Integer
```

Multidimensional arrays

The arrays created in the previous examples are all one-dimensional arrays. Think of one-dimensional arrays as a single line of values. Arrays you create in VBA can have as many as 60 dimensions — although you rarely need more than two or three dimensions in an array. The following example declares an 81-integer array with two dimensions:

```
Dim MyArray (1 To 9, 1 To 9) As Integer
```

You can think of this array as occupying a 9 x 9 matrix — perfect for storing all numbers in a soduku puzzle.

To refer to a specific element in this array, you need to specify two index numbers (similar to it's "row" and it's "column" in the matrix). The following example shows how you can assign a value to an element in this array:

```
MyArray (3, 4)= 125
```

This statement assigns a value to a single element in the array. If you're thinking of the array in terms of a 9 x 9 matrix, this assigns 125 to the element located in the third row and fourth column of the matrix.

Here's how to declare a three-dimensional array, with 1,000 elements:

```
Dim My3DArray (1 To 10, 1 To 10, 1 To 10) As Integer
```

You can think of a three-dimensional array as a cube. Visualizing an array of more than three dimensions is more difficult. Sorry, I haven't yet mastered the fourth dimension and beyond.

Dynamic arrays

You can also create *dynamic* arrays. A dynamic array doesn't have a preset number of elements. Declare a dynamic array with an empty set of parentheses:

```
Dim MyArray () As Integer
```

Before you can use this array, you must use the ReDim statement to tell VBA how many elements the array has. Usually, the number of elements in the array is determined while your code is running. You can use the ReDim statement any number of times, changing the array's size as often as needed. The following example demonstrates how to change the number of elements in a

dynamic array. It assumes that the NumElements variable contains a value, which your code calculated.

```
ReDim MyArray (1 To NumElements)
```

When you redimension an array by using ReDim, you wipe out any values currently stored in the array elements. You can avoid destroying the old values by using the Preserve keyword. The following example shows how you can preserve an array's values when you redimension the array:

```
ReDim Preserve MyArray(1 To NumElements)
```

If MyArray currently has ten elements and you execute the preceding statement with NumElements equaling 12, the first ten elements remain intact, and the array has room for two additional elements (up to the number contained in the variable NumElements). If NumElements equals 7 however, the first seven elements are retained but the remaining three elements meet their demise.

The topic of arrays comes up again in Chapter 10, when I discuss looping.

Using Labels

In early versions of BASIC, every line of code required a line number. For example, if you had written a BASIC program in the '70s (dressed, of course, in your bell bottoms), it may have looked something like this:

```
010: LET X=5
020: LET Y=3
030: LET Z=X*Y
040: PRINT Z
050: END
```

VBA permits the use of such line numbers, and it even permits text labels. You don't typically use a label for each line, but you may occasionally need to use a label. For example, insert a label if you use a GoTo statement (which I discuss in Chapter 10). A label must begin with the first nonblank character in a line and end with a colon.

The information in this chapter becomes clearer as you read subsequent chapters. If you want to find out more about VBA language elements, I refer you to the VBA Help system. You can find as much detail as you need, or care, to know.

Chapter 8

Working with Range Objects

. .

In This Chapter

▶ Finding out why Range objects are so important

▶ Understanding the various ways of referring to ranges

▶ Discovering some of the more useful Range object properties

▶ Uncovering some of the more useful Range object methods

. .

*I*n this chapter, I dig a bit deeper into Excel's dungeons and take a closer look at Range objects. Excel is all about cells, and the Range object is a container for cells. Why do you need to know so much about Range objects? Because much of the programming work you do in Excel focuses on Range objects. You can thank me later.

A Quick Review

A *Range object* represents a range contained in a Worksheet object. Range objects, like all other objects, have properties (which you can examine and change) and methods (which perform actions on the object).

A Range object can be as small as a single cell (for example, B4) or as large as every one of the 17,179,869,184 cells in a worksheet (A1:XFD1048576).

When you refer to a Range object, the address is always surrounded by double quotes, like this:

```
Range("A1:C5")
```

If the range consists of one cell, you still need the quotes:

```
Range("K9")
```

If the range happens to have a name (created by using Formulas➪Defined Names➪Define Name), you can use an expression like this:

```
Range("PriceList")
```

Unless you tell Excel otherwise by qualifying the range reference, it assumes that you're referring to a range on the active worksheet. If anything other than a worksheet is active (such as a chart sheet), the range reference fails, and your macro displays an error message.

As shown in the following example, you can refer to a range outside the active sheet by qualifying the range reference with a worksheet name from the active workbook:

```
Worksheets("Sheet1").Range("A1:C5")
```

If you need to refer to a range in a different workbook (that is, any workbook other than the active workbook), you can use a statement like this:

```
Workbooks("Budget.xlsx").Worksheets("Sheet1"). _
        Range("A1:C5")
```

A Range object can consist of one or more entire rows or columns. You can refer to an entire row (in this case, row 3) by using syntax like this:

```
Range("3:3")
```

You can refer to an entire column (column 4 in this example) like this:

```
Range("D:D")
```

In Excel, you select noncontiguous ranges by holding down the Ctrl key while selecting various ranges with your mouse. Figure 8-1 shows a noncontiguous range selection. You shouldn't be surprised that VBA also lets you work with noncontiguous ranges. The following expression refers to a two-area noncontiguous range. Notice that a comma separates the two areas.

```
Range("A1:B8,D9:G16")
```

Be aware that some methods and properties cause havoc with noncontiguous ranges. You may have to process each area separately by using a loop.

Figure 8-1:
A noncon-
tiguous
range
selection.

Other Ways to Refer to a Range

The more you work with VBA, the more you realize that it's a fairly well conceived language and is usually quite logical (despite what you may be thinking right now). Often, VBA provides multiple ways to perform an action. You can choose the most appropriate method for your problem. This section discusses some of the other ways to refer to a range.

This chapter barely scratches the surface for the Range object's properties and methods. As you work with VBA, you'll probably need to access other properties and methods. The Help system is the best place to find out about them, but it's also a good idea to record your actions and examine the code Excel generates.

The Cells property

Rather than use the VBA Range keyword, you can refer to a range via the Cells property.

Notice that I wrote Cells *property,* not Cells *object* or even Cells *collection.* Although Cells may seem like an object (or a collection), it's really not. Rather, Cells is a property that VBA evaluates. VBA then returns an object (more specifically, a Range object). If this seems strange, don't worry. Even Microsoft appears to be confused about this issue. In some earlier versions of Excel, the Cells property was known as the Cells method. Regardless of what it is, just understand that Cells is a handy way to refer to a range.

The Cells property takes two arguments: row and column. Both of these arguments are numbers, even though we usually refer to columns by using letters. For example, the following expression refers to cell C2 on Sheet2:

```
Worksheets("Sheet2").Cells(2, 3)
```

You can also use the Cells property to refer to a multi-cell range. The following example demonstrates the syntax you use:

```
Range(Cells(1, 1), Cells(10, 10))
```

This expression refers to a 100-cell range that extends from cell A1 (row 1, column 1) to cell J10 (row 10, column 10).

The following statements both produce the same result; they enter a value of 99 into a 10-by-10 range of cells. More specifically, these statements set the Value property of the Range object:

```
Range("A1:J10").Value = 99
Range(Cells(1, 1), Cells(10, 10)).Value = 99
```

The advantage of using the Cells method to refer to ranges becomes apparent when you use variables rather than actual numbers as the Cells arguments. And things really start to click when you understand looping, which I cover in Chapter 10.

The Offset property

The Offset property provides another handy means for referring to ranges. This property, which operates on a Range object and returns another Range object, lets you refer to a cell that is a particular number of rows and columns away from another cell.

Like the Cells property, the Offset property takes two arguments. The first argument represents the number of rows to offset; the second represents the number of columns to offset.

The following expression refers to a cell one row below cell A1 and two columns to the right of cell A1. In other words, this refers to the cell commonly known as C2:

```
Range("A1").Offset(1, 2)
```

The Offset method can also use negative arguments. A *negative* row offset refers to a row above the range. A negative column offset refers to a column to the left of the range. The following example refers to cell A1:

```
Range("C2").Offset(-1, -2)
```

And, as you may expect, you can use 0 as one or both of the arguments for Offset. The following expression refers to cell A1:

```
Range("A1").Offset(0, 0)
```

The Offset method is most useful when you use variables rather than actual values for the arguments. In Chapter 10, I present some examples that demonstrate this.

Referring to entire columns and rows

If you need to refer to a range that consists of one or more entire columns, you can use an expression like the following:

```
Columns("A:C")
```

And to refer to one or more complete rows, use an expression like this:

```
Rows("1:5")
```

Some Useful Range Object Properties

A Range object has dozens of properties. You can write VBA programs non-stop for the next 10 years and never use them all. In this section, I briefly describe some of the more commonly used Range properties. For complete details, consult the Help system in the VBE.

Some Range properties are *read-only* properties, which means that you can have your code look at their values, but you can't have it change them ("look, but don't touch"). For example, every Range object has an Address property (which holds the range's address). You can access this read-only property, but you can't change it.

By the way, the examples that follow are typically statements rather than complete procedures. If you'd like to try any of these (which you should), create a Sub procedure to do so. Also, many of these statements work properly only if a worksheet is the active sheet.

Assigning the values in a multi-cell range to a variable

I wasn't being fully truthful when I wrote "you can read the Value property only for a single-cell Range object." In fact, you can assign the values in a multi-cell range to a variable, as long as the variable is a variant. That's because a variant can act like an array. Here's an example:

```
Dim x As Variant
```

```
x = Range("A1:C3").Value
```

Then you can treat the x variable as if it were an array. This statement, for example, returns the value in cell B1:

```
MsgBox x(1, 2)
```

The Value property

The Value property represents the value contained in a cell. It's a read-write property, so your VBA code can either read or change the value.

The following statement displays a message box that shows the value in cell A1 on Sheet1:

```
MsgBox Worksheets("Sheet1").Range("A1").Value
```

It stands to reason that you can read the Value property only for a single-cell Range object. For example, the following statement generates an error:

```
MsgBox Worksheets("Sheet1").Range("A1:C3").Value
```

You can, however, change the Value property for a range of any size. The following statement enters the number 123 into each cell in a range:

```
Worksheets("Sheet1").Range("A1:C3").Value = 123
```

Value is the default property for a Range object. In other words, if you omit a property for a Range, Excel uses its Value property. The following statements both enter a value of 75 into cell A1 on Sheet1:

```
Worksheets("Sheet1").Range("A1").Value = 75
Worksheets("Sheet1").Range("A1") = 75
```

The Text property

The Text property returns a string that represents the text as displayed in a cell — the formatted value. The Text property is read-only. For example, suppose that cell A1 contains the value 12.3 and is formatted to display two decimals and a dollar sign ($12.30). The following statement displays a message box containing $12.30:

```
MsgBox Worksheets("Sheet1").Range("A1").Text
```

But the next statement displays a message box containing 12.3:

```
MsgBox Worksheets("Sheet1").Range("A1").Value
```

If the cell contains a formula, the Text property returns the result of the formula. If a cell contains text, then the Text property and the Value property will always return the same thing, because text (unlike a number) can't be formatted to display differently.

The Count property

The Count property returns the number of cells in a range. It counts all cells, not just the nonblank cells. Count is a read-only property (think about it for a second, and you'll understand why). The following statement accesses a range's Count property and displays the result (9) in a message box:

```
MsgBox Range("A1:C3").Count
```

The Column and Row properties

The Column property returns the column number of a single-cell range. It's sidekick, the Row property, returns the row number of a single-cell range. Both are read-only properties. For example, the following statement displays 6 because cell F3 is in the sixth column:

```
MsgBox Sheets("Sheet1").Range("F3").Column
```

The next expression displays 3 because cell F3 is in the third row:

```
MsgBox Sheets("Sheet1").Range("F3").Row
```

If the Range object consists of more than one cell, the Column property returns the column number of the first column in the range, and the Row property returns the row number of the first row in the range.

 Don't confuse the Column and Row properties with the Columns and Rows properties (discussed earlier in this chapter). The Column and Row properties return a single value. Columns and Rows properties return a Range object. What a difference an "s" makes.

The Address property

Address, a read-only property, displays the cell address for a Range object in absolute notation (a dollar sign before the column letter and before the row number). The following statement displays the message box shown in Figure 8-2.

```
MsgBox Range(Cells(1, 1), Cells(5, 5)).Address
```

Figure 8-2:
This message box displays the Address property of a 1-by-5 range.

The HasFormula property

The HasFormula property (which is read-only) returns True if the single-cell range contains a formula. It returns False if the cell does not have a formula. If the range consists of more than one cell, VBA returns True only if all cells in the range contain a formula, or False if all cells in the range don't have a formula. The property returns a Null if there is a mixture of formulas and nonformulas in the range. Null is kind of a no-man's land: The range contains a mixture of formulas and values.

 You need to be careful when you work with properties that can return Null. More specifically, the only data type that can deal with Null is Variant.

For example, assume that cell A1 contains a value and cell A2 contains a formula. The following statements generate an error because the range doesn't consist of all formulas or all nonformulas:

```
Dim FormulaTest As Boolean
FormulaTest = Range("A1:A2").HasFormula
```

The Boolean data type can handle only True or False. Null causes it to complain and throw up an error message. To fix this type of situation, the best thing to do is make sure that the FormulaTest variable is declared as a Variant rather than as a Boolean. The following example uses VBA's handy TypeName function (along with an If-Then statement) to determine the data type of the FormulaTest variable. If the range has a mixture of formulas and nonformulas, the message box displays *Mixed!*

```
Dim FormulaTest As Variant
FormulaTest = Range("A1:A2").HasFormula
If TypeName(FormulaTest) = "Null" Then MsgBox "Mixed!"
```

The Font property

As I note earlier in this chapter (see "The Cells property"), a property can return an object. The Font property of a Range object is another example of that concept at work. The Font property returns a Font object.

A Font object, as you may expect, has many accessible properties. To change some aspect of a range's font, you must first access the range's Font object and then manipulate the properties of that object. This may be confusing, but maybe this example will help.

The following statement uses the Font property of the Range object to return a Font object. Then the Bold property of the Font object is set to True. In plain English, this makes the cell display in boldface:

```
Range("A1").Font.Bold = True
```

Truth is, you don't really need to know that you're working with a special Font object that's contained in a Range object. As long as you use the proper syntax, it will work just fine. Often, recording your actions while you record a macro will tell you everything you need to know about the proper syntax.

See Chapter 6 for more information about recording macros.

The Interior property

Here's yet another example of a property that returns an object. A Range object's Interior property returns an Interior object (strange name, but that's what it's called). This type of object referencing works the same way as the Font property (which I describe in the preceding section).

For example, the following statement changes the Color property of the Interior object contained in the Range object:

```
Range("A1").Interior.Color = 8421504
```

In other words, this statement changes the cell's background to middle gray. What's that? You didn't know that 8421504 is middle gray? For some insights into Excel's wonderful world of color, see the sidebar, "A quick & dirty color primer."

The Formula property

The Formula property represents the formula in a cell. This is a read-write property, so you can access it to insert a formula into a cell. For example, the following statement enters a SUM formula into cell A13:

```
Range("A13").Formula = "=SUM(A1:A12)"
```

Notice that the formula is a text string and is enclosed in quotation marks.

If the formula itself contains quotation marks, things get a bit tricky. For example, let's say you want to insert this formula by using VBA:

```
=SUM(A1:A12)&" Stores"
```

This formula displays a value, followed by the word *Stores*. To make this formula acceptable, you need to replace every quotation mark in the formula with two quotation marks. Otherwise, VBA will get confused, and claim that there's a syntax error (because there is!). So here's a statement that will enter a formula that contains quotes:

```
Range("A13").Formula = "=SUM(A1:A12)&"" Stores"""
```

By the way, you can access a cell's Formula property even if the cell doesn't have a formula. If a cell has no formula, the Formula property returns the same as its Value property.

If you need to know whether a cell has a formula, use the HasFormula property.

Be aware that VBA "speaks" U.S. English. This means that in order to put a formula in a cell, you must use the U.S. syntax. To use your own locale formula syntax in VBA, check the FormulaLocal property.

A quick & dirty color primer

Prior to Excel 2007, Microsoft tried to convince us that 56 colors were good enough for a spreadsheet. But things have changed, and we can use more than 16 million colors in a workbook. 16,777,216 colors to be exact.

Many objects have a Color property, and that property accepts color values that range from 0 to 16777215. Nobody can remember that many color values, so (fortunately) there's an easier way to specify colors: use VBA's RGB function. This function takes advantage of the fact that any of these 16 million colors can be represented by various levels of red, green, and blue. The three arguments in the RGB function correspond to the color's red, green, and blue components, and each of these arguments can range from 0 to 255.

Note that 256 x 256 x 256 = 16,777,216 — which happens to be the number of colors. Don't you just love it when the math works out?

Following are a few examples that use the RGB function to change a cell's background color:

```
Range("A1").Interior.Color = RGB(0, 0, 0) 'black
Range("A1").Interior.Color = RGB(255, 0, 0) ' pure red
Range("A1").Interior.Color = RGB(0, 0, 255) ' pure blue
Range("A1").Interior.Color = RGB(200, 89, 18) ' orangy-brown
Range("A1").Interior.Color = RGB(128, 128, 128) ' middle gray
```

If you need to use standard colors, you may prefer to use one of the built-in color constants: vbBlack, vbRed, vbGreen, vbYellow, vbBlue, vbMagenta, vbCyan, or vbWhite. For example, the following statement makes cell A1 yellow:

```
Range("A1").Interior.Color = vbYellow
```

Excel 2007 also introduced "theme colors." These are the colors that appear when you use color control such as the Fill Color control in the Font group of the Home tab. Try recording a macro while you change colors, and you'll get something like this:

```
Range("A1").Interior.ThemeColor = xlThemeColorAccent4
Range("A1").Interior.TintAndShade = 0.399975585192419
```

Yep, two more color-related properties to deal with. Here we have a theme color (the basic color, specified as a built-in constant), plus a "tint and shade" value that represents how dark or light the color is. TintAndShade values range from −1.0 to +1.0. Positive values of the TintAndShade property make the color lighter, and negative values make the color darker. When you set a color using the ThemeColor property, the color will change if you apply a different document theme (using the Page Layout⇨Themes⇨Themes command).

The NumberFormat property

The NumberFormat property represents the number format (expressed as a text string) of the Range object. This is a read-write property, so your VBA code can change the number format. The following statement changes the number format of column A to a percent with two decimal places:

```
Columns("A:A").NumberFormat = "0.00%"
```

Follow these steps to see a list of other number formats. Better yet, turn on the macro recorder while you do this:

1. **Activate a worksheet.**

2. **Access the Format Cells dialog box by pressing Ctrl+1.**

3. **Click the Number tab.**

4. **Select the Custom category to view and apply some additional number format strings.**

Some Useful Range Object Methods

As you know, a VBA method performs an action. A Range object has dozens of methods but, again, you won't need most of these. In this section, I point out some of the more commonly used Range object methods.

The Select method

Use the Select method to select a range of cells. The following statement selects a range on the active worksheet:

```
Range("A1:C12").Select
```

Before selecting a range, it's often a good idea to use one additional statement to ensure that the correct worksheet is active. For example, if Sheet1 contains the range you want to select, use the following statements to select the range:

```
Sheets("Sheet1").Activate
Range("A1:C12").Select
```

Contrary to what you may expect, the following statement generates an error if Sheet1 is not already the active sheet. In other words, you must use two statements rather than just one: one to activate the sheet and another to select the range.

```
Sheets("Sheet1").Range("A1:C12").Select
```

If you use the GoTo method of the Application object to select a range, you can forget about selecting the right worksheet first. This statement activates Sheet1 and then selects the range:

```
Application.Goto Sheets("Sheet1").Range("A1:C12")
```

The GoTo method is the VBA equivalent of pressing F5 in Excel, which displays the GoTo dialog box.

The Copy and Paste methods

You can perform copy and paste operations in VBA by using the Copy and Paste methods. Note that two different objects come into play. The Copy method is applicable to the Range object, but the Paste method applies to the Worksheet object. It actually makes sense: You copy a range and paste it to a worksheet.

This short macro (courtesy of the macro recorder) copies range A1:A12 and pastes it to the same worksheet, beginning at cell C1:

```
Sub CopyRange()
    Range("A1:A12").Select
    Selection.Copy
    Range("C1").Select
    ActiveSheet.Paste
End Sub
```

Notice that in the preceding example, the ActiveSheet object is used with the Paste method. This is a special version of the Worksheet object that refers to the currently active worksheet. Also notice that the macro selects the range before copying it. However, you don't have to select a range before doing something with it. In fact, the following procedure accomplishes the same task as the preceding example by using a single statement:

```
Sub CopyRange2()
    Range("A1:A12").Copy Range("C1")
End Sub
```

This procedure takes advantage of the fact that the Copy method can use an argument that corresponds to the destination range for the copy operation.

The Clear method

The Clear method deletes the contents of a range, plus all of the cell formatting. For example, if you want to zap everything in column D, the following statement does the trick:

```
Columns("D:D").Clear
```

You should be aware of two related methods. The ClearContents method deletes the contents of the range but leaves the formatting intact. The ClearFormats method deletes the formatting in the range but not the cell contents.

The Delete method

Clearing a range differs from deleting a range. When you *delete* a range, Excel shifts the remaining cells around to fill up the range you deleted.

The following example uses the Delete method to delete row 6:

```
Rows("6:6").Delete
```

When you delete a range that's not a complete row or column, Excel needs to know how to shift the cells. (To see how this works, experiment with the Excel Home⇨Cells⇨Delete command.)

The following statement deletes a range and then fills the resulting gap by shifting the other cells to the left:

```
Range("C6:C10").Delete xlToLeft
```

The Delete method uses an argument that indicates how Excel should shift the remaining cells. In this case, I use a built-in constant (xlToLeft) for the argument. I could also use xlUp, another named constant.

Chapter 9

Using VBA and Worksheet Functions

*I*n previous chapters, I allude to the fact that you can use functions in your VBA expressions. There are three flavors of functions: those built into VBA, those built into Excel, and other functions written in VBA. I provide a full explanation in this chapter. Functions can make your VBA code perform some powerful feats, with little or no programming effort required. If you like that idea, this chapter's for you.

What Is a Function?

Except for a few people who think Excel is a word processor, all Excel users use worksheet functions in their formulas. The most common worksheet function is the SUM function, and you have hundreds of others at your disposal.

A *function* essentially performs a calculation and returns a single value. The SUM function, of course, returns the sum of a range of values. The same holds true for functions used in your VBA expressions: Each function does its thing and returns a single value.

The functions you use in VBA can come from three sources:

✔ Built-in functions provided by VBA

✔ Worksheet functions provided by Excel

✔ Custom functions that you (or someone else) write, using VBA

The rest of this chapter clarifies the differences and (I hope) convinces you of the value of using functions in your VBA code.

Using Built-In VBA Functions

VBA provides numerous built-in functions. Some of these functions take arguments and some do not.

VBA function examples

In this section, I present a few examples of using VBA functions in code. In many of these examples, I use the MsgBox function to display a value in a message box. Yes, MsgBox is a VBA function — a rather unusual one, but a function nonetheless. This useful function displays a message in a pop-up dialog box. For more details about the MsgBox function, see Chapter 15.

A workbook that contains all the examples is available at this book's Web site.

Displaying the system date or time

The first example uses VBA's Date function to display the current system date in a message box:

```
Sub ShowDate()
    MsgBox Date
End Sub
```

Notice that the Date function doesn't use an argument. Unlike worksheet functions, a VBA function with no argument doesn't require an empty set of parentheses. In fact, if you type an empty set of parentheses, the VBE will promptly remove them.

To get the system time, use the Time function. And if you want it all, use the Now function to return both the date and the time.

Finding a string length

The following procedure uses the VBA Len function, which returns the length of a text string. The Len function takes one argument: the string. When you execute this procedure, the message box displays 11 because the argument has 11 characters.

```
Sub GetLength()
    Dim MyString As String
    Dim StringLength As Integer
    MyString = "Hello World"
    StringLength = Len(MyString)
    MsgBox StringLength
End Sub
```

Excel also has a Len function, which you can use in your worksheet formulas. The Excel version and the VBA function work the same.

Displaying the integer part of a number

The following procedure uses the Fix function, which returns the *integer* portion of a value — the value without any decimal digits:

```
Sub GetIntegerPart()
    Dim MyValue As Double
    Dim IntValue As Integer
    MyValue = 123.456
    IntValue = Fix(MyValue)
    MsgBox IntValue
End Sub
```

In this case, the message box displays 123.

VBA has a similar function called Int. The difference between Int and Fix is how each deals with negative numbers. It's a subtle difference, but sometimes it's important.

✔ Int returns the first negative integer that's less than or equal to the argument. Fix (-123.456) returns -124.

✔ Fix returns the first negative integer that's greater than or equal to the argument. Fix (-123.456) returns -123.

Determining a file size

The following Sub procedure displays the size, in bytes, of the Excel executable file. It finds this value by using the FileLen function.

```
Sub GetFileSize()
    Dim TheFile As String
    TheFile = "C:\Program Files\Microsoft Office\Office14\
        Excel.exe"
    MsgBox FileLen(TheFile)
End Sub
```

Notice that this routine *hard codes* the filename (that is, it explicitly states the path). Generally, this isn't a good idea. The file might not be on the C drive, or the Excel folder may have a different name. The following statement shows a better approach:

```
TheFile = Application.Path & "\EXCEL.EXE"
```

Path is a property of the Application object. It simply returns the name of the folder in which the application (that is, Excel) is installed (without a trailing backslash).

Identifying the type of a selected object

The following procedure uses the TypeName function, which returns the type of the selection on the worksheet (as a string):

```
Sub ShowSelectionType()
    Dim SelType As String
    SelType = TypeName(Selection)
    MsgBox SelType
End Sub
```

This could be a Range, a Picture, a Rectangle, a ChartArea, or any other type of object that can be selected.

The TypeName function is very versatile. You can also use this function to determine the data type of a variable.

VBA functions that do more than return a value

A few VBA functions go above and beyond the call of duty. Rather than simply return a value, these functions have some useful side effects. Table 9-1 lists them.

Table 9-1	Functions with Useful Side Benefits
Function	*What It Does*
MsgBox	Displays a handy dialog box containing a message and buttons. The function returns a code that identifies which button the user clicks. See Chapter 15 for details.
InputBox	Displays a simple dialog box that asks the user for some input. The function returns whatever the user enters into the dialog box. I discuss this in Chapter 15.
Shell	Executes another program. The function returns the *task ID* (a unique identifier) of the other program (or an error if the function can't start the other program).

Discovering VBA functions

How do you find out which functions VBA provides? Good question. The best source is the Excel Visual Basic Help system. I compiled a partial list of functions, which I share with you in Table 9-2. I omitted some of the more specialized or obscure functions.

For complete details on a particular function, type the function name into a VBA module, move the cursor anywhere in the text, and press F1.

Table 9-2	VBA's Most Useful Built-In Functions
Function	*What It Does*
Abs	Returns a number's absolute value.
Array	Returns a variant containing an array.
Asc	Converts the first character of a string to its ASCII value.
Atn	Returns the arctangent of a number.
Choose	Returns a value from a list of items.
Chr	Converts an ANSI value to a string.
Cos	Returns a number's cosine.
CurDir	Returns the current path.
Date	Returns the current system date.
DateAdd	Returns a date to which a specified time interval has been added — for example, one month from a particular date.
DateDiff	Returns an integer showing the number of specified time intervals between two dates — for example, the number of months between now and your birthday.
DatePart	Returns an integer containing the specified part of a given date — for example, a date's day of the year.
DateSerial	Converts a date to a serial number.
DateValue	Converts a string to a date.
Day	Returns the day of the month from a date value.
Dir	Returns the name of a file or directory that matches a pattern.
Erl	Returns the line number that caused an error.
Err	Returns the error number of an error condition.
Error	Returns the error message that corresponds to an error number.
Exp	Returns the base of the natural logarithm (e) raised to a power.

(continued)

Table 9-2 *(continued)*

Function	What It Does
FileLen	Returns the number of bytes in a file.
Fix	Returns a number's integer portion.
Format	Displays an expression in a particular format.
GetSetting	Returns a value from the Windows registry.
Hex	Converts from decimal to hexadecimal.
Hour	Returns the hours portion of a time.
InputBox	Displays a box to prompt a user for input.
InStr	Returns the position of a string within another string.
Int	Returns the integer portion of a number.
IPmt	Returns the interest payment for an annuity or loan.
IsArray	Returns True if a variable is an array.
IsDate	Returns True if an expression is a date.
IsEmpty	Returns True if a variable has not been initialized.
IsError	Returns True if an expression is an error value.
IsMissing	Returns True if an optional argument was not passed to a procedure.
IsNull	Returns True if an expression contains no valid data.
IsNumeric	Returns True if an expression can be evaluated as a number.
IsObject	Returns True if an expression references an OLE Automation object.
LBound	Returns the smallest subscript for a dimension of an array.
LCase	Returns a string converted to lowercase.
Left	Returns a specified number of characters from the left of a string.
Len	Returns the number of characters in a string.
Log	Returns the natural logarithm of a number to base.
LTrim	Returns a copy of a string, with any leading spaces removed.
Mid	Returns a specified number of characters from a string.
Minute	Returns the minutes portion of a time value.
Month	Returns the month from a date value.
MsgBox	Displays a message box and (optionally) returns a value.
Now	Returns the current system date and time.
RGB	Returns a numeric RGB value representing a color.

Function	What It Does
Replace	Replaces a substring in a string with another substring.
Right	Returns a specified number of characters from the right of a string.
Rnd	Returns a random number between 0 and 1.
RTrim	Returns a copy of a string, with any trailing spaces removed.
Second	Returns the seconds portion of a time value.
Sgn	Returns an integer that indicates a number's sign.
Shell	Runs an executable program.
Sin	Returns a number's sine.
Space	Returns a string with a specified number of spaces.
Split	Splits a string into parts, using a delimiting character.
Sqr	Returns a number's square root.
Str	Returns a string representation of a number.
StrComp	Returns a value indicating the result of a string comparison.
String	Returns a repeating character or string.
Tan	Returns a number's tangent.
Time	Returns the current system time.
Timer	Returns the number of seconds since midnight.
TimeSerial	Returns the time for a specified hour, minute, and second.
TimeValue	Converts a string to a time serial number.
Trim	Returns a string without leading or trailing spaces.
TypeName	Returns a string that describes a variable's data type.
UBound	Returns the largest available subscript for an array's dimension.
UCase	Converts a string to uppercase.
Val	Returns the numbers contained in a string.
VarType	Returns a value indicating a variable's subtype.
Weekday	Returns a number representing a day of the week.
Year	Returns the year from a date value.

Using Worksheet Functions in VBA

Although VBA offers a decent assortment of built-in functions, you might not always find exactly what you need. Fortunately, you can also use most of Excel's worksheet functions in your VBA procedures. The only worksheet functions that you cannot use are those that have an equivalent VBA function.

VBA makes Excel's worksheet functions available through the WorksheetFunction object, which is contained in the Application object. Therefore, any statement that uses a worksheet function must use the Application.WorksheetFunction qualifier. In other words, you must precede the function name with **Application.WorksheetFunction** (with a dot separating the two). The following is an example:

```
Total = Application.WorksheetFunction.Sum(Range("A1:A12"))
```

You can omit the Application part or the WorksheetFunction part of the expression. In either case, VBA will figure out what you're doing. In other words, these three expressions all work exactly the same:

```
Total = Application.WorksheetFunction.Sum(Range("A1:A12"))
Total = WorksheetFunction.Sum(Range("A1:A12"))
Total = Application.Sum(Range("A1:A12"))
```

My personal preference is to use the WorksheetFunction part just to make it perfectly clear that the code is using an Excel function.

Worksheet function examples

In this section, I demonstrate how to use worksheet functions in your VBA expressions.

Finding the maximum value in a range

Here's an example that shows how to use Excel's MAX worksheet function in a VBA procedure. This procedure displays the maximum value in column A on the active worksheet:

```
Sub ShowMax()
    Dim TheMax As Double
    TheMax = WorksheetFunction.Max(Range("A:A"))
    MsgBox TheMax
End Sub
```

You can use the MIN function to get the smallest value in a range. And, as you might expect, you can use other worksheet functions in a similar manner. For example, you can use the LARGE function to determine the *k*th-largest value in a range. The following expression demonstrates this:

```
SecondHighest = WorksheetFunction.Large(Range("A:A"),2)
```

Notice that the LARGE function uses two arguments; the second argument represents the *k*th part — 2 in this case (the second-largest value).

Calculating a mortgage payment

The next example uses the PMT worksheet function to calculate a mortgage payment. I use three variables to store the data that's passed to the Pmt function as arguments. A message box displays the calculated payment.

```
Sub PmtCalc()
    Dim IntRate As Double
    Dim LoanAmt As Double
    Dim Periods As Integer
    IntRate = 0.0825 / 12
    Periods = 30 * 12
    LoanAmt = 150000
    MsgBox WorksheetFunction. _
        Pmt(IntRate, Periods, -LoanAmt)
End Sub
```

As the following statement shows, you can also insert the values directly as the function arguments:

```
MsgBox WorksheetFunction.Pmt(0.0825 /12, 360, -150000)
```

However, using variables to store the parameters makes the code easier to read and modify, if necessary.

Using a lookup function

The following example uses VBA's InputBox and MsgBox functions, plus Excel's VLOOKUP function. It prompts for a part number and then gets the price from a lookup table. In Figure 9-1, range A1:B13 is named PriceList.

```
Sub GetPrice()
    Dim PartNum As Variant
    Dim Price As Double
    PartNum = InputBox("Enter the Part Number")
    Sheets("Prices").Activate
    Price = WorksheetFunction. _
        VLookup(PartNum, Range("PriceList"), 2, False)
    MsgBox PartNum & " costs " & Price
End Sub
```

You can download this workbook from the book's Web site.

The procedure starts this way:

1. VBA's InputBox function asks the user for a part number.

2. This statement assigns the part number the user enters for the PartNum variable.

3. The next statement activates the Prices worksheet, just in case it's not already the active sheet.

4. The code uses the VLOOKUP function to find the part number in the table.

 Notice that the arguments you use in this statement are the same as those you would use with the function in a worksheet formula. This statement assigns the result of the function to the Price variable.

5. The code displays the price for the part via the MsgBox function.

Figure 9-1:
The range, named PriceList, contains prices for parts.

	A	B	C	D	E	F	G	H	I	J
1	Part	Price								
2	A-132	39.95								
3	A-183	12.95								
4	B-942	16.49				Get A Price				
5	C-832	3.99								
6	C-999	17.59								
7	D-873	19.99								
8	F-143	39.95				Microsoft Excel				
9	G-771	49.95								
10	K-873	129.95				Enter the Part Number		OK		
11	M-732	89.95						Cancel		
12	P-101	3.95								
13	R-932	13.95								
14						C-999				
15										
16										

This procedure doesn't have any error handling, and it fails miserably if you enter a nonexistent part number. (Try it.) If this were an actual application, you would want to add some error-handling statements for a more robust procedure. I discuss error handling in Chapter 12.

Entering worksheet functions

You can't use the Excel Paste Function dialog box to insert a worksheet function into a VBA module. Instead, enter such functions the old-fashioned way: by hand. However, you *can* use the Paste Function dialog box to identify the function you want to use and find out about its arguments.

You can also take advantage of the VBE's Auto List Members option, which displays a drop-down list of all worksheet functions. Just type **Application. WorksheetFunction**, followed by a period. Then you'll see a list of the function you can use.

If this feature isn't working, choose the VBE's Tools⇨Options command, click the Editor tab, and place a check mark next to Auto List Members.

More about Using Worksheet Functions

Newcomers to VBA often confuse VBA's built-in functions and Excel's workbook functions. A good rule to remember is that VBA doesn't try to reinvent the wheel. For the most part, VBA doesn't duplicate Excel worksheet functions.

For most worksheet functions that are unavailable as methods of the WorksheetFunction object, you can use an equivalent VBA built-in operator or function. For example, the MOD worksheet function is not available in the WorksheetFunction object because VBA has an equivalent, its built-in Mod operator.

Bottom line? If you need to use a function, first determine whether VBA has something that meets your needs. If not, check out the worksheet functions. If all else fails, you may be able to write a custom function by using VBA.

Using Custom Functions

I've covered VBA functions and Excel worksheet functions. The third category of functions you can use in your VBA procedures is custom functions. A *custom function* (also known as User Defined Function, UDF) is one you develop yourself by using (what else?) VBA. To use a custom function, you must define it in the workbook in which you use it.

Here's an example of defining a simple Function procedure and then using it in a VBA Sub procedure:

```
Function MultiplyTwo(num1, num2) As Double
    MultiplyTwo = num1 * num2
End Function

Sub ShowResult()
    Dim n1 As Double, n2 As Double
    Dim Result As Double
    n1 = 123
    n2 = 544
    Result = MultiplyTwo(n1, n2)
    MsgBox Result
End Sub
```

The custom function MultiplyTwo has two arguments. The ShowResult Sub procedure uses this Function procedure by passing two arguments to it (in parentheses). The ShowResult procedure then displays a message box showing the value returned by the MultiplyTwo function.

I probably don't have to tell you that the MultiplyTwo function is fairly use-less. It's much more efficient to perform the multiplication in the ShowResult Sub procedure. I include it simply to give you an idea of how a Sub procedure can make use of a custom function.

You can also use custom functions in your worksheet formulas. For example, if MultiplyTwo is defined in your workbook, you can write a formula such as this one:

```
=MultiplyTwo(A1,A2)
```

This formula returns the product of the values in cells A1 and A2.

Custom worksheet functions is an important (and very useful) topic. So important (and useful) that I devote an entire chapter to it. See Chapter 20.

Chapter 10

Controlling Program Flow and Making Decisions

• •

In This Chapter

▶ Discovering methods for controlling the flow of your VBA routines

▶ Finding out about the dreaded GoTo statement

▶ Using If-Then and Select Case structures

▶ Performing looping in your procedures

• •

Some VBA procedures start at the code's beginning and progress line by line to the end, never deviating from this top-to-bottom program flow. Macros that you record always work like this. In many cases, however, you need to control the flow of your code by skipping over some statements, executing some statements multiple times, and testing conditions to determine what the procedure does next. Hang on to your hat and enjoy the ride, because you're about to discover the essence of programming.

Going with the Flow, Dude

Some programming newbies can't understand how a dumb computer can make intelligent decisions. The secret is in several programming constructs that most programming languages support. Table 10-1 provides a quick summary of these constructs. (I explain all of these later in this chapter.)

Table 10-1	Programming Constructs for Making Decisions
Construct	*How It Works*
GoTo statement	Jumps to a particular statement.
If-Then structure	Does something if something else is true.
Select Case	Does any of several things, depending on something's value.
For-Next loop	Executes a series of statements a specified number of times.
Do-While loop	Does something as long as something else remains true.
Do-Until loop	Does something until something else becomes true.

The GoTo Statement

A GoTo statement offers the most straightforward means for changing a program's flow. The GoTo statement simply transfers program execution to a new statement, which is preceded by a label.

Your VBA routines can contain as many labels as you like. A *label* is just a text string followed by a colon.

The following procedure shows how a GoTo statement works:

```
Sub GoToDemo()
    UserName = InputBox("Enter Your Name: ")
    If UserName <> "Bill Gates" Then GoTo WrongName
    MsgBox ("Welcome Bill...")
'    ...[More code here] ...
    Exit Sub
WrongName:
    MsgBox "Sorry. Only Bill Gates can run this."
End Sub
```

The procedure uses the InputBox function to get the user's name. If the user enters a name other than Bill Gates, the program flow jumps to the WrongName label, displays an apologetic message, and the procedure ends. On the other hand, if Mr. Gates runs this procedure and uses his real name, the procedure displays a welcome message and then executes some additional code (not shown in the example). Notice that the Exit Sub statement ends the procedure before the second MsgBox function has a chance to work.

What is structured programming? Does it matter?

If you hang around with programmers, sooner or later you hear the term *structured programming*. This term has been around for decades, and programmers generally agree that structured programs are superior to unstructured programs. So, what is structured programming? And can you do that using VBA?

The basic premise of structured programming is that a routine or code segment should have only one entry point and one exit point. In other words, a block of code should be a stand-alone unit. A program cannot jump into the middle of this unit, nor can it exit at any point except the single exit point. When you write structured code, your program progresses in an orderly

manner and is easy to follow — unlike a program that jumps around in a haphazard fashion. This pretty much rules out using the GoTo statement.

In general, a structured program is easier to read and understand. More important, it's also easier to modify when the need arises.

VBA is indeed a structured language. It offers standard structured constructs such as If-Then-Else, For-Next loops, Do-Until loops, Do-While loops, and Select Case structures. Furthermore, it fully supports module code constructions. If you're new to programming, you should try to develop good structure-programming habits early on. End of lecture.

This simple routine works, but VBA provides several better (and more structured) alternatives than GoTo. In general, you should use GoTo only when you have no other way to perform an action. In real life, the only time you must use a GoTo statement is for trapping errors. (I cover this in Chapter 12.)

Many hard-core programming types have a deep-seated hatred for GoTo statements because using them tends to result in difficult-to-read (and difficult-to-maintain) "spaghetti code." Therefore, you should avoid this subject when talking with other programmers.

Decisions, decisions

In this section, I discuss two programming structures that can empower your VBA procedures with some impressive decision-making capabilities: If-Then and Select Case.

The If-Then structure

Okay, I'll say it: If-Then is VBA's most important control structure. You'll probably use this command on a daily basis (at least *I* do). As in many other aspects of life, effective decision-making is the key to success in writing Excel macros. If this book has the effect I intend, you'll soon share my philosophy

that a successful Excel application boils down to making decisions and acting upon them.

The If-Then structure has this basic syntax:

```
If condition Then statements [Else elsestatements]
```

Use the If-Then structure when you want to execute one or more statements conditionally. The optional Else clause, if included, lets you execute one or more statements if the condition you're testing is not true. Sound confusing? Don't worry; a few examples make this crystal clear.

If-Then examples

The following routine demonstrates the If-Then structure without the optional Else clause:

```
Sub GreetMe()
    If Time < 0.5 Then MsgBox "Good Morning"
End Sub
```

The GreetMe procedure uses VBA's Time function to get the system time. If the current system time is less than .5 (in other words, before noon), the routine displays a friendly greeting. If Time is greater than or equal to .5, the routine ends and nothing happens.

To display a different greeting if Time is greater than or equal to .5, add another If-Then statement after the first one:

```
Sub GreetMe2()
    If Time < 0.5 Then MsgBox "Good Morning"
    If Time >= 0.5 Then MsgBox "Good Afternoon"
End Sub
```

Notice that I used >= (greater than or equal to) for the second If-Then statement. This ensures that the entire day is covered. Had I used > (greater than), then no message would appear if this procedure were executed at precisely 12:00 noon. That's pretty unlikely, but with an important program like this, we don't want to take any chances.

An If-Then-Else example

Another approach to the preceding problem uses the Else clause. Here's the same routine recoded to use the If-Then-Else structure:

```
Sub GreetMe3()
    If Time < 0.5 Then MsgBox "Good Morning" Else _
        MsgBox "Good Afternoon"
End Sub
```

Notice that I use the line continuation character (underscore) in the preceding example. The If-Then-Else statement is actually a single statement. VBA provides a slightly different way of coding If-Then-Else constructs that use an End-If statement. Therefore, the GreetMe procedure can be rewritten as:

```
Sub GreetMe4()
    If Time < 0.5 Then
        MsgBox "Good Morning"
    Else
        MsgBox "Good Afternoon"
    End If
End Sub
```

In fact, you can insert any number of statements under the If part, and any number of statements under the Else part. I prefer to use this syntax because it's easier to read and makes the statements shorter.

What if you need to expand the GreetMe routine to handle three conditions: morning, afternoon, and evening? You have two options: Use three If-Then statements or use a *nested* If-Then-Else structure. *Nesting* means placing an If-Then-Else structure within another If-Then-Else structure. The first approach, the three statements, is simplest:

```
Sub GreetMe5()
  Dim Msg As String
  If Time < 0.5 Then Msg = "Morning"
  If Time >= 0.5 And Time < 0.75 Then Msg = "Afternoon"
  If Time >= 0.75 Then Msg = "Evening"
  MsgBox "Good " & Msg
End Sub
```

The Msg variable gets a different text value, depending on the time of day. The final MsgBox statement displays the greeting: Good Morning, Good Afternoon, or Good Evening.

The following routine performs the same action but uses an If-Then-End If structure:

```
Sub GreetMe6()
    Dim Msg As String
    If Time < 0.5 Then
        Msg = "Morning"
    End If
    If Time >= 0.5 And Time < 0.75 Then
        Msg = "Afternoon"
    End If
    If Time >= 0.75 Then
        Msg = "Evening"
    End If
    MsgBox "Good " & Msg
End Sub
```

How fast are loops?

You might be curious about how fast VBA can run through If-Then loops. Do some systems run code significantly faster than others? As an informal experiment, I posted the following VBA procedure at my blog, and asked others to post their result.

```
Sub TimeTest()
    '100 million random numbers, tests, and math operations
    Dim x As Long
    Dim StartTime As Single
    Dim i As Long
    x = 0
    StartTime = Timer
    For i = 1 To 100000000
        If Rnd <= 0.5 Then x = x + 1 Else x = x - 1
    Next i
    MsgBox Timer - StartTime & " seconds"
End Sub
```

The code loops 100 million times, and performs some operations inside the loop: It generates a random number, does an If-Then comparison, and performs a mathematical operation. When the loop is finished, the elapsed time is displayed in a message box. My system ran through this loop in 8.03 seconds. About 100 others posted their results, and times ranged from about 5 seconds up to about 30 seconds. In other words, some computers are about six times faster than others. That's good to know.

But the real question is, how long would it take me to do this task manually? I wrote 0 on a piece of paper, and I flipped a coin. If it came up heads, I added one to my tally. If it came up tails, I subtracted 1. I did this ten times and it took me 42 seconds. So, one time through my "loop" took 4.2 seconds. Using this information, I calculated that it would take me 799 years to perform this task 100 million times — but only if I work non-stop. The conclusion: My computer is about 52.3 million times faster than I am.

Using ElseIf

In the previous examples, every statement in the routine is executed — even in the morning. A more efficient structure would exit the routine as soon as a condition is found to be true. In the morning, for example, the procedure should display the Good Morning message and then exit — without evaluating the other superfluous conditions.

With a tiny routine like this, you don't have to worry about execution speed. But for larger applications in which speed is important, you should know about another syntax for the If-Then structure. The ElseIf syntax follows:

```
If condition Then
    [statements]
[ElseIf condition-n Then
    [elseifstatements]]
```

```
[Else
    [elsestatements]]
End If
```

Here's how you can rewrite the GreetMe routine by using this syntax:

```
Sub GreetMe7()
  Dim Msg As String
  If Time < 0.5 Then
    Msg = "Morning"
  ElseIf Time >= 0.5 And Time < 0.75 Then
    Msg = "Afternoon"
  Else
    Msg = "Evening"
  End If
  MsgBox "Good " & Msg
End Sub
```

When a condition is true, VBA executes the conditional statements and the If structure ends. In other words, VBA doesn't waste time evaluating the extraneous conditions, which makes this procedure a bit more efficient than the previous examples. The trade-off (there are always trade-offs) is that the code is more difficult to understand. (Of course, you already knew that.)

A workbook that contains all of the GreetMe examples can be downloaded from this book's Web site.

Another If-Then example

Here's another example that uses the simple form of the If-Then structure. This procedure prompts the user for a quantity and then displays the appropriate discount, based on the quantity the user enters:

```
Sub ShowDiscount()
    Dim Quantity As Integer
    Dim Discount As Double
    Quantity = InputBox("Enter Quantity:")
    If Quantity > 0 Then Discount = 0.1
    If Quantity >= 25 Then Discount = 0.15
    If Quantity >= 50 Then Discount = 0.2
    If Quantity >= 75 Then Discount = 0.25
    MsgBox "Discount: " & Discount
End Sub
```

A workbook that contains this section's examples can be downloaded from this book's Web site.

Notice that each If-Then statement in this routine is executed, and the value for Discount can change as the statements are executed. However, the routine ultimately displays the correct value for Discount because I put the If-Then statements in order of ascending Discount values.

The following procedure performs the same tasks by using the alternative ElseIf syntax. In this case, the routine ends immediately after executing the statements for a true condition.

```
Sub ShowDiscount2()
    Dim Quantity As Integer
    Dim Discount As Double
    Quantity = InputBox("Enter Quantity: ")
    If Quantity > 0 And Quantity < 25 Then
        Discount = 0.1
    ElseIf Quantity >= 25 And Quantity < 50 Then
        Discount = 0.15
    ElseIf Quantity >= 50 And Quantity < 75 Then
        Discount = 0.2
    ElseIf Quantity >= 75 Then
        Discount = 0.25
    End If
    MsgBox "Discount: " & Discount
End Sub
```

Personally, I find these multiple If-Then structures rather cumbersome. I generally use the If-Then structure for only simple binary decisions. When a decision involves three or more choices, the Select Case structure offers a simpler, more efficient approach.

The Select Case structure

The Select Case structure is useful for decisions involving three or more options (although it also works with two options, providing an alternative to the If-Then-Else structure).

The syntax for the Select Case structure follows:

```
Select Case testexpression
[Case expressionlist-n
    [statements-n]] . . .
[Case Else
    [elsestatements]]
End Select
```

Don't be scared off by this official syntax. Using the Select Case structure is quite easy.

A Select Case example

The following example shows how to use the Select Case structure. This also shows another way to code the examples presented in the previous section:

```
Sub ShowDiscount3()
    Dim Quantity As Integer
    Dim Discount As Double
    Quantity = InputBox("Enter Quantity: ")
    Select Case Quantity
        Case 0 To 24
            Discount = 0.1
        Case 25 To 49
            Discount = 0.15
        Case 50 To 74
            Discount = 0.2
        Case Is >= 75
            Discount = 0.25
    End Select
    MsgBox "Discount: " & Discount
End Sub
```

In this example, the Quantity variable is being evaluated. The routine is checking for four different cases (0–24, 25–49, 50–74, and 75 or greater).

Any number of statements can follow each Case statement, and they all are executed if the case is true. If you use only one statement, as in this example, you can put the statement on the same line as the Case keyword, preceded by a colon — the VBA statement separator character. In my opinion, this makes the code more compact and a bit clearer. Here's how the routine looks, using this format:

```
Sub ShowDiscount4 ()
    Dim Quantity As Integer
    Dim Discount As Double
    Quantity = InputBox("Enter Quantity: ")
    Select Case Quantity
        Case  0 To 24: Discount = 0.1
        Case 25 To 49: Discount = 0.15
        Case 50 To 74: Discount = 0.2
        Case Is >= 75: Discount = 0.25
    End Select
    MsgBox "Discount: " & Discount
End Sub
```

When VBA executes a Select Case structure, the structure is exited as soon as VBA finds a true case and executes the statements for that case.

A nested Select Case example

As demonstrated in the following example, you can nest Select Case structures. This routine examines the active cell and displays a message describing the cell's contents. Notice that the procedure has three Select Case structures and each has its own End Select statement.

```
Sub CheckCell()
    Dim Msg As String
    Select Case IsEmpty(ActiveCell)
        Case True
            Msg = "is blank."
        Case Else
            Select Case ActiveCell.HasFormula
                Case True
                    Msg = "has a formula"
                Case False
                    Select Case IsNumeric(ActiveCell)
                        Case True
                            Msg = "has a number"
                        Case Else
                            Msg = "has text"
                    End Select
            End Select
    End Select
    MsgBox "Cell " & ActiveCell.Address & " " & Msg
End Sub
```

This example is available at this book's Web site.

The logic goes something like this:

1. Find out whether the cell is empty.

2. If it's not empty, see whether it contains a formula.

3. If there's no formula, find out whether it contains a numeric value or text.

When the routine ends, the Msg variable contains a string that describes the cell's contents. As shown in Figure 10-1, the MsgBox function displays that message.

You can nest Select Case structures as deeply as you need to, but make sure that each Select Case statement has a corresponding End Select statement.

Figure 10-1:
A message
displayed
by the
CheckCell
procedure.

	A	B	C	D	E	F	G	H
1								
2	Jan	32						
3	Feb	0						
4	Mar	5						
5	Apr	43						
6	May	83						
7	Jun	122						
8	Total	285						
9								
10								
11								
12								

Microsoft Excel

Cell B8 has a formula

OK

If you've ever wondered why I indent the code I present here, the previous listing serves as a good example. The indentations really help to make the nesting levels clear (at least I think so). If you don't believe me, take a look at the same procedure without any indentation:

```
Sub CheckCell()
Dim Msg As String
Select Case IsEmpty(ActiveCell)
Case True
Msg = "is blank."
Case Else
Select Case ActiveCell.HasFormula
Case True
Msg = "has a formula"
Case False
Select Case IsNumeric(ActiveCell)
Case True
Msg = "has a number"
Case Else
Msg = "has text"
End Select
End Select
End Select
MsgBox "Cell " & ActiveCell.Address & " " & Msg
End Sub
```

Fairly incomprehensible, eh?

Knocking Your Code for a Loop

The term *looping* refers to repeating a block of VBA statements numerous times. In this section, I explain about several different types of loops.

There are two types of loops: good loops and bad loops. (Good loops get rewarded, and bad loops get sent to their room.)

The following code demonstrates a bad loop. The procedure simply enters consecutive numbers into a range. It starts by prompting the user for two values: a starting value and the total number of cells to fill. (Because InputBox returns a string, I convert the strings to integers by using the CInt function.) This loop uses the GoTo statement to control the flow. The CellCount variable keeps track of how many cells are filled. If this value is less than the number requested by the user, program control loops back to DoAnother.

```
Sub BadLoop()
    Dim StartVal As Long
    Dim NumToFill As Long
    Dim CellCount As Long
    StartVal = InputBox("Enter the starting value: ")
    NumToFill = InputBox("How many cells? ")
    ActiveCell = StartVal
    CellCount = 1
DoAnother:
    ActiveCell.Offset(CellCount, 0) = StartVal + CellCount
    CellCount = CellCount + 1
    If CellCount < NumToFill Then GoTo DoAnother _
        Else Exit Sub
End Sub
```

This routine works as intended, but I'm not particularly proud of it. So why is
it an example of bad looping? As I mention earlier in this chapter, avoid using
a GoTo statement unless it's absolutely necessary. Using GoTo statements to
perform looping

✔ Is contrary to the concept of structured programming. (See the side-
 bar earlier in this chapter, "What is structured programming? Does it
 matter?")

✔ Makes the code more difficult to read.

✔ Is more prone to errors than using structured looping procedures.

VBA has enough structured looping commands that you almost never have
to rely on GoTo statements for your decision-making. Again, the exception is
for error handling.

Now you can move on to a discussion of good looping structures.

For-Next loops

The simplest type of loop is a For-Next loop. Here's the syntax for this
structure:

```
For counter = start To end [Step stepval]
    [statements]
    [Exit For]
    [statements]
Next [counter]
```

The looping is controlled by a counter variable, which starts at one value and
stops at another value. The statements between the For statement and the

Next statement are the statements that get repeated in the loop. To see how this works, keep reading.

A For-Next example

The following example shows a For-Next loop that doesn't use the optional Step value or the optional Exit For statement. This routine loops 20 times and uses the VBA Rnd function to enter a random number into 20 cells, beginning with the active cell:

```
Sub FillRange()
    Dim Count As Long
    For Count = 0 To 19
        ActiveCell.Offset(Count, 0) = Rnd
    Next Count
End Sub
```

In this example, Count (the loop counter variable) starts with a value of 0 and increases by 1 each time through the loop. Because I didn't specify a Step value, VBA uses the default value (1). The Offset method uses the value of Count as an argument. The first time through the loop, Count is 0 and the procedure enters a number into the active cell offset by zero rows. The second time through (Count = 1), the procedure enters a number into the active cell offset by one row, and so on.

Because the loop counter is a normal variable, you can write code to change its value within the block of code between the For and the Next statements. This, however, is a *very bad* practice. Changing the counter within the loop can have unpredictable results. Take special precautions to ensure that your code does not directly change the value of the loop counter.

A For-Next example with a Step

You can use a Step value to skip some values in a For-Next loop. Here's the same procedure as in the preceding section, rewritten to insert random numbers into every other cell:

```
Sub FillRange2()
    Dim Count As Long
    For Count = 0 To 19 Step 2
        ActiveCell.Offset(Count, 0) = Rnd
    Next Count
End Sub
```

This time, Count starts out as 0 and then takes on a value of 2, 4, 6, and so on. The final Count value is 18. The Step value determines how the counter is incremented. Notice that the upper loop value (19) is not used because the highest value of Count after 18 would be 20, and 20 is larger than 19.

Figure 10-2 shows the result of running FillRange2 when cell B2 is the active cell.

Earlier in this chapter, you saw the BadLoop example, which uses a GoTo statement. Here's the same example, which is available on this book's Web site, converted into a good loop by using the For-Next structure:

```
Sub GoodLoop()
    Dim StartVal As Long
    Dim NumToFill As Long
    Dim CellCount As Long
    StartVal = InputBox("Enter the starting value: ")
    NumToFill = InputBox("How many cells? ")
    For CellCount = 1 To NumToFill
        ActiveCell.Offset(CellCount - 1, 0) = _
            StartVal + CellCount - 1
    Next CellCount
End Sub
```

	A	B	C	D	E
1					
2		0.045353			
3					
4		0.414033			
5					
6		0.862619			
7					
8		0.79048			
9					
10		0.373536			
11					
12		0.961953			
13					
14		0.871446			
15					
16		0.056237			
17					
18		0.949557			
19					
20		0.364019			
21					
22					

Figure 10-2: Using a loop to generate random numbers.

A For-Next example with an Exit For statement

A For-Next loop can also include one or more Exit For statements within the loop. When VBA encounters this statement, the loop terminates immediately.

The following example, available on the book's Web site, demonstrates the Exit For statement. This routine identifies which of the active worksheet's cells in column A has the largest value:

```
Sub ExitForDemo()
    Dim MaxVal As Double
    Dim Row As Long
    MaxVal = WorksheetFunction.Max(Range("A:A"))
    For Row = 1 To Rows.Count
```

```
        If Range("A1").Offset(Row-1, 0).Value = MaxVal Then
            Range("A1").Offset(Row-1, 0).Activate
            MsgBox "Max value is in Row " & Row
            Exit For
        End If
    Next Row
End Sub
```

The routine calculates the maximum value in the column by using Excel's MAX function and assigns the result to the MaxVal variable. The For-Next loop then checks each cell in the column. If the cell being checked is equal to MaxVal, the routine doesn't need to continue looping (its job is finished), so the Exit For statement terminates the loop.

Now you might shout "Hey, but you said something about always using a single point of exit!" Well, you're right, and obviously you're getting the hang of this structured programming business. But in some cases, ignoring that rule is a wise decision. In this example it will greatly speed up your code because there's no reason to continue the loop after the value is found.

Before terminating the loop, the procedure activates the cell with the maximum value and informs the user of its location.

Notice that I use Rows.Count in the For statement. The count property of the Rows object returns the number of rows in the worksheet. Therefore, you can use this procedure with earlier versions of Excel (which have fewer rows).

A nested For-Next example

So far, all this chapter's examples use relatively simple loops. However, you can have any number of statements in the loop and nest For-Next loops inside other For-Next loops.

The following example uses a nested For-Next loop to insert random numbers into a 12-row-x-5-column range of cells, as shown in Figure 10-3. Notice that the routine executes the *inner loop* (the loop with the Row counter) once for each iteration of the *outer loop* (the loop with the Col counter). In other words, the routine executes the Cells(Row, Col) = Rnd statement 60 times.

```
Sub FillRange2()
    Dim Col As Long
    Dim Row As Long
    For Col = 1 To 5
        For Row = 1 To 12
            Cells(Row, Col) = Rnd
        Next Row
    Next Col
End Sub
```

	A	B	C	D	E	F	G	H	I
1	0.705548	0.862619	0.4687	0.695116	0.28448				
2	0.533424	0.79048	0.298165	0.980003	0.045649				
3	0.579519	0.373536	0.622697	0.243931	0.295773				
4	0.289562	0.961953	0.647821	0.533873	0.382011		Fill Range		
5	0.301948	0.871446	0.263793	0.10637	0.30097				
6	0.77474	0.056237	0.279342	0.999415	0.948571				
7	0.014018	0.949557	0.829802	0.676176	0.979829				
8	0.760724	0.364019	0.824602	0.015704	0.401374				
9	0.81449	0.524868	0.589163	0.575184	0.27828				
10	0.709038	0.767112	0.986093	0.100052	0.160442				
11	0.045353	0.053505	0.910964	0.103023	0.162822				
12	0.414033	0.592458	0.226866	0.798884	0.646587				
13									

Figure 10-3:
These cells were filled by using a nested For-Next loop.

The next example uses nested For-Next loops to initialize a three-dimensional array with the value 100. This routine executes the statement in the middle of all the loops (the assignment statement) 1,000 times (10 * 10 * 10), each time with a different combination of values for i, j, and k:

```
Sub NestedLoops()
    Dim MyArray(10, 10, 10)
    Dim i As Integer
    Dim j As Integer
    Dim k As Integer
    For i = 1 To 10
        For j = 1 To 10
            For k = 1 To 10
                MyArray(i, j, k) = 100
            Next k
        Next j
    Next i
    ' Other statements go here
End Sub
```

Refer to Chapter 7 for information about arrays.

Do-While loop

VBA supports another type of looping structure known as a Do-While loop. Unlike a For-Next loop, a Do-While loop continues until a specified condition is met. Here's the Do-While loop syntax:

```
Do [While condition]
    [statements]
    [Exit Do]
    [statements]
Loop
```

The following example uses a Do-While loop. This routine uses the active cell as a starting point and then travels down the column, multiplying each cell's value by 2. The loop continues until the routine encounters an empty cell.

```
Sub DoWhileDemo()
    Do While ActiveCell.Value <> Empty
        ActiveCell.Value = ActiveCell.Value * 2
        ActiveCell.Offset(1, 0).Select
    Loop
End Sub
```

Some people prefer to code a Do-While loop as a Do-Loop While loop. This example performs exactly as the previous procedure but uses a different loop syntax:

```
Sub DoLoopWhileDemo()
    Do
        ActiveCell.Value = ActiveCell.Value * 2
        ActiveCell.Offset(1, 0).Select
    Loop While ActiveCell.Value <> Empty
End Sub
```

Here's the key difference between the Do-While and Do-Loop While loops: The Do-While loop always performs its conditional test first. If the test is not true, the instructions inside the loop are never executed. The Do-Loop While loop, on the other hand, always performs its conditional test after the instructions inside the loop are executed. Thus, the loop instructions are always executed at least once, regardless of the test. This difference can sometimes have a big effect on how your program functions.

Do-Until loop

The Do-Until loop structure is similar to the Do-While structure. The two structures differ in their handling of the tested condition. A program continues to execute a Do-While loop *while* the condition remains true. In a Do-Until loop, the program executes the loop *until* the condition is true.

Here's the Do-Until syntax:

```
Do [Until condition]
    statements]
    [Exit Do]
    [statements]
Loop
```

The following example is the same one presented for the Do-While loop but recoded to use a Do-Until loop:

```
Sub DoUntilDemo()
    Do Until IsEmpty(ActiveCell.Value)
        ActiveCell.Value = ActiveCell.Value * 2
        ActiveCell.Offset(1, 0).Select
    Loop
End Sub
```

Just like with the Do-While loop, you may encounter a different form of the
Do-Until loop — a Do-Loop Until loop. The following example, which has the
same effect as the preceding procedure, demonstrates an alternate syntax for
this type of loop:

```
Sub DoLoopUntilDemo()
    Do
        ActiveCell.Value = ActiveCell.Value * 2
        ActiveCell.Offset(1, 0).Select
    Loop Until IsEmpty(ActiveCell.Value)
End Sub
```

There is a subtle difference in how the Do-Until loop and the Do-Loop Until
loop operate. In the former, the test is performed at the beginning of the loop,
before anything in the body of the loop is executed. This means that it is pos-
sible that the code in the loop body will not be executed if the test condition
is met. In the latter version, the condition is tested at the end of the loop.
Therefore, at a minimum, the Do-Loop Until loop always results in the body of
the loop being executed once.

Another way to think about it is like this: The Do-While loop keeps looping as
long as the condition is True. The Do-Until loop keeps looping as long as the
condition is False.

Looping through a Collection

VBA supports yet another type of looping — looping through each object in a
collection of objects. Recall that a collection consists of a number of objects
of the same type. For example, Excel has a collection of all open workbooks
(the Workbooks collection), and each workbook has a collection of work-
sheets (the Worksheets collection).

When you need to loop through each object in a collection, use the For Each-
Next structure. The syntax is

```
For Each element In collection
    [statements]
    [Exit For]
    [statements]
Next [element]
```

The following example loops through each worksheet in the active workbook and deletes the first row of each worksheet:

```
Sub DeleteRow1()
    Dim WkSht As Worksheet
    For Each WkSht In ActiveWorkbook.Worksheets
        WkSht.Rows(1).Delete
    Next WkSht
End Sub
```

In this example, the variable WkSht is an object variable that represents each worksheet in the workbook. Nothing is special about the variable name WkSht — you can use any variable name that you like.

The example that follows loops through the cells in a range, and checks each cell. The code switches the sign of the values (negative values are made positive; positive values are made negative). It does this by multiplying each value times –1. Note that I used an If-Then construct, along with the VBA IsNumeric function, to ensure that the cell contains a numeric value:

```
Sub ChangeSign()
    Dim Cell As Range
    For Each Cell In Range("A1:E50")
        If IsNumeric(Cell.Value) Then
            Cell.Value = Cell.Value * -1
        End If
    Next Cell
End Sub
```

The preceding code sample has a problem: It changes any formulas in the range it loops through to values, zapping your formulas. That's probably not what you want. Here's another version of the Sub that skips formula cells. It checks whether the cell has a formula by accessing the HasFormula property:

```
Sub ChangeSign2()
    Dim Cell As Range
    For Each Cell In Range("A1:E50")
        If Not Cell.HasFormula Then
            If IsNumeric(Cell.Value) Then
                Cell.Value = Cell.Value * -1
            End If
        End If
    Next Cell
End Sub
```

And here's one more For Each-Next example. This procedure loops through each chart on Sheet1 (that is, each member of the ChartObjects collection) and changes each chart to a line chart. In this example, Cht is a variable that represents each ChartObject. If Sheet1 has no ChartObjects, nothing happens.

```
Sub ChangeCharts()
    Dim Cht As ChartObject
    For Each Cht In Sheets("Sheet1").ChartObjects
        Cht.Chart.ChartType = xlLine
    Next Cht
End Sub
```

To write a procedure like ChangeCharts, you need to know something about the object model for charts. You can get that information by recording a macro to find out which objects are involved and then checking the Help system for details.

Excel 2007 users are out of luck here: The macro recorder in Excel 2007 does not record all chart changes you make.

Chapter 11

Automatic Procedures and Events

. .

In This Chapter

▶ Knowing the event types that can trigger an execution

▶ Finding out where to place your event-handler VBA code

▶ Executing a macro when a workbook is opened or closed

▶ Executing a macro when a workbook or worksheet is activated

. .

*Y*ou have a number of ways to execute a VBA Sub procedure. One way is to arrange for the Sub to be executed automatically. In this chapter, I cover the ins and outs of this potentially useful feature, explaining how to set things up so that a macro is executed automatically when a particular event occurs. (No, this chapter is not about capital punishment.)

Preparing for the Big Event

What types of events am I talking about here? Good question. An *event* is basically something that happens in Excel. Following are a few examples of the types of events that Excel can deal with:

✔ A workbook is opened or closed.

✔ A window is activated.

✔ A worksheet is activated or deactivated.

✔ Data is entered into a cell or the cell is edited.

✔ A workbook is saved.

✔ A worksheet is calculated.

✔ An object, such as a button, is clicked.

✔ A particular key or key combination is pressed.

✔ A particular time of day occurs.

✔ An error occurs.

Most Excel programmers never need to worry about most of the events in this list. You should, however, at least know that these events exist because they may come in handy someday. In this chapter, I discuss the most commonly used events. To simplify things, I talk about two types of events: workbook and worksheet.

Table 11-1 lists most of the workbook-related events. If, for some reason, you need to see the complete list of workbook-related events, you'll find it in the Help system.

Table 11-1	Workbook Events
Event	*When It's Triggered*
Activate	The workbook is activated.
AddinInstall	An add-in is installed (relevant only for add-ins).
AddinUninstall	The add-in is uninstalled (relevant only for add-ins).
BeforeClose	The workbook is closed.
BeforePrint	The workbook is printed.
BeforeSave	The workbook is saved.
Deactivate	The workbook is deactivated.
NewSheet	A new sheet is added to the workbook.
Open	The workbook is opened.
SheetActivate	A sheet in the workbook is activated.
SheetBefore DoubleClick	A cell in the workbook is double-clicked.
SheetBefore RightClick	A cell in the workbook is right-clicked.
SheetCalculate	A sheet in the workbook is recalculated.
SheetChange	A change is made to a cell in the workbook.
SheetDeactivate	A sheet in the workbook is deactivated.
SheetFollowHyperlink	A hyperlink in a worksheet is clicked.
SheetSelectionChange	The selection is changed.
WindowActivate	The workbook window is activated.
WindowDeactivate	The workbook window is deactivated.
WindowResize	The workbook window is resized.

Table 11-2 lists most of the worksheet-related events.

Table 11-2	Worksheet Events
Event	*When It's Triggered*
Activate	The worksheet is activated.
BeforeDoubleClick	A cell in the worksheet is double-clicked.
BeforeRightClick	A cell in the worksheet is right-clicked.
Calculate	The worksheet is recalculated.
Change	A change is made to a cell in the worksheet.
Deactivate	The worksheet is deactivated.
FollowHyperlink	A hyperlink is activated.
SelectionChange	The selection is changed.

Are events useful?

At this point, you may be wondering how these events can be useful. Here's a quick example.

Suppose you have a workbook in which you enter data in column A. Your boss tells you that he needs to know exactly when each data point was entered. Entering data is an event — a WorksheetChange event. You can write a macro that responds to this event. That macro kicks in whenever the worksheet is changed. If the change was made in column A, the macro puts the date and time in column B, next to the data point that was entered.

In case you're curious, here's what such a macro would look like. (It should be in the Code module for the worksheet.) Probably a lot simpler than you thought it would be, eh?

```
Private Sub Worksheet_Change(ByVal Target As Range)
    If Target.Column = 1 Then
        Target.Offset(0, 1) = Now
    End If
End Sub
```

Just because your workbook contains procedures that respond to events doesn't guarantee that those procedures will actually run. As you know, it's possible to open a workbook with macros disabled. In such a case, all macros (even procedures that respond to events) are turned off. Keep this fact in mind when you create workbooks that rely on event-handler procedures.

Programming event-handler procedures

A VBA procedure that executes in response to an event is called an *event-handler procedure*. These are always Sub procedures (as opposed to Function procedures). Writing these event-handlers is relatively straightforward after you understand how the process works. It boils down to a few steps, all of which I explain later:

1. **Identify the event you want to trigger the procedure.**
2. **Press Alt+F11 to Activate the Visual Basic Editor.**
3. **In the VBE Project Window, double-click the appropriate object listed under Microsoft Excel Objects.**

 For workbook-related events, the object is ThisWorkbook. For a worksheet-related event, the object is a Worksheet object (such as Sheet1).

4. **In the Code window for the object, write the event-handler procedure that is executed when the event occurs.**

 This procedure will have a special name that identifies it as an event-handler procedure.

These steps become clearer as you progress through the chapter. Trust me.

Where Does the VBA Code Go?

It's very important to understand where your event-handler procedures go. They must reside in the Code window of an Object module. They do not go in a standard VBA module. If you put your event-handler procedure in the wrong place, it simply won't work. And you won't see any error messages either.

Figure 11-1 shows the VBE window with one project displayed in the Project window. (Refer to Chapter 3 for some background on the VBE.) Notice that the VBA project for Book1 is fully expanded and consists of several objects:

- ✔ One object for each worksheet in the workbook (in this case, three Sheet objects)
- ✔ An object labeled ThisWorkbook
- ✔ A VBA module that I inserted manually by using the Insert⇨Module command

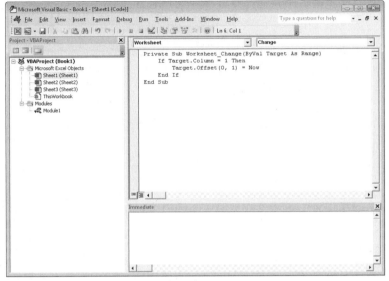

Double-clicking any of these objects displays the code associated with the item, if any.

The event-handler procedures that you write go into the Code window for the ThisWorkbook item (for workbook-related events) or one of the Sheet objects (for worksheet-related events).

In Figure 11-1, the Code window for the Sheet1 object is displayed, and it happens to have a single event-handler procedure defined. Notice the two drop-down controls at the top of the Code module? Keep reading to find out why those are useful.

Writing an Event-Handler Procedure

The VBE helps you out when you're ready to write an event-handler procedure; it displays a list of all events for the selected object.

At the top of each Code window, you find two drop-down lists:

- ✔ The Object drop-down list (the one on the left)
- ✔ The Procedure drop-down list (the one on the right)

By default, the Object drop-down list in the Code window displays General. If you're writing an event-handler for the ThisWorkbook object, you need to choose Workbook from the Object drop-down (it's the only other choice).

If you're writing an event-handler for a Sheet object, you need to choose Worksheet (again, the only other choice).

After you've made your choice from the Object drop-down list, then you can choose the event from the Procedure drop-down list. Figure 11-2 shows the choices for a workbook-related event.

Figure 11-2:
Choosing an event in the Code window for the ThisWork-book object.

When you select an event from the list, VBE automatically starts creating an event-handler procedure for you. This is a very useful feature, because you can verify that the proper arguments are used.

Here's a little quirk. When you first selected Workbook from the Object list, VBE always assumes that you want to create an event-handler procedure for the Open event and creates it for you. If you're actually creating a Workbook_ Open procedure, that's fine. But if you're creating a different event-procedure, you need to delete the empty Workbook_Open Sub that Excel created.

VBE's help goes only so far, however. It writes the Sub statement and the End Sub statement. Writing the VBA code that goes between these two state-ments is your job.

You don't really have to use those two drop-downs, but it makes your job easier because the name of the event-handler procedure is critically impor-tant. If you don't get the name exactly right, it won't work. Plus, some event-handler procedures use one or more arguments in the Sub statement. There's no way you can remember what those arguments are. For example, if you select SheetActivate from the event list for a Workbook object, VBE writes the following Sub statement:

```
Private Sub Workbook_SheetActivate(ByVal Sh As Object)
```

In this case, Sh is the argument passed to the procedure and is a variable that represents the sheet in the activated workbook. Examples in this chapter clarify this point.

Introductory Examples

In this section, I provide a few examples so that you can get the hang of this event-handling business.

The Open event for a workbook

One of the most commonly used events is the Workbook Open event. Assume that you have a workbook that you use every day. The Workbook_Open procedure in this example is executed every time the workbook is opened. The procedure checks the day of the week; if it's Friday, the code displays a reminder message for you.

To create the procedure that is executed whenever the Workbook Open event occurs, follow these steps:

1. **Open the workbook.**

 Any workbook will do.

2. **Press Alt+F11 to activate the VBE.**

3. **Locate the workbook in the Project window.**

4. **Double-click the project name to display its items, if necessary.**

5. **Double-click the ThisWorkbook item.**

 The VBE displays an empty Code window for the ThisWorkbook object.

6. **In the Code window, select Workbook from the Object (left) drop-down list.**

 The VBE enters the beginning and ending statements for a Workbook_ Open procedure.

7. **Enter the following statements, so the complete event-procedure looks like this:**

```
Private Sub Workbook_Open()
    Dim Msg As String
    If WeekDay(Now) = 6 Then
        Msg = "Today is Friday. Make sure that you "
        Msg = Msg & "do your weekly backup!"
        MsgBox Msg
    End If
End Sub
```

The Code window should look like Figure 11-3.

Figure 11-3:
The event-
handler
procedure
is executed
when the
workbook is
opened.

Workbook_Open is executed automatically whenever the workbook is opened. It uses VBA's WeekDay function to determine the day of the week. If it's Friday (day 6), a message box reminds the user to perform a weekly file backup. If it's not Friday, nothing happens.

If today isn't Friday, you might have a hard time testing this procedure. Here's a chance to test your own skill at VBA. You can modify this procedure any way you like. For example, the following version displays a message every time the workbook is opened. This gets annoying after a while, trust me.

```
Private Sub Workbook_Open()
    Msg = "This is Frank's cool workbook!"
    MsgBox Msg
End Sub
```

A Workbook_Open procedure can do almost anything. These event-handlers are often used for the following:

✔ Displaying welcome messages (such as in Frank's cool workbook)

✔ Opening other workbooks

✔ Activating a particular worksheet in the workbook

✔ Setting up custom shortcut menus

The BeforeClose event for a workbook

Here's an example of the Workbook_BeforeClose event-handler procedure, which is executed automatically immediately before the workbook is closed. This procedure is located in the Code window for a ThisWorkbook object:

```
Private Sub Workbook_BeforeClose(Cancel As Boolean)
    Dim Msg As String
    Dim Ans As Integer
    Dim FName As String
    Msg = "Would you like to make a backup of this file?"
    Ans = MsgBox(Msg, vbYesNo)
    If Ans = vbYes Then
        FName = "F:\BACKUP\" & ThisWorkbook.Name
        ThisWorkbook.SaveCopyAs FName
    End If
End Sub
```

This routine uses a message box to ask the user whether he would like to make a backup copy of the workbook. If the answer is yes, the code uses the SaveCopyAs method to save a backup copy of the file on drive F. If you adapt this procedure for your own use, you probably need to change the drive and path.

Excel programmers often use a Workbook_BeforeClose procedure to clean up after themselves. For example, if you use a Workbook_Open procedure to change some settings when you open a workbook (hiding the status bar, for example), it's only appropriate that you return the settings to their original state when you close the workbook. You can perform this electronic house-keeping with a Workbook_BeforeClose procedure.

There is an unfortunate caveat with the Workbook_BeforeClose event. If you close Excel and any open file has been changed since the last save, Excel will show its usual "Do you want to save changes" message box. Clicking the Cancel button cancels the entire closing process. But the Workbook_BeforeClose event will have been executed anyway.

The BeforeSave event for a workbook

The BeforeSave event, as its name implies, is triggered before a workbook is saved. This event occurs when you use either the File⇨Save or File⇨Save As command.

The following procedure, which is placed in the Code window for a ThisWorkbook object, demonstrates the BeforeSave event. The routine updates the value in a cell (cell A1 on Sheet1) every time the workbook is saved. In other words, cell A1 serves as a counter to keep track of the number of times the file was saved.

```
Private Sub Workbook_BeforeSave(ByVal SaveAsUI _
    As Boolean, Cancel As Boolean)
        Sheets("Sheet1").Range("A1").Value = _
            Sheets("Sheet1").Range("A1").Value +1
End Sub
```

Notice that the Workbook_BeforeSave procedure has two arguments, SaveAsUI and Cancel. To demonstrate how these arguments work, examine the following macro, which is executed before the workbook is saved. This procedure prevents the user from saving the workbook with a different name. If the user chooses the File⇨Save As command, then the SaveAsUI argument is True.

When the code executes, it checks the SaveAsUI value. If this variable is True, the procedure displays a message and sets Cancel to True, which cancels the Save operation.

```
Private Sub Workbook_BeforeSave(ByVal SaveAsUI _
    As Boolean, Cancel As Boolean)
        If SaveAsUI Then
            MsgBox "You cannot save a copy of this workbook!"
            Cancel = True
        End If
End Sub
```

Keep in mind that this procedure won't really prevent anyone from saving a copy with a different name. If someone really wants to do it, they can just open the workbook with macros disabled. When macros are disabled, event-handler procedures are also disabled — which makes sense because they are, after all, macros.

Examples of Activation Events

Another category of events consists of activating and deactivating objects — specifically, sheets and workbooks.

Activate and deactivate events in a sheet

Excel can detect when a particular sheet is activated or deactivated and execute a macro when either of these events occurs. These event-handler procedures go in the Code window for the Sheet object.

You can quickly access a sheet's code window by right-clicking on the sheet's tab and selecting View Code.

The following example shows a simple procedure that is executed whenever a particular sheet is activated. This code simply pops up a message box that displays the name of the active sheet:

```
Private Sub Worksheet_Activate()
    MsgBox "You just activated " & ActiveSheet.Name
End Sub
```

Here's another example that activates cell A1 whenever the sheet is activated:

```
Private Sub Worksheet_Activate()
    Range("A1").Activate
End Sub
```

Although the code in these two procedures is about as simple as it gets, event-handler procedures can be as complex as you like.

The following procedure (which is stored in the Code window for the Sheet1 object) uses the Deactivate event to prevent a user from activating any other sheet in the workbook. If Sheet1 is deactivated (that is, another sheet is activated), the user gets a message and Sheet1 is activated.

```
Private Sub Worksheet_Deactivate()
    MsgBox "You must stay on Sheet1"
    Sheets("Sheet1").Activate
End Sub
```

By the way, I don't recommend using procedures, such as this one, that attempt to take over Excel. These so-called "dictator" applications can be very frustrating and confusing for the user. Rather, I recommend training the user how to use your application correctly.

Activate and deactivate events in a workbook

The previous examples use events associated with a specific worksheet. The ThisWorkbook object also handles events that deal with sheet activation and deactivation. The following procedure, which is stored in the Code window for the ThisWorkbook object, is executed when *any* sheet in the workbook is activated. The code displays a message with the name of the activated sheet.

```
Private Sub Workbook_SheetActivate(ByVal Sh As Object)
    MsgBox Sh.Name
End Sub
```

The Workbook_SheetActivate procedure uses the Sh argument. Sh is a variable that represents the active Sheet object. The message box displays the Sheet object's Name property. The next example is contained in a ThisWorkbook Code window. It consists of two event-handler procedures:

- Workbook_SheetDeactivate: Executed when any sheet in the workbook is deactivated. It stores the sheet that is deactivated in an object variable. (The Set keyword creates an object variable.)

- Workbook_SheetActivate: Executed when any sheet in the workbook is activated. It checks the type of sheet that is activated (using the TypeName function). If the sheet is a chart sheet, the user gets a message (see Figure 11-4). When the OK button in the message box is clicked, the *previous* sheet (which is stored in the OldSheet variable) is reactivated.

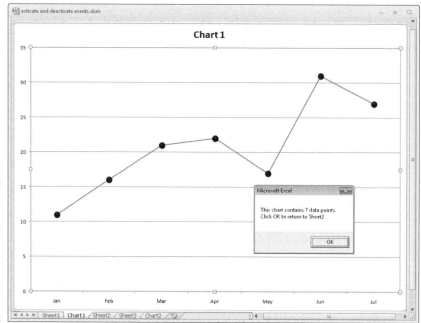

Figure 11-4: When a chart sheet is activated, the user sees a message like this.

A workbook that contains this code is available at this book's Web site.

```
Dim OldSheet As Object

Private Sub Workbook_SheetDeactivate(ByVal Sh As Object)
    Set OldSheet = Sh
End Sub

Private Sub Workbook_SheetActivate(ByVal Sh As Object)
    Dim Msg As String
    If TypeName(Sh) = "Chart" Then
        Msg = "This chart contains "
        Msg = Msg & ActiveChart.SeriesCollection(1).
            Points.Count
        Msg = Msg & " data points." & vbNewLine
        Msg = Msg & "Click OK to return to " & OldSheet.
            Name
        MsgBox Msg
        OldSheet.Activate
    End If
End Sub
```

Workbook activation events

Excel also recognizes the event that occurs when you activate or deactivate a particular workbook. The following code, which is contained in the Code window for the ThisWorkbook object, is executed whenever the workbook is activated. The procedure simply maximizes the workbook's window.

```
Private Sub Workbook_Activate()
    ActiveWindow.WindowState = xlMaximized
End Sub
```

The Workbook_Deactivate code, shown next, is executed when a workbook is deactivated. Here's an example procedure that copies the selected range. It might be useful if you're copying data from lots of different areas and pasting them to a different workbook. Select the range, activate the other workbook, select the destination, and press Ctrl+V to paste the copied data.

```
Private Sub Workbook_Deactivate()
    ThisWorkbook.Windows(1).RangeSelection.Copy
End Sub
```

Simple as it is, this procedure required some experimentation before I got it to work correctly. First I tried this:

```
Selection.Copy
```

This statement didn't work as I had intended. It copied the range from the second workbook (the one I activated after deactivating the first workbook). That's because the second workbook became the active workbook after the deactivation event occurred.

This statement didn't work either. In fact, it gave me a runtime error:

```
ThisWorkbook.ActiveSheet.Selection.Copy
```

I eventually remembered the RangeSelection property of a Window object. And that one did the trick.

Other Worksheet-Related Events

In the preceding section, I present examples for worksheet activation and deactivation events. In this section, I discuss three additional events that occur in worksheets: double-clicking a cell, right-clicking a cell, and changing a cell.

The BeforeDoubleClick event

You can set up a VBA procedure to be executed when the user double-clicks a cell. In the following example (which is stored in the Code window for a Sheet object), double-clicking a cell in that sheet makes the cell bold (if it's not bold) or not bold (if it is bold):

```
Private Sub Worksheet_BeforeDoubleClick _
    (ByVal Target As Excel.Range, Cancel As Boolean)
    Target.Font.Bold = Not Target.Font.Bold
    Cancel = True
End Sub
```

The Worksheet_BeforeDoubleClick procedure has two arguments: Target and Cancel. Target represents the cell (a Range object) that was double-clicked. If Cancel is set to True, the default double-click action doesn't occur.

The default action for double-clicking a cell is to put Excel into cell edit mode. I didn't want that to happen, so I set Cancel to True.

The BeforeRightClick event

The BeforeRightClick event is similar to the BeforeDoubleClick event, except that it consists of right-clicking a cell. The following procedure checks to see whether the cell that was right-clicked contains a numeric value. If so, the

code displays the Format Number dialog box and sets the Cancel argument to True (avoiding the normal shortcut menu display). If the cell does not contain a numeric value, nothing special happens — the shortcut menu is displayed as usual.

```
Private Sub Worksheet_BeforeRightClick _
    (ByVal Target As Excel.Range, Cancel As Boolean)
    If IsNumeric(Target) And Not IsEmpty(Target) Then
        Application.CommandBars.ExecuteMso _
            ("NumberFormatsDialog")
        Cancel = True
    End If
End Sub
```

Notice that the code, which is available on this book's Web site, makes an additional check to see if the cell is not empty. This is because VBA considers empty cells to be numeric. Don't ask me why; it just does.

The Change event

The Change event occurs whenever any cell on the worksheet is changed. In the following example, the Worksheet_Change procedure effectively prevents a user from entering a nonnumeric value into cell A1. This code is stored in the Code window for a Sheet object.

```
Private Sub Worksheet_Change(ByVal Target As Range)
    If Target.Address = "$A$1" Then
        If Not IsNumeric(Target) Then
            MsgBox "Enter a number in cell A1."
            Range("A1").ClearContents
            Range("A1").Activate
        End If
    End If
End Sub
```

The single argument for the Worksheet_Change procedure (Target) represents the range that was changed. The first statement sees whether the cell's address is A1. If so, the code uses the IsNumeric function to determine whether the cell contains a numeric value. If not, a message appears, and the cell's value is erased. Cell A1 is then activated — useful if the cell pointer moved to a different cell after the entry was made. If the change occurs in any cell except A1, nothing happens.

Why not use data validation?

You may be familiar with the Data⇨Data Tools⇨Data Validation command. This is a handy feature that makes it easy to ensure that only data of the proper type is entered into a particular cell or range. Although the

Data⇨Data Tools⇨Data Validation command is useful, it's definitely not foolproof. To demonstrate, start with a blank worksheet and perform the following steps:

1. **Select the range A1:C12.**

2. **Choose Data⇨Data Tools⇨Data Validation.**

3. **Set up your validation criteria to accept only whole numbers between 1 and 12, as shown in Figure 11-5.**

Figure 11-5: These settings allow only whole numbers between 1 and 12.

Now, enter some values in the range A1:C12. The data validation works as it should. But to see it fall apart at the seams, try this:

1. **Enter –1 into any cell outside the validation range (any cell not in A1:C12).**

2. **Press Ctrl+C to copy the negative number to the Clipboard.**

3. **Select any cell in the validation range.**

4. **Press Ctrl+V to paste the copied value.**

You find that the paste operation is allowable. Look a little closer, however, and you find that the cell into which you pasted the negative value no longer has any validation criteria. Pasting wipes out the data validation criteria! The severity of this flaw depends on your application. In the next section, I describe how to use the Change event to provide for better validating.

Pasting wipes out data validation because Excel considers validation a format for a cell. Therefore, it is in the same classification as font size, color, or other similar attributes. When you paste a cell, you are replacing the formats in the target cell with those of the source cell. Unfortunately, those formats also include your validation rules.

Preventing data validation from being destroyed

The procedure in this section demonstrates how to prevent users from copying data and wiping out data validation rules. This example assumes that the worksheet has a range named InputArea, and this input area contains data validation rules (set up by using the Data⇨Data Tools⇨Data Validation command). The range can have any validation rules you want.

A workbook that contains this code is available at this book's Web site:

```
Private Sub Worksheet_Change(ByVal Target As Range)
    Dim VT As Long
    'Do all cells in the validation range
    'still have validation?
    On Error Resume Next
    VT = Range("InputRange").Validation.Type
    If Err.Number <> 0 Then
        Application.Undo
        MsgBox "Your last operation was canceled." & _
        "It would have deleted data validation rules.", _
        vbCritical
    End If
End Sub
```

The procedure is executed whenever a cell is changed. It checks the validation type of the range (named InputRange) that is *supposed* to contain the data validation rules. If the VT variable contains an error, that means that one or more cells in the InputRange no longer have data validation (the user probably copied some data over it). If that's the case, the code executes the Undo method of the Application object and reverses the user's action. Then it displays a message box.

The net effect? It's impossible to wipe out the validation rules by copying data. When Excel is broken, use VBA to fix it.

Events Not Associated with Objects

The events that I discuss previously in this chapter are associated with either a workbook object or a worksheet object. In this section, I discuss two types of events that are not associated with objects: time and keypresses.

Because time and keypresses aren't associated with a particular object such as a workbook or a worksheet, you program these events in a normal VBA module (unlike the other events discussed in this chapter).

The OnTime event

The OnTime event occurs when a particular time of day occurs. The following example demonstrates how to get Excel to execute a procedure when the 3:00 p.m. event occurs. In this case, a robot voice tells you to wake up, accompanied by a message box:

```
Sub SetAlarm()
    Application.OnTime 0.625, "DisplayAlarm"
End Sub

Sub DisplayAlarm()
    Application.Speech.Speak ("Hey, wake up")
    MsgBox " It's time for your afternoon break!"
End Sub
```

In this example, I use the OnTime method of the Application object. This method takes two arguments: the time (0.625 or 3:00 p.m.) and the name of the Sub procedure to execute when the time event occurs (DisplayAlarm).

This procedure is quite useful if you tend to get so wrapped up in your work that you forget about meetings and appointments. Just set an OnTime event to remind yourself.

Most people (this author included) find it difficult to think of time in terms of the Excel numbering system. Therefore, you may want to use the VBA TimeValue function to represent the time. TimeValue converts a string that looks like a time into a value that Excel can handle. The following statement shows an easier way to program an event for 3:00 p.m.:

```
Application.OnTime TimeValue("3:00:00 pm"), "DisplayAlarm"
```

If you want to schedule an event relative to the current time — for example, 20 minutes from now — you can use a statement like this:

```
Application.OnTime Now + TimeValue("00:20:00"),
        "DisplayAlarm"
```

You can also use the OnTime method to run a VBA procedure on a particular day. You must make sure that your computer keeps running and that the workbook with the procedure is kept open. The following statement runs the DisplayAlarm procedure at 5:00 p.m. on December 31, 2010:

```
Application.OnTime DateValue("12/31/2010 5:00 pm"), _
        "DisplayAlarm"
```

This particular code line could come in handy to warn you that you need to go home and get ready for the New Year's Eve festivities.

Here's another example that uses the OnTime event. Executing the UpdateClock procedures writes the time to cell A1 and also programs another event five seconds later. This event reruns the UpdateClock procedure. The net effect is that cell A1 is updated with the current time every five seconds. To stop the events, execute the StopClock procedure (which cancels the event). Note that NextTick is a module-level variable that stores the time for the next event.

```
Dim NextTick As Date

Sub UpdateClock()
'    Updates cell A1 with the current time
     ThisWorkbook.Sheets(1).Range("A1") = Time
'    Set up the next event five seconds from now
     NextTick = Now + TimeValue("00:00:05")
     Application.OnTime NextTick, "UpdateClock"
End Sub

Sub StopClock()
'    Cancels the OnTime event (stops the clock)
     On Error Resume Next
     Application.OnTime NextTick, "UpdateClock", , False
End Sub
```

The OnTime event persists even after the workbook is closed. In other words, if you close the workbook without running the StopClock procedure, the workbook will reopen itself in five seconds (assuming that Excel is still running). To prevent this, use a Workbook_BeforeClose event procedure that contains the following statement:

```
Call StopClock
```

The OnTime method has two additional arguments. If you plan to use this method, you should refer to the online help for complete details.

If you'd like to see a rather complicated application, download a copy of my analog clock workbook, shown in Figure 11-6. The clock face is actually a chart, and the chart is updated every second to display the time of day. Useless, but fun.

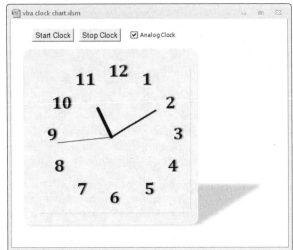

Figure 11-6:
My analog
clock
application.

Keypress events

While you work, Excel constantly monitors what you type. Because of this, you can set up a keystroke or a key combination to execute a procedure.

Here's an example that reassigns the PgDn and PgUp keys:

```
Sub Setup_OnKey()
    Application.OnKey "{PgDn}", "PgDn_Sub"
    Application.OnKey "{PgUp}", "PgUp_Sub"
End Sub

Sub PgDn_Sub()
    On Error Resume Next
      ActiveCell.Offset(1, 0).Activate
End Sub

Sub PgUp_Sub()
    On Error Resume Next
      ActiveCell.Offset(-1, 0).Activate
End Sub
```

After setting up the OnKey events by executing the Setup_OnKey procedure, pressing PgDn moves you down one row. Pressing PgUp moves you up one row.

Notice that the key codes are enclosed in braces, not in parentheses. For a complete list of keyboard codes, consult the Help system. Search for *OnKey*.

In this example, I use On Error Resume Next to ignore any errors that are generated. For example, if the active cell is in the first row, trying to move up one row causes an error that can safely be ignored. And if a chart sheet is active, there is no active cell.

By executing the following routine, you cancel the OnKey events:

```
Sub Cancel_OnKey()
    Application.OnKey "{PgDn}"
    Application.OnKey "{PgUp}"
End Sub
```

Using an empty string as the second argument for the OnKey method does *not* cancel the OnKey event. Rather, it causes Excel to simply ignore the keystroke. For example, the following statement tells Excel to ignore Alt+F4. The percent sign represents the Alt key:

```
Application.OnKey "%{F4}", ""
```

Although you can use the OnKey method to assign a shortcut key for executing a macro, you should use the Macro Options dialog box for this task. For more details, see Chapter 5.

If you close the workbook that contains the code and leave Excel open, the OnKey method will not be reset. As a consequence, pressing the shortcut key will cause Excel to automatically open the file with the macro. To prevent this from happening, you should include code in your Workbook_BeforeClose event code (shown earlier in this chapter) to reset the Onkey event.

Chapter 12

Error-Handling Techniques

*T*o err is human. To anticipate errors is divine. When working with VBA, you should be aware of two broad classes of errors: programming errors and *run-time errors*. (I cover programming errors, also known as *bugs,* in Chapter 13.) A well-written program handles errors the way Fred Astaire danced: gracefully. Fortunately, VBA includes several tools to help you identify errors — and then handle them gracefully.

Types of Errors

If you've tried any of the examples in this book, you have probably encountered one or more error messages. Some of these errors result from bad VBA code. For example, you may spell a keyword incorrectly or type a statement with the wrong syntax. If you make such an error, you won't even be able to execute the procedure until you correct it.

This chapter does not deal with those types of errors. Instead, I discuss run-time errors — the errors that occur while Excel executes your VBA code. More specifically, this chapter covers the following fascinating topics:

✔ Identifying errors

✔ Doing something about the errors that occur

✔ Recovering from errors

✔ Creating intentional errors (Yes, sometimes an error can be a good thing.)

The ultimate goal of error handling is to write code that avoids displaying Excel's error messages as much as possible. In other words, you want to anticipate potential errors and deal with them before Excel has a chance to rear its ugly head with a (usually) less-than-informative error message.

An Erroneous Example

To get things started, I developed a short VBA macro. Activate the VBE, insert a module, and enter the following code:

```
Sub EnterSquareRoot()
    Dim Num As Double
'   Prompt for a value
    Num = InputBox("Enter a value")

'   Insert the square root
    ActiveCell.Value = Sqr(Num)
End Sub
```

As shown in Figure 12-1, this procedure asks the user for a value. It then performs a magical calculation and enters the square root of that value into the active cell.

Figure 12-1:
The
InputBox
function
displays a
dialog box
that asks
the user for
a value.

You can execute this procedure directly from the VBE by pressing F5. Alternatively, you may want to add a button to a worksheet (use Developer⇨ Controls⇨Insert and select the Form controls button to do this) and then assign the macro to the button. (Excel prompts you for the macro to assign.) Then you can run the procedure by simply clicking the button.

The macro's not quite perfect

Execute the code a couple of times to try it out. It works pretty well, doesn't it? Now try entering a negative number when you are prompted for a value. Oops. Trying to calculate the square root of a negative number is illegal on this planet. Excel responds with the message shown in Figure 12-2, indicating that your code generated a run-time error. For now, just click the End button. If you click the Debug button, Excel suspends the macro so you can use the debugging tools to help track down the error. (I describe the debugging tools in Chapter 13.)

Figure 12-2:
Excel
displays
this error
message
when the
procedure
attempts to
calculate
the square
root of a
negative
number.

Most folks don't find the Excel error messages (for example, *Invalid procedure call or argument*) very helpful. To improve the procedure, you need to anticipate this error and handle it more gracefully. In other words, you need to add some error-handling code.

Here's a modified version of EnterSquareRoot:

```
Sub EnterSquareRoot2()
    Dim Num As Double
'   Prompt for a value
    Num = InputBox("Enter a value")

'   Make sure the number is nonnegative
    If Num < 0 Then
        MsgBox "You must enter a positive number."
        Exit Sub
    End If

'   Insert the square root
    ActiveCell.Value = Sqr(Num)
End Sub
```

An If-Then structure checks the value contained in the Num variable. If Num is less than 0, the procedure displays a message box containing information that humans can actually understand. The procedure ends with the Exit Sub statement, so the run-time error never has a chance to occur.

The macro is still not perfect

So the modified EnterSquareRoot procedure is perfect, right? Not really. Try entering text rather than a value. Or click the Cancel button in the input box. Both of these actions generate an error *(Type mismatch)*. This simple little procedure needs still more error-handling code.

The following modified code uses the IsNumeric function to make sure that Num contains a numeric value. If the user doesn't enter a number, the procedure displays a message and then stops. Also, notice that the Num variable is now defined as a Variant. If it were defined as a Double, the code would generate an unhandled error if the user entered a nonnumeric value into the input box.

```
Sub EnterSquareRoot3()
    Dim Num As Variant
'   Prompt for a value
    Num = InputBox("Enter a value")

'   Make sure Num is a number
    If Not IsNumeric(Num) Then
        MsgBox "You must enter a number."
        Exit Sub
    End If

'    Make sure the number is nonnegative
    If Num < 0 Then
        MsgBox "You must enter a positive number."
        Exit Sub
    End If

'   Insert the square root
    ActiveCell.Value = Sqr(Num)
End Sub
```

Is the macro perfect yet?

Now this code is absolutely perfect, right? Not quite. Try running the procedure while the active sheet is a chart sheet. Yikes, another run-time error; this time it's the dreaded Number 91 (see Figure 12-3). This error occurs because there is no active cell when a chart sheet is active, or when something other than a range is selected.

Figure 12-3:
Running the
procedure
when a
chart is
selected
generates
this error.

```
Microsoft Visual Basic

Run-time error '91':

Object variable or With block variable not set

    Continue        End        Debug        Help
```

The following listing uses the TypeName function to make sure that the selection is a range. If anything other than a range is selected, this procedure displays a message and then exits:

```
Sub EnterSquareRoot4()
    Dim Num As Variant
'   Make sure a worksheet is active
    If TypeName(Selection) <> "Range" Then
        MsgBox "Select a cell for the result."
        Exit Sub
    End If

'   Prompt for a value
    Num = InputBox("Enter a value")

'   Make sure Num is a number
    If Not IsNumeric(Num) Then
        MsgBox "You must enter a number."
        Exit Sub
    End If

'   Make sure the number is nonnegative
    If Num < 0 Then
        MsgBox "You must enter a positive number."
        Exit Sub
    End If

'   Insert the square root
    ActiveCell.Value = Sqr(Num)
End Sub
```

Giving up on perfection

By now, this procedure simply *must* be perfect. Think again, pal. Protect the worksheet (using the Review➪Changes➪Protect Sheet command) and then run the code. Yep, a protected worksheet generates yet another error. And I probably haven't thought of all the other errors that can occur. Keep reading for another way to deal with errors — even those you can't anticipate.

Handling Errors Another Way

How can you identify and handle every possible error? Often you can't. Fortunately, VBA provides another way to deal with errors.

Revisiting the EnterSquareRoot procedure

Examine the following code. I modified the routine from the previous section by adding an all-purpose On Error statement to trap all errors and then checking to see whether the InputBox was cancelled.

```
Sub EnterSquareRoot5()
    Dim Num As Variant
    Dim Msg As String

'   Set up error handling
    On Error GoTo BadEntry

'   Prompt for a value
    Num = InputBox("Enter a value")

'   Exit if cancelled
    If Num = "" Then Exit Sub

'   Insert the square root
    ActiveCell.Value = Sqr(Num)
    Exit Sub

BadEntry:
    Msg = "An error occurred." & vbNewLine & vbNewLine
    Msg = Msg & "Make sure a range is selected, "
    Msg = Msg & "the sheet is not protected, "
    Msg = Msg & "and you enter a nonnegative value."
    MsgBox Msg, vbCritical
End Sub
```

This routine traps *any* type of run-time error. After trapping a run-time error, the revised EnterSquareRoot procedure displays the message box shown in Figure 12-4. This message box describes the most likely causes for the error.

On Error not working?

If an On Error statement isn't working as advertised, you need to change one of your settings.

1. Activate the VBE.

2. Choose the Tools⇨Options command.

3. Click the General tab of the Options dialog box.

4. Make sure that the Break On All Errors setting is deselected.

If this setting is selected, Excel essentially ignores any On Error statements. You normally want to keep the Error Trapping options set to Break on Unhandled Errors.

Figure 12-4:
A run-time
error in the
procedure
generates
this helpful
error
message.

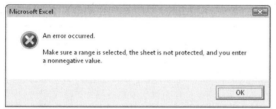

About the On Error statement

Using an On Error statement in your VBA code lets you bypass Excel's built-in error handling and use your own error-handling code. In the previous example, a run-time error causes macro execution to jump to the statement labeled BadEntry. As a result, you avoid Excel's unfriendly error messages, and you can display your own (friendlier, I hope) message to the user.

Notice that the example uses an Exit Sub statement right before the BadEntry label. This statement is necessary because you don't want to execute the error-handling code if an error does *not* occur.

Handling Errors: The Details

You can use the On Error statement in three ways, as shown in Table 12-1.

Table 12-1	Using the On Error Statement
Syntax	*What It Does*
On Error GoTo label	After executing this statement, VBA resumes execution at the specified line. You must include a colon after the label so that VBA recognizes it as a label.
On Error Resume Next	After executing this statement, VBA simply ignores all errors and resumes execution with the next statement.
On Error GoTo 0	After executing this statement, VBA resumes its normal error-checking behavior. Use this statement after using one of the other On Error statements, or when you want to remove error handling in your procedure.

Resuming after an error

In some cases, you simply want the routine to end gracefully when an error occurs. For example, you may display a message describing the error and then exit the procedure. (The EnterSquareRoot5 example uses this technique.) In other cases, you want to recover from the error, if possible.

To recover from an error, you must use a Resume statement. This clears the error condition and lets you continue execution at some location. You can use the Resume statement in three ways, as shown in Table 12-2.

Table 12-2	Using the Resume Statement
Syntax	*What It Does*
Resume	Execution resumes with the statement that caused the error. Use this if your error-handling code corrects the problem and it's okay to continue.
Resume Next	Execution resumes with the statement immediately following the statement that caused the error. This essentially ignores the error.
Resume *label*	Execution resumes at the *label* you specify.

The following example uses a Resume statement after an error occurs:

```
Sub EnterSquareRoot6()
    Dim Num As Variant
    Dim Msg As String
    Dim Ans As Integer
TryAgain:
'   Set up error handling
    On Error GoTo BadEntry

'   Prompt for a value
    Num = InputBox("Enter a value")
    If Num = "" Then Exit Sub

'   Insert the square root
    ActiveCell.Value = Sqr(Num)

    Exit Sub

BadEntry:
    Msg = Err.Number & ": " & Error(Err.Number)
    Msg = Msg & vbNewLine & vbNewLine
    Msg = Msg & "Make sure a range is selected, "
    Msg = Msg & "the sheet is not protected, "
    Msg = Msg & "and you enter a nonnegative value."
    Msg = Msg & vbNewLine & vbNewLine & "Try again?"
    Ans = MsgBox(Msg, vbYesNo + vbCritical)
    If Ans = vbYes Then Resume TryAgain
End Sub
```

This procedure has another label: TryAgain. If an error occurs, execution continues at the BadEntry label, and the code displays the message shown in Figure 12-5. If the user responds by clicking Yes, the Resume statement kicks in and execution jumps back to the TryAgain label. If the user clicks No, the procedure ends.

Notice that the error message also includes the error number, along with the "official" error description. I threw that in because I write about it later. See "Identifying specific errors."

Figure 12-5:
If an error occurs, the user can decide whether to try again.

Remember that the Resume statement clears the error condition before continuing. To see what I mean, try substituting the following statement for the second-to-last statement in the preceding example:

```
If Ans = vbYes Then GoTo TryAgain
```

The code doesn't work correctly if you use GoTo rather than Resume. To demonstrate, enter a negative number: You get the error prompt. Click Yes to try again and then enter *another* negative number. This second error is not trapped because the original error condition was not cleared.

This example is available on this book's Web site.

Error handling in a nutshell

To help you keep all this error-handling business straight, I've prepared a quick-and-dirty summary. A block of error-handling code has the following characteristics:

- ✔ It begins immediately after the label specified in the On Error statement.
- ✔ It should be reached by your macro only if an error occurs. This means that you must use a statement such as Exit Sub or Exit Function immediately before the label.
- ✔ It may require a Resume statement. If you choose not to abort the procedure when an error occurs, you must execute a Resume statement before returning to the main code.

Knowing when to ignore errors

In some cases, it's perfectly okay to ignore errors. That's when the On Error Resume Next statement comes into play.

The following example loops through each cell in the selected range and converts the value to its square root. This procedure generates an error message if any cell in the selection contains a negative number or text:

```
Sub SelectionSqrt()
    Dim cell As Range
    If TypeName(Selection) <> "Range" Then Exit Sub
    For Each cell In Selection
        cell.Value = Sqr(cell.Value)
    Next cell
End Sub
```

In this case, you may want to simply skip any cell that contains a value you can't convert to a square root. You can create all sorts of error-checking capabilities by using If-Then structures, but you can devise a better (and simpler) solution by simply ignoring the errors that occur.

The following routine accomplishes this by using the On Error Resume Next statement:

```
Sub SelectionSqrt()
    Dim cell As Range
    If TypeName(Selection) <> "Range" Then Exit Sub
    On Error Resume Next
    For Each cell In Selection
        cell.Value = Sqr(cell.Value)
    Next cell
End Sub
```

In general, you can use an On Error Resume Next statement if you consider the errors inconsequential to your task.

Identifying specific errors

All errors are not created equal. Some are serious and some are less serious. Although you may ignore errors you consider inconsequential, you must deal with other, more serious errors. In some cases, you need to identify the specific error that occurred.

When an error occurs, Excel stores the error number in an Error object named Err. This object's Number property contains the error number. You can get a description of the error by using the VBA Error function. For example, the following statement displays the error number and a description:

```
MsgBox Err.Number & ": " & Error(Err.Description)
```

Figure 12-5, earlier in this chapter, shows an example of this. Keep in mind, however, that the Excel error messages are not always very useful — but you already know that.

The following procedure demonstrates how to determine which error occurred. In this case, you can safely ignore errors caused by trying to get the square root of a nonpositive number (that is, error 5) or errors caused by trying to get the square root of a nonnumeric value (error 13). On the other hand, you need to inform the user if the worksheet is protected and the selection contains one or more locked cells. (Otherwise, the user may think the macro worked when it really didn't.) This event causes error 1004.

```
Sub SelectionSqrt()
    Dim cell As Range
    Dim ErrMsg As String
    If TypeName(Selection) <> "Range" Then Exit Sub
    On Error GoTo ErrorHandler
    For Each cell In Selection
        cell.Value = Sqr(cell.Value)
    Next cell
    Exit Sub

ErrorHandler:
    Select Case Err.Number
        Case 5 'Negative number
          Resume Next
        Case 13 'Type mismatch
          Resume Next
        Case 1004 'Locked cell, protected sheet
          MsgBox "Cell is locked. Try again.", vbCritical,
            cell.Address
          Exit Sub
        Case Else
          ErrMsg = Error(Err.Number)
          MsgBox "ERROR: " & ErrMsg, vbCritical, cell.
            Address
          Exit Sub
    End Select
End Sub
```

When a run-time error occurs, execution jumps to the code beginning at the ErrorHandler label. The Select Case structure (I discuss that structure in Chapter 10) tests for three common error numbers. If the error number is 5 or 13, execution resumes at the next statement. (In other words, the error is ignored.) But if the error number is 1004, the routine advises the user and then ends. The last case, a catchall for unanticipated errors, traps all other errors and displays the actual error message.

An Intentional Error

Sometimes you can use an error to your advantage. For example, suppose you have a macro that works only if a particular workbook is open. How can you determine whether that workbook is open? One way is to write code that loops through the Workbooks collection checking to determine if the workbook you're interested in is in that collection.

Here's an easier way: a general-purpose function that accepts one argument (a workbook name) and returns True if the workbook is open, False if it's not.

Here's the function:

```
Function WorkbookIsOpen(book As String) As Boolean
    Dim WBName As String
    On Error GoTo NotOpen
    WBName = Workbooks(book).Name
    WorkbookIsOpen = True
    Exit Function
NotOpen:
    WorkbookIsOpen = False
End Function
```

This function takes advantage of the fact that Excel generates an error if you refer to a workbook that is not open. For example, the following statement generates an error if a workbook named MyBook.xlsx is not open:

```
WBName = Workbooks("MyBook.xlsx").Name
```

In the WorkbookIsOpen function, the On Error statement tells VBA to resume the macro at the NotOpen statement if an error occurs. Therefore, an error means that the workbook is not open, and the function returns False. If the workbook is open, no error occurs and the function returns True.

Here's another variation on the WorkbookIsOpen function. This version uses On Error Resume Next to ignore the error. But the code checks Err's Number property. If Err.Number is 0, no error occurred and the workbook is open. If Err.Number is anything else, it means that an error occurred (and the workbook is not open).

```
Function WorkbookIsOpen(book) As Boolean
    Dim WBName As String
    On Error Resume Next
    WBName = Workbooks(book).Name
    If Err.Number = 0 Then WorkbookIsOpen = True _
       Else WorkbookIsOpen = False
End Function
```

The following example demonstrates how to use this function in a Sub procedure:

```
Sub UpdatePrices()
    If Not WorkbookIsOpen("Prices.xlsx") Then
        MsgBox "Please open the Prices workbook first!"
        Exit Sub
    End If
'   [Other code goes here]
End Sub
```

The UpdatePrices procedure (which must be in the same workbook as WorkbookIsOpen) calls the WorkbookIsOpen function and passes the workbook name (Prices.xlsx) as an argument. The WorkbookIsOpen function returns either True or False. Therefore, if the workbook is not open, the procedure informs the user of that fact. If the workbook is open, the macro continues.

Error handling can be a tricky proposition — after all, many different errors can occur, and you can't anticipate all of them. In general, you should trap errors and correct the situation before Excel intervenes, if possible. Writing effective error-trapping code requires a thorough knowledge of Excel and a clear understanding of how the VBA error handling works. Subsequent chapters contain more examples of error handling.

Chapter 13

Bug Extermination Techniques

● ●

● ●

1 f the word *bugs* conjures up an image of a cartoon rabbit, this chapter can
set you straight. Simply put, a bug is an error in your programming. Here
I cover the topic of programming bugs — how to identify them and how to
wipe them off the face of your module.

Species of Bugs

Welcome to Entomology 101. The term *program bug,* as you probably know,
refers to a problem with software. In other words, if software doesn't perform
as expected, it has a bug. Fact is, all major software programs have bugs —
lots of bugs. Excel itself has hundreds (if not thousands) of bugs. Fortunately,
the vast majority of these bugs are relatively obscure and appear in only very
specific circumstances.

When you write non-trivial VBA programs, your code probably will have
bugs. This is a fact of life and not necessarily a reflection of your program-
ming ability. The bugs may fall into any of the following categories:

- **Logic flaws in your code:** You can often avoid these bugs by carefully
 thinking through the problem your program addresses.

- **Incorrect context bugs:** This type of bug surfaces when you attempt to
 do something at the wrong time. For example, you may try to write data
 to cells in the active sheet when the active sheet is actually a chart sheet
 (which has no cells).

- **Extreme-case bugs:** These bugs rear their ugly heads when you encoun-
 ter data you didn't anticipate, such as very large or very small numbers.

✔ **Wrong data type bugs:** This type of bug occurs when you try to process data of the wrong type, such as attempting to take the square root of a text string.

✔ **Wrong version bugs:** This type of bug involves incompatibilities between different Excel versions. For example, you may develop a workbook with Excel 2010 and then find out that the workbook doesn't work with Excel 2003. You can usually avoid such problems by not using version-specific features. Often, the easiest approach is to develop your application by using the lowest version number of Excel that users might have. In all cases, however, you should test your work on all versions you expect it will be used with.

✔ **Beyond-your-control bugs:** These are the most frustrating. An example occurs when Microsoft upgrades Excel and makes a minor, undocumented change that causes your macro to bomb. Even security updates have been known to cause problems.

Debugging is the process of identifying and correcting bugs in your program. Developing debugging skills takes time, so don't be discouraged if this process is difficult at first.

It's important to understand the distinction between *bugs* and *syntax errors.* A syntax error is a language error. For example, you might misspell a keyword, omit the Next statement in a For-Next loop, or have a mismatched parenthesis. Before you can even execute the procedure, you must correct these syntax errors. A program bug is much subtler. You can execute the routine, but it doesn't perform as expected.

Identifying Bugs

Before you can do any debugging, you must determine whether a bug actually exists. You can tell that your macro contains a bug if it doesn't work the way it should. (Gee, this book is just filled with insight, isn't it?) Usually, but not always, you can easily discern this.

A bug often (but not always) becomes apparent when Excel displays a run-time error message. Figure 13-1 shows an example. Notice that this error message includes a button labeled Debug. More about this later in the "About the Debugger" section.

A key fact known to all programmers is that bugs often appear when you least expect them. For example, just because your macro works fine with one data set doesn't mean you can assume it will work equally as well with all data sets.

Figure 13-1:
An error
message
like this
often means
that your
VBA code
contains a
bug.

The best debugging approach is to start with thorough testing, under a variety of real-life conditions. And because any workbook changes made by your VBA code cannot be undone, it is always a good idea to use a backup copy of the workbook that you use for testing. I usually copy some files into a temporary folder and use those files for my testing.

Debugging Techniques

In this section, I discuss the four most common methods for debugging Excel VBA code:

- ✔ Examining the code
- ✔ Inserting MsgBox functions at various locations in your code
- ✔ Inserting Debug.Print statements
- ✔ Using the Excel built-in debugging tools

Examining your code

Perhaps the most straightforward debugging technique is simply taking a close look at your code to see whether you can find the problem. If you're lucky, the error jumps right out, and you slap your forehead and say, "Doh!" When the forehead pain diminishes, you can fix the problem.

Notice I said, "If you're lucky." That's because often you discover errors when you have been working on your program for eight hours straight, it is 2 a.m., and you are running on caffeine and willpower. At times like that, you are lucky if you can even see your code, let alone find the bugs. Thus, don't be surprised if simply examining your code isn't enough to make you find and expunge all the bugs it contains.

Using the MsgBox function

A common problem in many programs involves one or more variables not taking on the values you expect. In such cases, monitoring the variable(s) while your code runs is a helpful debugging technique. One way to do this is by inserting temporary MsgBox functions into your routine. For example, if you have a variable named CellCount, you can insert the following statement:

```
MsgBox CellCount
```

When you execute the routine, the MsgBox function displays CellCount's value.

It's often helpful to display the values of two or more variables in the message box. The following statement displays the current value of two variables: LoopIndex (1) and CellCount (72), as shown in Figure 13-2:

```
MsgBox LoopIndex & " " & CellCount
```

Figure 13-2:
Using a
message
box to
display the
value of two
variables.

Figure 13-2: Using a message box to display the value of two variables.

Notice that I combine the two variables with the concatenation operator (&) and insert a space character between them. Otherwise, the message box strings the two values together, making them look like a single value. You can also use the built-in constant, vbNewLine, in place of the space character. vbNewLine inserts a line-feed break, which displays the text on a new line. The following statement displays three variables, each on a separate line:

```
MsgBox LoopIndex & vbNewLine & CellCount & _
    vbNewLine & MyVal
```

This technique isn't limited to monitoring variables. You can use a message box to display all sorts of useful information while your code is running. For example, if your code loops through a series of sheets, the following statement displays the name and type of the active sheet:

```
MsgBox ActiveSheet.Name & " " & TypeName(ActiveSheet)
```

If your message box shows something unexpected, hit control-break, and you see a dialog box that tells you, "Code execution has been interrupted." As shown in Figure 13-3, you have four choices:

✔ Click the Continue button, and the code continues executing.

✔ Click the End button, and execution stops.

✔ Click the Debug button, and the VBE goes into Debug mode (which is explained a bit later).

✔ Click the Help button, and a help screen tells you that you pressed Ctrl+Break. In other words, it's not very helpful.

Figure 13-3:
Pressing
Ctrl+Break
halts
execution of
your code
and gives
you some
choices.

Feel free to use MsgBox functions frequently when you debug your code. Just make sure that you remove them after you identify and correct the problem.

Inserting Debug.Print statements

As an alternative to using MsgBox functions in your code, you can insert one or more temporary Debug.Print statements. Use these statements to print the value of one or more variables in the Immediate window. Here's an example that displays the value of three variables:

```
Debug.Print LoopIndex, CellCount, MyVal
```

Notice that the variables are separated with commas. You can display as many variables as you like with a single Debug.Print statement. If VBE's Immediate window is not visible, press Ctrl+G.

Unlike MsgBox, Debug.Print statements do not halt your code. So you'll need to keep an eye on the Immediate window to see what's going on.

After you've debugged your code, be sure to remove all the Debug.Print statements. Even big companies like Microsoft occasionally forget to remove their Debug.Print statements. In several previous versions of Excel, every time the Analysis ToolPak add-in was opened, you'd see several strange messages in the Immediate window (as shown in Figure 13-4). That problem was fixed in Excel 2007.

```
Immediate

[auto_open] <
[SetupFunctionIDs] <
[SetupFunctionIDs] >
[PickPlatform] <
[PickPlatform] >
[VerifyOpen] <
[VerifyOpen] > 1
[RegisterFunctionIDs] <
[RegisterFunctionIDs] >
[auto_open] >
|
```

Using the VBA debugger

The Excel designers are intimately familiar with the concept of bugs. consequently, Excel includes a set of debugging tools that can help you correct problems in your VBA code. The VBA debugger is the topic of the next section.

About the Debugger

In this section, I discuss the gory details of using the Excel debugging tools. These tools are much more powerful than the techniques I discuss in the previous section. But along with power comes responsibility. Using the debugging tools takes a bit of setup work.

Setting breakpoints in your code

Earlier in this chapter, I discuss using MsgBox functions in your code to monitor the values of certain variables. Displaying a message box essentially halts your code in mid-execution, and clicking the OK button resumes execution.

Wouldn't it be nice if you could halt a routine's execution, take a look at the value of *any* of your variables, and then continue execution? Well, that's exactly what you can do by setting a breakpoint. You can set a breakpoint in your VBA code in several ways:

✔ Move the cursor to the statement at which you want execution to stop; then press F9.

✔ Click in the gray margin to the left of the statement at which you want execution to stop.

✔ Position the insertion point in the statement at which you want execution to stop. Then use the Debug➪Toggle Breakpoint command.

✔ Right-click a statement and choose Toggle➪Breakpoint from the shortcut menu.

The results of setting a breakpoint are shown in Figure 13-5. Excel highlights the line to remind you that you set a breakpoint there; it also inserts a large dot in the gray margin.

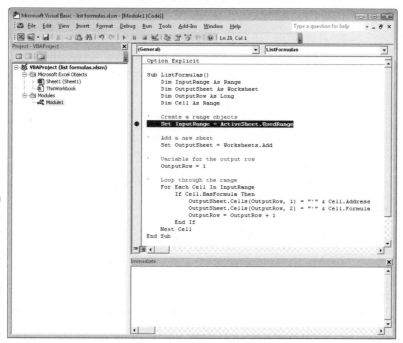

Figure 13-5: The highlighted statement marks a breakpoint in this procedure.

When you execute the procedure, Excel goes into *Break mode* before the line with the breakpoint is executed. In Break mode, the word [break] is displayed in the VBE title bar. To get out of Break mode and continue execution, press F5 or click the Run Sub/UserForm button in the VBE toolbar. See "stepping through your code" later in this chapter to find out more.

To quickly remove a breakpoint, click the large dot in the gray margin or move the cursor to the highlighted line and press F9. To remove all breakpoints in the module, press Ctrl+Shift+F9.

VBA also has a keyword that forces Break mode:

```
Stop
```

When your code reaches the Stop keyword, VBA enters Break mode. The handy thing about this Stop word is that if your code is protected, it will be ignored.

What is Break mode? You can think of it as a state of suspended animation. Your VBA code stops running, and the current statement is highlighted in bright yellow. In Break mode, you can

- ✔ Type VBA statements in the Immediate window. (See the next section for details.)
- ✔ Press F8 to step through your code one line at a time to check various things while the program is paused.
- ✔ Move the mouse pointer over a variable to display its value in a small pop-up window.
- ✔ Skip the next statement(s) and continue execution there (or even go back a couple of statements).
- ✔ Edit a statement and then continue.

Figure 13-6 shows some debugging action. A breakpoint is set (notice the big dot), and I'm using the F8 key to step through the code line by line (notice the arrow that points to the current statement). I used the Immediate window to check a few things, the mouse pointer is hovering over the OutputRow variable, and the VBE displays its current value.

Using the Immediate window

The Immediate window may not be visible in the VBE. You can display the VBE's Immediate window at any time by pressing Ctrl+G.

In Break mode, the Immediate window is particularly useful for finding the current value of any variable in your program. For example, if you want to know the current value of a variable named CellCount, enter the following in the Immediate window and press Enter:

```
Print CellCount
```

You can save a few milliseconds by using a question mark in place of the word *Print,* like this:

```
? CellCount
```

Figure 13-6:
A typical
scene in
Break mode.

The Immediate window lets you do other things besides check variable values. For example, you can change the value of a variable, activate a different sheet, or even open a new workbook. Just make sure that the command you enter is a valid VBA statement.

You can also use the Immediate window when Excel is not in Break mode. I often use the Immediate window to test small code snippets (whatever I can cram on a single line) before incorporating them into my procedures.

Stepping through your code

While in Break mode, you can also step through your code line by line. One statement is executed each time you press F8. Throughout this line-by-line execution of your code, you can activate the Immediate window at any time to check the status of your variables.

You can use your mouse to change which statement VBA will execute next. If you put your mouse pointer in the gray margin to the left of the currently highlighted statement (which will usually be yellow), your pointer changes to a right-pointing arrow. Simply drag your mouse to the statement you want done next and watch that statement turn yellow.

Using the Watch window

In some cases, you may want to know whether a certain variable or expression takes on a particular value. For example, suppose that a procedure loops through 1,000 cells. You notice that a problem occurs during the 900th iteration of the loop. Well, you could insert a breakpoint in the loop, but that would mean responding to 899 prompts before the code finally gets to the iteration you want to see (and that gets boring real fast). A more efficient solution involves setting a *watch expression*.

For example, you can create a watch expression that puts the procedure into Break mode whenever a certain variable takes on a specific value — for example, Counter=900. To create a watch expression, choose Debug⇨Add Watch to display the Add Watch dialog box. See Figure 13-7.

Figure 13-7:
The Add Watch dialog box lets you specify a condition that causes a break.

The Add Watch dialog has three parts:

- ✔ **Expression:** Enter a valid VBA expression or a variable here. For example, *Counter=900* or just *Counter*.

- ✔ **Context:** Select the procedure and the module you want to watch. Note that you can select All Procedures and All Modules.

- ✔ **Watch Type:** Select the type of watch by clicking an option button. Your choice here depends on the expression you enter. The first choice, Watch Expression, does not cause a break; it simply displays the expression's value when a break occurs.

Execute your procedure after setting up your watch expression(s). Things run normally until your watch expression is satisfied (based on the Watch Type you specified). When that happens, Excel enters Break mode (you did set the Watch Type to "Break When Value Is True," didn't you?). From there, you can step through the code or use the Immediate window to debug your code.

When you create a watch, VBE displays the Watches window shown in Figure 13-8. This window displays the value of all watches that you've defined. In this figure, the value of Counter hit 900, which caused Excel to enter Break mode.

Figure 13-8:
The
Watches
window
displays all
watches.

The best way to understand how this Watch business works is to use it and try various options. Before long, you'll probably wonder how you ever got along without it.

Using the Locals Window

Another useful debugging aid is the Locals window. You can show this window by choosing View⇨Locals Window from the VBE's menu. When you are in Break mode, this window will show you a list of all variables that are local to the current procedure (see Figure 13-9). The nice thing about this window is that you don't have to add a load of watches manually if you want to look at the content of many variables. The VBE has done all the hard work for you.

Figure 13-9:
The Locals
window
displays
all local
variables
and their
content.

Bug Reduction Tips

I can't tell you how to completely eliminate bugs in your programs. Finding bugs in software can be a profession by itself, but I can provide a few tips to help you keep those bugs to a minimum:

✔ **Use an Option Explicit statement at the beginning of your modules.** This statement requires you to define the data type for every variable you use. This creates a bit more work for you, but you avoid the common error of misspelling a variable name. And it has a nice side benefit: Your routines run a bit faster.

✔ **Format your code with indentation.** Using indentations helps delineate different code segments. If your program has several nested For-Next loops, for example, consistent indentation helps you keep track of them all.

✔ **Be careful with the On Error Resume Next statement.** As I discuss in Chapter 12, this statement causes Excel to ignore any errors and continue executing the routine. In some cases, using this statement causes Excel to ignore errors that it shouldn't ignore. Your code may have bugs, and you may not even realize it.

✔ **Use lots of comments.** Nothing is more frustrating than revisiting code you wrote six months ago and not having a clue as to how it works. By adding a few comments to describe your logic, you can save lots of time down the road.

✔ **Keep your Sub and Function procedures simple.** By writing your code in small modules, each of which has a single, well-defined purpose, you simplify the debugging process.

✔ **Use the macro recorder to help identify properties and methods.** When I can't remember the name or the syntax of a property or method, I often simply record a macro and look at the recorded code.

✔ **Understand Excel's debugger.** Although it can be a bit daunting at first, the Excel debugger is a useful tool. Invest some time and get to know it.

Debugging code is not one of my favorite activities (it ranks right up there with getting audited by the IRS), but it's a necessary evil that goes along with programming. As you gain more experience with VBA, you spend less time debugging and, when you have to debug, are more efficient at doing so.

Chapter 14

VBA Programming Examples

My philosophy for figuring out how to write Excel macros places heavy emphasis on examples. I find that a good example often communicates a concept much better than a lengthy description of the underlying theory. Because you're reading this book, you probably agree with me. This chapter presents several examples that demonstrate common VBA techniques.

I organize these examples into the following categories:

- ✔ Working with ranges
- ✔ Changing Excel settings
- ✔ Working with charts
- ✔ Speeding up your VBA code

Although you may be able to use some of the examples directly, in most cases you must adapt them to your own needs.

Working with Ranges

Most of your VBA programming probably involves worksheet ranges. (For a refresher course on Range objects, refer to Chapter 8.) When you work with Range objects, keep the following points in mind:

- ✔ Your VBA doesn't need to *select* a range to work with it.
- ✔ If your code does select a range, its worksheet must be active.
- ✔ The macro recorder doesn't always generate the most efficient code. Often, you can create your macro by using the recorder and then edit the code to make it more efficient.

✔ It's a good idea to use named ranges in your VBA code. For example, using Range("Total") is better than using Range("D45"). In the latter case, if you add a row above row 45, you need to modify the macro so that it uses the correct range address (D46). Note that you name a range of cells by choosing Formulas⇨Defined Names⇨Define Name.

✔ When running a macro that works on the current range selection, the user might select entire columns or rows. In most cases, you don't want to loop through every cell in the selection (that could take a long time). Your macro should create a subset of the selection consisting of only the nonblank cells.

✔ Excel allows multiple selections. For example, you can select a range, press Ctrl, and select another range with your mouse. Your code can test for a multiple selection and take appropriate actions.

The examples in this section, which are available at this book's Web site, demonstrate these points.

If you prefer to enter these examples yourself, press Alt+F11 to activate the VBE. Then insert a VBA module and type the code. Make sure that the workbook is set up properly. For instance, if the example uses two sheets named Sheet1 and Sheet2, make sure that the workbook has sheets with those names.

Copying a range

Copying a range ranks right up there as one of the most favorite Excel activities of all time. When you turn on the macro recorder and copy a range from A1:A5 to B1:B5, you get this VBA macro:

```
Sub CopyRange()
    Range("A1:A5").Select
    Selection.Copy
    Range("B1").Select
    ActiveSheet.Paste
    Application.CutCopyMode = False
End Sub
```

Notice the last statement. This statement was generated by pressing Esc, which cancels the marching ants display that appears in the worksheet when you copy a range.

This macro works fine, but you can copy a range more efficiently than this. You can produce the same result with the following one-line macro, which doesn't select any cells:

```
Sub CopyRange2()
    Range("A1:A5").Copy Range("B1")
End Sub
```

This procedure takes advantage of the fact that the Copy method can use an argument that specifies the destination. I found that by consulting the VBA Help system. This example also demonstrates that the macro recorder doesn't always generate the most efficient code.

Copying a variable-sized range

In many cases, you need to copy a range of cells but don't know the exact row and column dimensions. For example, you might have a workbook that tracks weekly sales. The number of rows changes as you add new data.

Figure 14-1 shows a range on a worksheet. This range consists of several rows, and the number of rows can change from day to day. Because you don't know the exact range address at any given time, writing a macro to copy the range can be challenging. Are you up for the challenge?

	A	B	C	D	E	F
1	Date	Units	Amount			
2	15-Nov	132	$2,737			
3	16-Nov	143	$154			
4	17-Nov	133	$109			
5	18-Nov	169	$614			
6	19-Nov	102	$2,744			
7	20-Nov	143	$5,164			
8	21-Nov	109	$4,314			
9	22-Nov	122	$4,448			
10	23-Nov	156	$4,657			
11	24-Nov	187	$6,989			
12	25-Nov	140	$2,014			
13	26-Nov	132	$1,070			
14						
15						

Figure 14-1: This range can consist of any number of rows.

The following macro demonstrates how to copy this range from Sheet1 to Sheet2 (beginning at cell A1). It uses the CurrentRegion property, which returns a Range object that corresponds to the block of cells around a particular cell. In this case, that cell is A1.

```
Sub CopyCurrentRegion()
    Range("A1").CurrentRegion.Copy
    Sheets("Sheet2").Select
    Range("A1").Select
    ActiveSheet.Paste
    Sheets("Sheet1").Select
    Application.CutCopyMode = False
End Sub
```

Using the CurrentRegion property is equivalent to choosing Home⇨Editing⇨ Find & Select⇨Goto Special (which displays the Go To Special dialog box), and choosing the Current Region option. To see how this works, record your actions while issuing that command. Generally, the CurrentRegion consists of a rectangular block of cells surrounded by one or more blank rows or columns.

You can make this macro even more efficient by not selecting the destination. The following macro takes advantage of the fact that the Copy method can use an argument for the destination range:

```
Sub CopyCurrentRegion2()
    Range("A1").CurrentRegion.Copy _
        Sheets("Sheet2").Range("A1")
    Application.CutCopyMode = False
End Sub
```

Selecting to the end of a row or column

You're probably in the habit of using key combinations such as Ctrl+Shift+Right Arrow and Ctrl+Shift+Down Arrow to select a range that consists of everything from the active cell to the end of a row or a column. Not surprisingly, you can write macros that perform these types of selections.

You can use the CurrentRegion property to select an entire block of cells. But what if you want to select, say, one column from a block of cells? Fortunately, VBA can accommodate this type of action. The following VBA procedure selects the range beginning at the active cell and extending down to the cell just above the first blank cell in the column. After selecting the range, you can do whatever you want with it — copy it, move it, format it, and so on.

```
Sub SelectDown()
    Range(ActiveCell, ActiveCell.End(xlDown)).Select
End Sub
```

You can make this type of selection manually: Select the first cell, hold down the Shift key, press End, and then press Down Arrow.

This example uses the End method of the ActiveCell object, which returns a Range object. The End method takes one argument, which can be any of the following constants:

- xlUp
- xlDown
- xlToLeft
- xlToRight

Keep in mind that it's not necessary to select a range before doing some-
thing with it. The following macro applies bold formatting to a variable-sized
(single column) range without selecting the range:

```
Sub MakeBold()
    Range(ActiveCell, ActiveCell.End(xlDown)) _
        .Font.Bold = True
End Sub
```

Selecting a row or column

The following procedure demonstrates how to select the column that con-
tains the active cell. It uses the EntireColumn property, which returns a
Range object that consists of a full column:

```
Sub SelectColumn()
    ActiveCell.EntireColumn.Select
End Sub
```

As you may expect, VBA also offers an EntireRow property, which returns a
Range object that consists of an entire row.

Moving a range

You move a range by cutting it to the Clipboard and then pasting it in
another area. If you record your actions while performing a move operation,
the macro recorder generates code like the following:

```
Sub MoveRange()
    Range("A1:C6").Select
    Selection.Cut
    Range("A10").Select
    ActiveSheet.Paste
End Sub
```

As with the copying example earlier in this chapter, this is not the most effi-
cient way to move a range of cells. In fact, you can move a range with a single
VBA statement, as follows:

```
Sub MoveRange2()
    Range("A1:C6").Cut Range("A10")
End Sub
```

This macro takes advantage of the fact that the Cut method can use an argument that specifies the destination. Notice also that the range was not selected. The cell pointer remains in its original position.

Looping through a range efficiently

Many macros perform an operation on each cell in a range, or they might perform selected actions based on each cell's content. These macros usually include a For-Next loop that processes each cell in the range.

The following example demonstrates how to loop through a range of cells. In this case, the range is the current selection. An object variable named Cell refers to the cell being processed. Within the For-Next loop, the single statement evaluates the cell and applies bold formatting if the cell contains a positive value.

```
Sub ProcessCells()
    Dim Cell As Range
    For Each Cell In Selection
        If Cell.Value > 0 Then Cell.Font.Bold = True
    Next Cell
End Sub
```

This example works, but what if the selection consists of an entire column or row? This is not uncommon because Excel lets you perform operations on entire columns or rows. In such a case, the macro seems to take forever because it loops through each cell (all 1,048,576 of them) in the column — even the blank cells. To make the macro more efficient, you need a means for processing only the nonblank cells.

The following routine does just that by using the SpecialCells method. (Refer to the VBA Help system for specific details about its arguments.) This routine uses the Set keyword to create two new Range objects: the selection's subset that consists of cells with constants and the selection's subset that consists of cells with formulas. The routine processes each of these subsets, with the net effect of skipping all blank cells. Pretty slick, eh?

```
Sub SkipBlanks()
    Dim ConstantCells As Range
    Dim FormulaCells As Range
    Dim cell As Range
'    Ignore errors
    On Error Resume Next
```

```
'       Process the constants
        Set ConstantCells = Selection _
            .SpecialCells(xlConstants)
        For Each cell In ConstantCells
            If cell.Value > 0 Then
                cell.Font.Bold = True
            End If
        Next cell

'       Process the formulas
        Set FormulaCells = Selection _
            .SpecialCells(xlFormulas)
        For Each cell In FormulaCells
            If cell.Value > 0 Then
                cell.Font.Bold = True
            End If
        Next cell
End Sub
```

The SkipBlanks procedure works equally fast, regardless of what you select. For example, you can select the range, all columns in the range, all rows in the range, or even the entire worksheet. It's a vast improvement over the ProcessCells procedure presented earlier in this section.

Notice that I use the following statement in this code:

```
On Error Resume Next
```

This statement tells Excel to ignore any errors that occur and simply process the next statement (see Chapter 12 for a discussion of error handling). This statement is necessary because the SpecialCells method produces an error if no cells qualify.

Using the SpecialCells method is equivalent to choosing the Home⇨Editing⇨ Find & Select⇨Goto Special command, and selecting the Constants option or the Formulas option. To get a feel for how this works, record your actions while you issue that command and select various options.

Looping through a range efficiently (Part II)

And now, the sequel. This section demonstrates another way of processing cells in an efficient manner. It takes advantage of the UsedRange property — which returns a Range object that consists only of the used area of the worksheet. It also uses the Intersect method, which returns a Range object that consists of cells that two ranges have in common.

Here's a variation of the SkipBlanks procedure from the previous section:

```
Sub SkipBlanks2()
    Dim WorkRange As Range
    Dim cell As Range
    Set WorkRange = Intersect _
        (Selection, ActiveSheet.UsedRange)
    For Each cell In WorkRange
        If cell.Value > 0 Then
            cell.Font.Bold = True
        End If
    Next cell
End Sub
```

The WorkRange object variable consists of cells that are common to the user's selection, and the worksheet's used range. Therefore, if an entire column is selected, WorkRange contains only the cells that are within the used area of the worksheet. Fast and efficient, with no CPU cycles wasted on processing cells that are outside of the worksheet's used area.

Prompting for a cell value

As shown in Figure 14-2, you can use VBA's InputBox function to get a value from the user. Then you can insert that value into a cell. The following procedure demonstrates how to ask the user for a value and place the value in cell A1 of the active worksheet, using only one statement:

```
Sub GetValue()
    Range("A1").Value = InputBox _
        ("Enter the value for cell A1")
End Sub
```

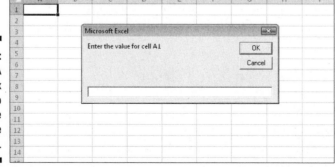

Figure 14-2:
Use the VBA
InputBox
function to
get a value
from the
user.

If you try this example, you'll find that clicking the Cancel button in the Input Box erases the current value in cell A1. Erasing the user's data isn't a very good programming practice. The following macro demonstrates a better approach: using a variable (x) to store the value entered by the user. If the value is not empty (that is, the user didn't click Cancel), the value of x is placed into cell A1. Otherwise, nothing happens.

```
Sub GetValue2()
    Dim x as Variant
    x = InputBox("Enter the value for cell A1")
    If x <> "" Then Range("A1").Value = x
End Sub
```

The variable x is defined as a Variant data type because it could be a number or an empty string (if the user clicks Cancel).

Determining the selection type

If you design your macro to work with a range selection, the macro must be able to determine whether a range is actually selected. If something other than a range is selected (such as a chart or a shape), the macro will probably bomb. The following procedure uses the VBA TypeName function to identify the type of object that is currently selected:

```
Sub SelectionType()
    MsgBox TypeName(Selection)
End Sub
```

If a Range object is selected, the MsgBox displays Range. If your macro works only with ranges, you can use an If statement to ensure that a range is selected. This example displays a message and exits the procedure if the current selection is not a Range object:

```
Sub CheckSelection()
    If TypeName(Selection) <> "Range" Then
        MsgBox "Select a range."
        Exit Sub
    End If
'   ... [Other statements go here]
End Sub
```

Identifying a multiple selection

As you know, Excel allows multiple selections by pressing Ctrl while choosing objects or ranges. This can cause problems with some macros. For example, you can't copy a multiple selection that consists of nonadjacent cells. If you attempt to do so, Excel scolds you with the message shown in Figure 14-3.

Figure 14-3:
Excel
doesn't like
it if you try
to copy a
multiple
selection.

The following macro demonstrates how to determine whether the user made a multiple selection so your macro can take appropriate action:

```
Sub MultipleSelection()
    If Selection.Areas.Count > 1 Then
        MsgBox "Multiple selections not allowed."
        Exit Sub
    End If
'    ... [Other statements go here]
End Sub
```

This example uses the Areas method, which returns a collection of all objects in the selection. The Count property returns the number of objects in the collection.

Changing Excel Settings

Some of the most useful macros are simple procedures that change one or more of Excel's settings. For example, if you find yourself making frequent trips to the Excel Options dialog box to change a setting, that's a good candidate for a simple time-saving macro.

This section presents two examples that show you how to change settings in Excel. You can apply the general principles demonstrated by these examples to other operations that change settings.

Changing Boolean settings

Like a light switch, a *Boolean* setting is either on or off. For example, you might want to create a macro that turns the worksheet page break display on and off. After you print or preview a worksheet, Excel displays dashed lines to indicate the page breaks. Some people (author included) find these dashed lines very annoying. Unfortunately, the only way to get rid of the page break display is to open the Excel Options dialog box, click the Advanced tab, and scroll down until you find the Show Page Breaks check box. If you turn on the macro recorder when you change that option, Excel generates the following code:

```
ActiveSheet.DisplayPageBreaks = False
```

On the other hand, if page breaks are not visible when you record the macro, Excel generates the following code:

```
ActiveSheet.DisplayPageBreaks = True
```

This may lead you to suspect that you need two macros: one to turn on the page break display and one to turn it off. Not true. The following procedure uses the Not operator, which turns True to False and False to True. Executing the TogglePageBreaks procedure is a simple way to toggle the page break display from True to False and from False to True:

```
Sub TogglePageBreaks()
    On Error Resume Next
    ActiveSheet.DisplayPageBreaks = Not _
      ActiveSheet.DisplayPageBreaks
End Sub
```

The first statement ignores an error that occurs if the active sheet is a chart sheet. (Chart sheets don't display page breaks.)

You can use this technique to toggle any settings that have Boolean (True or False) values.

Changing non-Boolean settings

Use a Select Case structure for non-Boolean settings. This example toggles the calculation mode between manual and automatic and displays a message indicating the current mode:

```
Sub ToggleCalcMode()
  Select Case Application.Calculation
    Case xlManual
        Application.Calculation = xlCalculationAutomatic
        MsgBox "Automatic Calculation Mode"
    Case xlAutomatic
        Application.Calculation = xlCalculationManual
        MsgBox "Manual Calculation Mode"
  End Select
End Sub
```

You can adapt this technique for changing other non-Boolean settings.

Working with Charts

Charts are jam-packed with different objects, so manipulating charts with VBA can be a bit of a challenge. The challenge increases with Excel 2007, because Microsoft decided to omit recording macros for all the new and fancy chart formatting stuff. Fortunately, this serious problem was corrected in Excel 2010.

I fired up Excel 2010, entered some numbers in A1:A3 and selected that range. Then I turned on the macro recorder and created a basic column chart with three data points. I deleted the chart's legend and added a shadow effect to the columns. Here's the macro:

```
Sub Macro1()
    ActiveSheet.Shapes.AddChart.Select
    ActiveChart.ChartType = xlColumnClustered
    ActiveChart.SetSourceData Source:=Range _
        ("'Sheet1'!$A$1:$A$3")
    ActiveChart.Legend.Select
    Selection.Delete
    ActiveSheet.ChartObjects("Chart 1").Activate
    ActiveChart.SeriesCollection(1).Select
    Selection.Format.Shadow.Type = msoShadow21
End Sub
```

If you record this macro in Excel 2007, the last statement (which applies the shadow) is not even generated. That's just one example of how Excel 2007 ignores chart formatting commands when recording a macro.

This macro, by the way, will probably generate an error because it hard-codes the chart's name in the macro. When you run this macro, the chart that's created is not necessarily named Chart 1. If you happen to have a chart named Chart 1, the shadow formatting will be applied to that one — not the

one that the macro created. Also, the chart's data range is hard-coded, so you couldn't use this for a general-purpose chart-creator macro.

However, examining the recorded code does reveal a few things that may be helpful in writing your own chart-related macros. If you're curious, here's a hand-crafted version of that macro that creates a chart from the selected range:

```
Sub CreateAChart()
    Dim ChartData As Range
    Dim ChartShape As Shape
    Dim NewChart As Chart

'    Create object variables
    Set ChartData = ActiveWindow.RangeSelection
    Set ChartShape = ActiveSheet.Shapes.AddChart
    Set NewChart = ChartShape.Chart

'    Adjust the chart
    With NewChart
      .ChartType = xlColumnClustered
      .SetSourceData Source:=Range(ChartData.Address)
      .Legend.Delete
      .SeriesCollection(1).Format.Shadow.Type = _
          msoShadow21
    End With
End Sub
```

If you need to write VBA macros that manipulate charts, you must understand some terminology. An *embedded chart* on a worksheet is a ChartObject object. You can activate a ChartObject much like you activate a sheet. The following statement activates the ChartObject named Chart 1:

```
ActiveSheet.ChartObjects("Chart 1").Activate
```

After you activate the chart, you can refer to it in your VBA code as the ActiveChart. If the chart is on a separate chart sheet, it becomes the active chart as soon as you activate that chart sheet.

A ChartObject is also a Shape, which can be a bit confusing. In fact, when your VBA code creates a chart, it starts by adding a new Shape. You can also activate a chart by selecting the Shape object that holds the chart:

```
ActiveSheet.Shapes("Chart 1").Select
```

I prefer to use the ChartObject object in my code, just to make it perfectly clear that I'm working with a chart.

When you click an embedded chart, Excel actually selects an object *inside* the ChartObject object. You can select the ChartObject itself by pressing Ctrl while clicking the embedded chart.

Modifying the chart type

Here's a confusing statement for you: A ChartObject object acts as a container for a Chart object. Read that a few times, and it might actually make sense.

To modify a chart with VBA, you don't have to activate the chart. Rather, the Chart method can return the chart contained in the ChartObject. Are you thoroughly confused yet? The following two procedures have the same effect — they change the chart named Chart 1 to an area chart. The first procedure activates the chart first and then works with the active chart. The second procedure doesn't activate the chart. Rather it uses the Chart property to return the Chart object contained in the ChartObject object.

```
Sub ModifyChart1()
    ActiveSheet.ChartObjects("Chart 1").Activate
    ActiveChart.Type = xlArea
End Sub
```

```
Sub ModifyChart2()
    ActiveSheet.ChartObjects("Chart 1") _
        .Chart.Type = xlArea
End Sub
```

Looping through the ChartObjects collection

This example changes the chart type of every embedded chart on the active sheet. The procedure uses a For-Next loop to cycle through each object in the ChartObjects collection, access the Chart object in each, and change its Type property.

```
Sub ChartType()
    Dim cht As ChartObject
    For Each cht In ActiveSheet.ChartObjects
        cht.Chart.Type = xlArea
    Next cht
End Sub
```

The following macro performs the same function but works on all the chart sheets in the active workbook:

```
Sub ChartType2()
    Dim cht As Chart
    For Each cht In ActiveWorkbook.Charts
        cht.Type = xlArea
    Next cht
End Sub
```

Modifying chart properties

The following example changes the Legend font for all charts on the active sheet. It uses a For-Next loop to process all ChartObject objects:

```
Sub LegendMod()
    Dim cht As ChartObject
    For Each cht In ActiveSheet.ChartObjects
        With cht.Chart.Legend.Font
            .Name = "Calibri"
            .FontStyle = "Bold"
            .Size = 12
        End With
    Next cht
End Sub
```

Note that the Font object is contained in the Legend object, which is contained in the Chart object, which is contained in the ChartObjects collection. Now do you understand why it's called an *object hierarchy?*

Applying chart formatting

This example applies several different types of formatting to the active chart. I created this macro by recording my actions as I formatted a chart. Then I cleaned up the recorded code by removing irrelevant lines.

```
Sub ChartMods()
    ActiveChart.Type = xlArea
    ActiveChart.ChartArea.Font.Name = "Calibri"
    ActiveChart.ChartArea.Font.FontStyle = "Regular"
    ActiveChart.ChartArea.Font.Size = 9
    ActiveChart.PlotArea.Interior.ColorIndex = xlNone
    ActiveChart.Axes(xlValue).TickLabels.Font.Bold = True
    ActiveChart.Axes(xlCategory).TickLabels.Font.Bold = _
        True
    ActiveChart.Legend.Position = xlBottom
End Sub
```

You must activate a chart before executing the ChartMods macro. Activate an embedded chart by clicking it. To activate a chart on a chart sheet, activate the chart sheet.

To ensure that a chart is selected, you can add a statement to determine if a chart is active. Here's the modified macro, which displays a message (and ends) if a chart is not activated:

```
Sub ChartMods2()
    If ActiveChart Is Nothing Then
        MsgBox "Activate a chart."
        Exit Sub
    End If
    ActiveChart.Type = xlArea
    ActiveChart.ChartArea.Font.Name = "Calibri"
    ActiveChart.ChartArea.Font.FontStyle = "Regular"
    ActiveChart.ChartArea.Font.Size = 9
    ActiveChart.PlotArea.Interior.ColorIndex = xlNone
    ActiveChart.Axes(xlValue).TickLabels.Font.Bold = True
    ActiveChart.Axes(xlCategory).TickLabels.Font.Bold = _
        True
    ActiveChart.Legend.Position = xlBottom
End Sub
```

Here's another version that uses the With-End With construct to save some typing and make the code a bit clearer. Once again, I'm getting ahead of myself. Flip ahead a few pages to read about the With End-With structure.

```
Sub ChartMods3()
    If ActiveChart Is Nothing Then
        MsgBox "Activate a chart."
        Exit Sub
    End If
    With ActiveChart
      .Type = xlArea
      .ChartArea.Font.Name = "Calibri"
      .ChartArea.Font.FontStyle = "Regular"
      .ChartArea.Font.Size = 9
      .PlotArea.Interior.ColorIndex = xlNone
      .Axes(xlValue).TickLabels.Font.Bold = True
      .Axes(xlCategory).TickLabels.Font.Bold = True
      .Legend.Position = xlBottom
    End With
End Sub
```

When it comes to using VBA to work with charts, this short section barely scratched the surface. There's a lot more to it, of course, but at least this basic introduction will get you headed in the right direction.

VBA Speed Tips

VBA is fast, but it's not always fast enough. (Computer programs are never fast enough.) This section presents some programming examples you can use to speed up your macros.

Turning off screen updating

When executing a macro, you can sit back and watch all the on-screen action that occurs in the macro. Although doing this can be instructive, after getting the macro working properly, it's often annoying and can slow down the course of your macro considerably. Fortunately, you can disable the screen updating that normally occurs when you execute a macro. To turn off screen updating, use the following statement:

```
Application.ScreenUpdating = False
```

If you want the user to see what's happening at any point during the macro, use the following statement to turn screen updating back on:

```
Application.ScreenUpdating = True
```

To demonstrate the difference in speed, execute this simple macro, which fills a range with numbers:

```
Sub FillRange()
    Dim r as Long, c As Long
    Dim Number as Long
    Number = 0
    For r = 1 To 50
        For c = 1 To 50
            Number = Number + 1
            Cells(r, c).Select
            Cells(r, c).Value = Number
        Next c
    Next r
End Sub
```

You see each cell being selected, and the value being entered into the cells. Now insert the following statement at the beginning of the procedure and execute it again:

```
Application.ScreenUpdating = False
```

The range is filled up much faster, and you don't see the end result until the macro is finished running.

When debugging code, sometimes program execution ends somewhere in the middle, without having turned Screen updating back on (and yes, this happens to me, too). This sometimes causes Excel's application window to become totally unresponsive. The way out of this frozen state is simple: Go back to the VBE and execute the following statement in the Immediate window:

```
Application.ScreenUpdating = True
```

Turning off automatic calculation

If you have a worksheet with many complex formulas, you may find that you can speed things up considerably by setting the calculation mode to manual while your macro is executing. When the macro finishes, set the calculation mode back to automatic.

The following statement sets the Excel calculation mode to manual:

```
Application.Calculation = xlCalculationManual
```

Execute the next statement to set the calculation mode to automatic:

```
Application.Calculation = xlCalculationAutomatic
```

If your code uses cells with formula results, remember that turning off calculation means that the cells will not be recalculated unless you explicitly tell Excel to do so!

Eliminating those pesky alert messages

As you know, a macro can automatically perform a series of actions. In many cases, you can start a macro and then go hang out in the mail room while Excel does its thing. Some Excel operations, however, display messages that require a human response. For example, if your macro deletes a nonempty sheet, your code comes to a screeching halt while Excel waits for your response to the message shown in Figure 14-4. These types of messages mean that you can't leave Excel unattended while it executes your macro — unless you know the secret trick.

Figure 14-4:
You can
instruct
Excel to
not display
these types
of alerts
while run-
ning a
macro.

The secret trick: To avoid these alert messages, insert the following VBA statement in your macro:

```
Application.DisplayAlerts = False
```

Excel executes the default operation for these types of messages. In the case of deleting a sheet, the default operation is Delete (which is just what you want to happen). If you're not sure what the default operation is, perform a test and see what happens.

When the procedure ends, Excel automatically resets the DisplayAlerts property to True (its normal state). If you need to turn the alerts back on before the procedure ends, use this statement:

```
Application.DisplayAlerts = True
```

Simplifying object references

As you probably already know, references to objects can become very lengthy. For example, a fully qualified reference to a Range object may look like this:

```
Workbooks("MyBook.xlsx").Worksheets("Sheet1") _
    .Range("InterestRate")
```

If your macro frequently uses this range, you may want to create an object variable by using the Set command. For example, the following statement assigns this Range object to an object variable named Rate:

```
Set Rate = Workbooks("MyBook.xlsx") _
    .Worksheets("Sheet1").Range("InterestRate")
```

After defining this object variable, you can use the variable Rate rather than the lengthy reference. For example, you can change the value of the cell named InterestRate:

```
Rate.Value = .085
```

This is much easier to type (and understand) than the following statement:

```
Workbooks("MyBook.xlsx").Worksheets("Sheet1"). _
    Range("InterestRate") = .085
```

In addition to simplifying your coding, using object variables also speeds up your macros considerably. After creating object variables, I've seen some macros execute twice as fast as before.

Declaring variable types

You don't usually have to worry about the type of data you assign to a variable. Excel handles all the details for you behind the scenes. For example, if you have a variable named MyVar, you can assign a number of any type to that variable. You can even assign a text string to it later in the procedure.

But if you want your procedures to execute as fast as possible (and avoid some potentially nasty problems), tell Excel what type of data will be assigned to each of your variables. This is known as *declaring* a variable's type. (Refer to Chapter 7 for complete details.) Get into the habit of declaring all variables that you use.

In general, you should use the data type that requires the smallest number of bytes yet can still handle all the data assigned to it. When VBA works with data, execution speed depends on the number of bytes VBA has at its disposal. In other words, the fewer bytes data uses, the faster VBA can access and manipulate the data.

If you use an object variable (as described in the preceding section), you can declare the variable as a particular object type. Here's an example:

```
Dim Rate as Range
Set Rate = Workbooks("MyBook.xlsx") _
    .Worksheets("Sheet1").Range("InterestRate")
```

Using the With-End With structure

Do you need to set a number of properties for an object? Your code runs faster if you use the With-End With structure. An additional benefit is that your code may be easier to read.

The following code does not use With-End With:

```
Selection.HorizontalAlignment = xlCenter
Selection.VerticalAlignment = xlCenter
Selection.WrapText = True
Selection.Orientation = 0
Selection.ShrinkToFit = False
Selection.MergeCells = False
```

Here's the same code, rewritten to use With-End With:

```
With Selection
    .HorizontalAlignment = xlCenter
    .VerticalAlignment = xlCenter
    .WrapText = True
    .Orientation = 0
    .ShrinkToFit = False
    .MergeCells = False
End With
```

If this structure seems familiar to you, it's probably because the macro recorder uses With-End With whenever it can. And I presented another example earlier in this chapter.

Part IV
Communicating with Your Users

The 5th Wave By Rich Tennant

"I've used several spreadsheet programs, but this is the best one for designing quilt patterns."

In this part . . .

The five chapters in this part show you how to develop custom dialog boxes (also known as UserForms). This VBA feature is fairly easy to use after you get a few basic concepts under your belt. And, if you're like me, you may actually *enjoy* creating dialog boxes.

Chapter 15

Simple Dialog Boxes

. .

. .

You can't use Excel very long without being exposed to dialog boxes. They seem to pop up almost every time you select a command. Excel — like most Windows programs — uses dialog boxes to obtain information, clarify commands, and display messages. If you develop VBA macros, you can create your own dialog boxes that work just like those built into Excel. Those custom dialog boxes are called UserForms in VBA.

This chapter doesn't tell you anything about creating UserForms. Rather, it describes some techniques you might be able to use in place of UserForms. Chapters 16 through 18, however, do cover UserForms.

UserForm Alternatives

Some of the VBA macros you create behave the same every time you execute them. For example, you may develop a macro that enters a list of your employees into a worksheet range. This macro always produces the same result and requires no additional user input.

You might develop other macros, however, that behave differently under various circumstances or that offer the user options. In such cases, the macro may benefit from a custom dialog box. A custom dialog box provides a simple means for getting information from the user. Your macro then uses that information to determine what it should do.

UserForms can be quite useful, but creating them takes time. Before I cover the topic of creating UserForms in the next chapter, you need to know about some potentially timesaving alternatives.

VBA lets you display several different types of dialog boxes that you can sometimes use in place of a UserForm. You can customize these built-in dialog boxes in some ways, but they certainly don't offer the options available in a UserForm. In some cases, however, they're just what the doctor ordered.

In this chapter you read about

- ✔ The MsgBox function
- ✔ The InputBox function
- ✔ The GetOpenFilename method
- ✔ The GetSaveAsFilename method
- ✔ The FileDialog method

I also describe how to use VBA to display the Excel built-in dialog boxes — the dialog boxes that Excel uses to get information from you.

The MsgBox Function

You're probably already familiar with the VBA MsgBox function — I use it quite a bit in the examples throughout this book. The MsgBox function, which accepts the arguments shown in Table 15-1, is handy for displaying information and getting simple user input. It's able to get user input because it's a function. A function, as you recall, returns a value. In the case of the Msgbox function, it uses a dialog box to get the value that it returns. Keep reading to see exactly how it works.

Here's a simplified version of the syntax for the MsgBox function:

```
MsgBox(prompt[, buttons][, title])
```

Table 15-1	MsgBox Function Arguments
Argument	*What It Does*
prompt	The text Excel displays in the message box
buttons	A number that specifies which buttons (along with what icon) appear in the message box (optional)
title	The text that appears in the message box's title bar (optional) Displaying a simple message box

You can use the MsgBox function in two ways:

- **To simply show a message to the user.** In this case, you don't care about the result returned by the function.

- **To get a response from the user.** In this case, you do care about the result returned by the function. The result depends on the button that the user clicks.

If you use the MsgBox function by itself, don't include parentheses around the arguments. The following example simply displays a message and does not return a result. When the message is displayed, the code stops until the user clicks OK.

```
Sub MsgBoxDemo()
    MsgBox "Click OK to begin printing."
    Sheets("Results").PrintOut
End Sub
```

Figure 15-1 shows how this message box looks.

Figure 15-1:
A simple message box.

Getting a response from a message box

If you display a message box that has more than just an OK button, you'll probably want to know which button the user clicks. You're in luck. The MsgBox function can return a value that represents which button is clicked. You can assign the result of the MsgBox function to a variable.

In the following code, I use some built-in constants (which I describe later in Table 15-2) that make it easy to work with the values returned by MsgBox:

```
Sub GetAnswer()
    Dim Ans As Integer
    Ans = MsgBox("Did you eat lunch yet?", vbYesNo)
    Select Case Ans
        Case vbYes
'           ...[code if Ans is Yes]...
        Case vbNo
'           ...[code if Ans is No]...
    End Select
End Sub
```

Figure 15-2 shows how it looks. When you execute this procedure, the Ans variable is assigned a value of either vbYes or vbNo, depending on which button the user clicks. The Select Case statement uses the Ans value to determine which action the code should perform.

Figure 15-2:
A simple
message
box, with
two buttons.

You can also use the MsgBox function result without using a variable, as the following example demonstrates:

```
Sub GetAnswer2()
    If MsgBox("Continue?", vbYesNo) = vbYes Then
'        ...[code if Yes is clicked]...
    Else
'        ...[code if Yes is not clicked]...
    End If
End Sub
```

Customizing message boxes

The flexibility of the buttons argument makes it easy to customize your message boxes. You can specify which buttons to display, determine whether an icon appears, and decide which button is the default (the default button is "clicked" if the user presses Enter).

Table 15-2 lists some of the built-in constants you can use for the buttons argument. If you prefer, you can use the value rather than a constant (but I think using the built-in constants is a lot easier).

Table 15-2	Constants Used in the MsgBox Function	
Constant	**Value**	**What It Does**
vbOKOnly	0	Displays OK button only.
vbOKCancel	1	Displays OK and Cancel buttons.
vbAbortRetryIgnore	2	Displays Abort, Retry, and Ignore buttons.
vbYesNoCancel	3	Displays Yes, No, and Cancel buttons.
vbYesNo	4	Displays Yes and No buttons.

Constant	Value	What It Does
vbRetryCancel	5	Displays Retry and Cancel buttons.
vbCritical	16	Displays Critical Message icon.
vbQuestion	32	Displays Warning Query icon.
vbExclamation	48	Displays Warning Message icon.
vbInformation	64	Displays Information Message icon.
vbDefaultButton1	0	First button is default.
vbDefaultButton2	256	Second button is default.
vbDefaultButton3	512	Third button is default.
vbDefaultButton4	768	Fourth button is default.

To use more than one of these constants as an argument, just connect them with a + operator. For example, to display a message box with Yes and No buttons and an exclamation icon, use the following expression as the second MsgBox argument:

```
vbYesNo + vbExclamation
```

Or, if you prefer to make your code less understandable, use a value of 52 (that is, 4 + 48).

The following example uses a combination of constants to display a message box with a Yes button and a No button (vbYesNo) as well as a question mark icon (vbQuestion). The constant vbDefaultButton2 designates the second button (No) as the default button — that is, the button that is clicked if the user presses Enter. For simplicity, I assign these constants to the Config variable and then use Config as the second argument in the MsgBox function:

```
Sub GetAnswer3()
    Dim Config As Integer
    Dim Ans As Integer
    Config = vbYesNo + vbQuestion + vbDefaultButton2
    Ans = MsgBox("Process the monthly report?", Config)
    If Ans = vbYes Then RunReport
End Sub
```

Figure 15-3 shows the message box Excel displays when you execute the GetAnswer3 procedure. If the user clicks the Yes button, the routine executes the procedure named RunReport (which is not shown). If the user clicks the No button (or presses Enter), the routine ends with no action. Because I omitted the title argument in the MsgBox function, Excel uses the default title, Microsoft Excel.

Figure 15-3:
The MsgBox
function's
buttons
argument
determines
what
appears in
the mes-
sage box.

The following routine provides another example of using the MsgBox function:

```
Sub GetAnswer4()
    Dim Msg As String, Title As String
    Dim Config As Integer, Ans As Integer
    Msg = "Do you want to process the monthly report?"
    Msg = Msg & vbNewLine & vbNewLine
    Msg = Msg & "Processing the monthly report will "
    Msg = Msg & "take approximately 15 minutes. It "
    Msg = Msg & "will generate a 30-page report for "
    Msg = Msg & "all sales offices for the current "
    Msg = Msg & "month."
    Title = "XYZ Marketing Company"
    Config = vbYesNo + vbQuestion
    Ans = MsgBox(Msg, Config, Title)
    If Ans = vbYes Then RunReport
End Sub
```

This example demonstrates an efficient way to specify a longer message in a message box. I use a variable (Msg) and the concatenation operator (&) to build the message in a series of statements. The vbNewLine constant inserts a line break character that starts a new line (use it twice to insert a blank line). I also use the title argument to display a different title in the message box. Figure 15-4 shows the message box Excel displays when you execute this procedure.

Previous examples have used constants (such as vbYes and vbNo) for the return value of a MsgBox function. Besides these two constants, Table 15-3 lists a few others.

And that's pretty much all you need to know about the MsgBox function. Use message boxes with caution, though. There's usually no reason to display message boxes that serve no purpose. For example, people tend to get annoyed when they see a message box every day that reads, "Good morning, thanks for loading the Budget Projection workbook."

Figure 15-4:
This dialog
box, dis-
played by
the MsgBox
function, dis-
plays a title,
an icon, and
two buttons.

Table 15-3 Constants Used as Return Values for the MsgBox Function

Constant	Value	What It Means
vbOK	1	User clicked OK.
vbCancel	2	User clicked Cancel.
vbAbort	3	User clicked Abort.
vbRetry	4	User clicked Retry.
vbIgnore	5	User clicked Ignore.
vbYes	6	User clicked Yes.
vbNo	7	User clicked No.

The InputBox Function

The VBA InputBox function is useful for obtaining a single piece of informa-tion from the user. That information could be a value, a text string, or even a range address. This is a good alternative to developing a UserForm when you need to get only one value.

InputBox syntax

Here's a simplified version of the syntax for the InputBox function:

```
InputBox(prompt[, title][, default])
```

The InputBox function accepts the arguments listed in Table 15-4.

Table 15-4	InputBox Function Arguments
Argument	*What It Means*
Prompt	The text displayed in the input box
Title	The text displayed in the input box's title bar (optional)
Default	The default value for the user's input (optional)

An InputBox example

Here's an example showing how you can use the InputBox function:

```
TheName = InputBox("What is your name?", "Greetings")
```

When you execute this VBA statement, Excel displays the dialog box shown in Figure 15-5. Notice that this example uses only the first two arguments and does not supply a default value. When the user enters a value and clicks OK, the routine assigns the value to the variable TheName.

Figure 15-5: The InputBox function displays this dialog box.

The following example uses the third argument and provides a default value. The default value is the username stored by Excel (the Application object's UserName property).

```
Sub GetName()
    Dim DefName As String
    Dim TheName As String
    DefName = Application.UserName
    TheName = InputBox("What is your name?", _
        "Greetings", DefName)
End Sub
```

The input box always displays a Cancel button. If the user clicks Cancel, the InputBox function returns an empty string.

VBA's InputBox function always returns a string, so if you need to get a value, your code will need to do some additional checking. The following example uses the InputBox function to get a number. It uses the IsNumeric function to check whether the string is a number. If the string does contain a number, all is fine. If the user's entry cannot be interpreted as a number, the code displays a message box.

```
Sub GetName2AddSheet()
    Dim Prompt As String
    Dim Caption As String
    Dim DefValue As Integer
    Dim NumSheets As String

    Prompt = "How many sheets do you want to add?"
    Caption = "Tell me..."
    DefValue = 1
    NumSheets = InputBox(Prompt, Caption, DefValue)

    If NumSheets = "" Then Exit Sub 'Canceled
    If IsNumeric(NumSheets) Then
        If NumSheets > 0 Then Sheets.Add Count:=NumSheets
    Else
        MsgBox "Invalid number"
    End If
End Sub
```

Figure 15-6 shows the dialog box that this routine produces.

Figure 15-6:
Another
example of
using the
InputBox
function.

The information presented in this section applies to VBA's InputBox function. In addition, you have access to the InputBox method, which is a method of the Application object.

One big advantage of using the InputBox method is that your code can prompt for a range selection. The user can then select the range in the worksheet by highlighting the cells. Here's a quick example that prompts the user to select a range:

```
Sub GetRange()
    Dim Rng As Range
    On Error Resume Next
    Set Rng = Application.InputBox _
      (prompt:="Specify a range:", Type:=8)
    If Rng Is Nothing Then Exit Sub
    MsgBox "You selected range " & Rng.Address
End Sub
```

In this simple example, the code tells the user the address of the range that was selected. In real life, your code would actually do something useful with the selected range.

The Application.InputBox method is similar to VBA's InputBox function, but it also has some differences. Check the Help system for complete details.

The GetOpenFilename Method

If your VBA procedure needs to ask the user for a filename, you *could* use the InputBox function. An input box usually isn't the best tool for this job, however, because most users find it difficult to remember paths, backslashes, filenames, and file extensions. In other words, it's far too easy to make a typographical error when typing a filename.

For a better solution to this problem, use the GetOpenFilename method of the Application object, which ensures that your code gets its hands on a valid filename, including its complete path. The GetOpenFilename method displays the familiar Open dialog box (a dead ringer for the dialog box Excel displays when you choose File⇨Open).

The GetOpenFilename method doesn't actually open the specified file. This method simply returns the user-selected filename as a string. Then you can write code to do whatever you want with the filename.

The syntax for the GetOpenFilename method

The official syntax for the GetOpenFilename method is as follows:

```
object.GetOpenFilename ([fileFilter], [filterIndex],
    [title],[buttonText], [multiSelect])
```

The GetOpenFilename method takes the optional arguments shown in Table 15-5.

Table 15-5	GetOpenFilename Method Arguments
Argument	*What It Does*
FileFilter	Determines the types of files that appear in the dialog box (for example, *.TXT). You can specify several different filters from which the user can choose.
FilterIndex	Determines which of the file filters the dialog box displays by default.
Title	Specifies the caption for the dialog box's title bar.
ButtonText	Ignored (used only for the Macintosh version of Excel).
MultiSelect	If True, the user can select multiple files.

A GetOpenFilename example

The fileFilter argument determines what appears in the dialog box's Files of Type drop-down list. This argument consists of pairs of file filter strings followed by the wild card file filter specification, with commas separating each part and pair. If omitted, this argument defaults to the following:

```
All Files (*.*), *.*
```

Notice that this string consists of two parts:

```
All Files (*.*)
```

and

```
*.*
```

The first part of this string is the text displayed in the Files of Type drop-down list. The second part determines which files the dialog box displays. For example, *.* means *all files*.

The code in the following example brings up a dialog box that asks the user for a filename. The procedure defines five file filters. Notice that I use the VBA line continuation sequence to set up the Filter variable; doing so helps simplify this rather complicated argument.

```
Sub GetImportFileName ()
    Dim Finfo As String
    Dim FilterIndex As Integer
    Dim Title As String
    Dim FileName As Variant

'   Set up list of file filters
    FInfo = "Text Files (*.txt),*.txt," & _
            "Lotus Files (*.prn),*.prn," & _
            "Comma Separated Files (*.csv),*.csv," & _
            "ASCII Files (*.asc),*.asc," & _
            "All Files (*.*),*.*"

'   Display *.* by default
    FilterIndex = 5

'   Set the dialog box caption
    Title = "Select a File to Import"

'   Get the filename
    FileName = Application.GetOpenFilename (FInfo, _
        FilterIndex, Title)

'   Handle return info from dialog box
    If FileName = False Then
        MsgBox "No file was selected."
    Else
        MsgBox "You selected " & FileName
    End If
End Sub
```

Figure 15-7 shows the dialog box Excel displays when you execute this procedure. In a real application, you would do something more meaningful with the filename. For example, you might want to open it by using a statement such as this:

```
Workbooks.Open FileName
```

Notice that the FileName variable is declared as a Variant data type. If the user clicks Cancel, that variable contains a Boolean value (False). Otherwise, FileName is a string. Therefore, using a Variant data type handles both possibilities.

By the way, the dialog box may look different, depending on which version of Windows you use.

Figure 15-7: The GetOpenFilename method displays a customizable dialog box and returns the selected file's path and name. It does not open the file.

Selecting multiple files

If the MultiSelect argument for the GetOpenFilename method is True, the user can select multiple files in the dialog box by pressing Ctrl while clicking the files. In this case, the GetOpenFilename method returns an array of filenames. Your code must loop through the array to identify each selected filename, as the following example demonstrates:

```
Sub GetImportFileName2()
    Dim FileNames As Variant
    Dim Msg As String
    Dim I As Integer
    FileNames = Application.GetOpenFilename _
        (MultiSelect:=True)
    If IsArray(FileNames) Then
'       Display full path and name of the files
        Msg = "You selected:" & vbNewLine

        For I = LBound(FileNames) To UBound(FileNames)
            Msg = Msg & FileNames(i) & vbNewLine
        Next i
        MsgBox Msg
    Else
'       Cancel button clicked
        MsgBox "No files were selected."
    End If
End Sub
```

Figure 15-8 shows the result of running this procedure. The message box displays the filenames that were selected.

Figure 15-8:
Select
multiple
filenames
by using the
GetOpen-
Filename
method.

Notice that I use a named argument for the GetOpenFilename method. I also set the MultiSelect argument to True. The other arguments are omitted, so they take on their default values. Using named arguments eliminates the need to specify arguments that aren't used.

The FileNames variable is defined as a Variant data type. I use the IsArray function to determine whether FileName contains an array. If so, the code uses the VBA LBound and UBound functions to determine the array's lower and upper bounds and build a message that consists of each array element. If FileNames is not an array, that means the user clicked the Cancel button (the FileNames variable contains an array even if only one file is selected).

The GetSaveAsFilename Method

The Excel GetSaveAsFilename method works just like the GetOpenFilename method, but it displays the Excel Save As dialog box rather than its Open dialog box. The GetSaveAsFilename method gets a path and filename from the user but doesn't do anything with it. It's up to you to write code that actually saves the file.

The syntax for this method follows:

```
object.GetSaveAsFilename ([InitialFilename], [FileFilter],
        [FilterIndex], [Title], [ButtonText])
```

The GetSaveAsFilename method takes Table 15-6's arguments, all of which are optional.

Table 15-6	GetSaveAsFilename Method Arguments
Argument	**What It Does**
InitialFileName	Specifies a default filename that appears in the File Name box.
FileFilter	Determines the types of files Excel displays in the dialog box (for example, *.TXT). You can specify several different filters from which the user can choose.
FilterIndex	Determines which of the file filters Excel displays by default.
Title	Defines a caption for the dialog box's title bar.

Getting a Folder Name

Sometimes, you don't need to get a filename; you just need to get a folder name. If that's the case, the FileDialog object is just what the doctor ordered.

The following procedure displays a dialog box that allows the user to select a directory. The selected directory name (or "Canceled") is then displayed by using the MsgBox function.

```
Sub GetAFolder()
    With Application.FileDialog(msoFileDialogFolderPicker)
        .InitialFileName = Application.DefaultFilePath & "\"
        .Title = "Please select a location for the backup"
        .Show
        If .SelectedItems.Count = 0 Then
            MsgBox "Canceled"
        Else
            MsgBox .SelectedItems(1)
        End If
    End With
End Sub
```

The FileDialog object lets you specify the starting directory by specifying a value for the InitialFileName property. In this case, the code uses Excel's default file path as the starting directory.

Displaying Excel's Built-in Dialog Boxes

One way to look at VBA is that it's a tool that lets you mimic Excel commands. For example, consider this VBA statement:

```
Range("A1:A12").Name = "MonthNames"
```

Executing this VBA statement has the same effect as choosing Formulas⇨ Defined Names⇨Define Name to display the New Name dialog box, and then typing MonthNames in the Name box and A1:A12 in the Refers to box, and clicking OK.

When you execute the VBA statement, the New Name dialog box does not appear. This is almost always what you want to happen; you don't want dialog boxes flashing across the screen while your macro executes.

In some cases, however, you may want your code to display one of Excel's many built-in dialog boxes and let the user make the choices in the dialog box. You can do this by using VBA to execute a Ribbon command. Here's an example that displays the New Name dialog box (see Figure 15-9).

```
Application.CommandBars.ExecuteMso ("NameDefine")
```

Figure 15-9:
Displaying one of Excel's dialog boxes by using VBA.

Your VBA code can't get any information from the dialog box. For example, if you execute the code to display the New Name dialog box, your code can't get the name entered by the user, or the range that's being named.

The ExecuteMso is a method of the CommandBars object, and accepts one argument, an idMso parameter that represents a Ribbon control. Unfortunately, these parameters are not listed in the Help system. Code that uses the ExecuteMso method is not compatible with versions prior to Excel 2007.

You can download a file from this book's Web site that lists all of the Excel Ribbon command parameter names.

Here's another example of using the ExecuteMso method. This statement, when executed, displays the Font tab of the Format Cells dialog box:

```
Application.CommandBars.ExecuteMso("FormatCellsFontDialog")
```

If you try to display a built-in dialog box in an incorrect context, Excel displays an error message. For example, here's a statement that displays the Format Number dialog box:

```
Application.CommandBars.ExecuteMso ("NumberFormatsDialog")
```

If you execute this statement when it's not appropriate (for example, a Shape is selected), Excel displays an error message because that dialog box is appropriate only for worksheet cells.

Chapter 16

UserForm Basics

In This Chapter

▶ Finding out when to use UserForms

▶ Understanding UserForm objects

▶ Displaying a UserForm

▶ Creating a UserForm that works with a useful macro

A UserForm is useful if your VBA macro needs to get information from a user. For example, your macro may have some options that can be specified in a UserForm. If only a few pieces of information are required (for example, a Yes/No answer or a text string), one of the techniques I describe in Chapter 15 may do the job. But if you need to obtain more information, you must create a UserForm. In this chapter, I introduce you to UserForms. You'll be pleased to make their acquaintance.

Knowing When to Use a UserForm

This section describes a situation in which a UserForm is useful. The following macro changes the text in each cell in the selection to uppercase letters. It does this by using the VBA built-in UCase function.

```
Sub ChangeCase()
    Dim WorkRange As Range

'   Exit if a range is not selected
    If TypeName(Selection) <> "Range" Then Exit Sub

'   Process only text cells, no formulas
    On Error Resume Next
    Set WorkRange = Selection.SpecialCells _
        (xlCellTypeConstants, xlCellTypeConstants)
    For Each cell In WorkRange
        cell.Value = UCase(cell.Value)
    Next cell
End Sub
```

You can make this macro even more useful. For example, it would be nice if the macro could also change the text in the cells to either lowercase or proper case (capitalizing the first letter in each word). One approach is to create two additional macros — one for lowercase and one for proper case. Another approach is to modify the macro to handle the other options. If you use the second approach, you need some method of asking the user which type of change to make to the cells.

The solution is to display a dialog box like the one shown in Figure 16-1. You create this dialog box on a UserForm in the VBE and display it by using a VBA macro. In the next section, I provide step-by-step instructions for creating this dialog box. Before I get into that, I set the stage with some introductory material.

Figure 16-1:
You can get information from the user by displaying a UserForm.

In VBA, the official name for a dialog box is a UserForm. But a UserForm is really an object that contains what's commonly known as a *dialog box.* This distinction isn't important, so I tend to use these terms interchangeably.

Creating UserForms: An Overview

To create a UserForm, you usually take the following general steps:

1. **Determine how the dialog box will be used and where it will be displayed in your VBA macro.**

2. **Press Alt+F11 to activate the VBE and insert a new UserForm object.**

 A UserForm object holds a single UserForm.

3. **Add controls to the UserForm.**

 Controls include items such as text boxes, buttons, check boxes, and list boxes.

4. **Use the Properties window to modify the properties for the controls or for the UserForm itself.**

5. **Write event-handler procedures for the controls (for example, a macro that executes when the user clicks a button in the dialog box).**

 These procedures are stored in the Code window for the UserForm object.

6. **Write a procedure (stored in a VBA module) that displays the dialog box to the user.**

Don't worry if some of these steps seem foreign. I provide more details in the following sections, along with step-by-step instructions for creating a UserForm.

When you are designing a UserForm, you are creating what developers call the Graphical User Interface (GUI) to your application. Take some time to consider what your form should look like and how your users are likely to want to interact with the elements on the UserForm. Try to guide them through the steps they need to take on the form by carefully considering the arrangement and wording of the controls. Like most things VBA-related, the more you do it, the easier it gets.

Working with UserForms

Each dialog box that you create is stored in its own UserForm object — one dialog box per UserForm. You create and access these UserForms in the Visual Basic Editor.

Inserting a new UserForm

Insert a UserForm object with the following steps:

1. **Activate the VBE by pressing Alt+F11.**

2. **Select the workbook in the Project window.**

3. **Choose Insert⇨UserForm.**

 The VBE inserts a new UserForm object, which contains an empty dialog box.

Figure 16-2 shows a UserForm — an empty dialog box, in need of some controls.

Figure 16-2:
A new
UserForm
object.

Adding controls to a UserForm

When you activate a UserForm, the VBE displays the Toolbox in a floating window, as shown in Figure 16-2. You use the tools in the Toolbox to add controls to your UserForm. If the Toolbox doesn't appear when you activate your UserForm, choose View⇨Toolbox.

To add a control, just click the desired control in the Toolbox and drag it into the dialog box to create the control. After you add a control, you can move and resize it by using standard techniques.

Table 16-1 indicates the various tools, as well as their capabilities. To determine which tool is which, hover your mouse pointer over the control and read the small pop-up description.

Table 16-1	Toolbox Controls
Control	*What It Does*
Label	Shows text.
TextBox	Allows the user to enter text.
ComboBox	Displays a drop-down list.
ListBox	Displays a list of items.
CheckBox	Useful for on/off or yes/no options.
OptionButton	Used in groups; allows the user to select one of several options.
ToggleButton	A button that is either on or off.
Frame	A container for other controls.

Control	What It Does
CommandButton	A clickable button.
TabStrip	Displays tabs.
MultiPage	A tabbed container for other objects.
ScrollBar	A draggable bar.
SpinButton	A clickable button often used for changing a value.
Image	Contains an image.
RefEdit	Allows the user to select a range.

Changing properties for a UserForm control

Every control you add to a UserForm has a number of properties that determine how the control looks or behaves. In addition, the UserForm itself also has its own set of properties. You can change these properties with the Properties window. Figure 16-3 shows the properties window when a CommandButton control is selected.

The Properties window appears when you press F4, and the properties shown in this window depend on what is selected. If you select a different control, the properties change to those appropriate for that control. To hide the Properties window, click the close button in its title bar.

Figure 16-3:
Use the Properties windows to change the properties of UserForm controls.

Properties for controls include the following:

- ✔ Name
- ✔ Width
- ✔ Height
- ✔ Value
- ✔ Caption

Each control has its own set of properties (although many controls have some common properties). To change a property using the Properties window:

1. **Make sure that the correct control is selected in the UserForm.**

2. **Make sure the Properties window is visible (press F4 if it's not).**

3. **In the Properties window, click on the property that you want to change.**

4. **Make the change in the right portion of the Properties window.**

If you select the UserForm itself (not a control on the UserForm), you can use the Properties window to adjust UserForm properties.

Chapter 17 tells you everything you need to know about working with dialog box controls.

Some of the UserForm properties serve as default settings for new controls you drag onto the UserForm. For example, if you change the Font property for a UserForm, controls that you add will use that same font. Controls that are already on the UserForm are not affected.

Viewing the UserForm Code window

Every UserForm object has a Code module that holds the VBA code (the event-handler procedures) executed when the user works with the dialog box. To view the Code module, press F7. The Code window is empty until you add some procedures. Press Shift+F7 to return to the dialog box.

Here's another way to switch between the Code window and the UserForm display: Use the View Code and View Object buttons in the Project window's title bar. Or right-click the UserForm and choose View Code. If you're viewing code, double-click the UserForm name in the Project window to return to the UserForm.

Displaying a UserForm

You display a UserForm by using the UserForm's Show method in a VBA procedure.

The macro that displays the dialog box must be in a VBA module — not in the Code window for the UserForm.

The following procedure displays the dialog box named UserForm1:

```
Sub ShowDialog()
    UserForm1.Show
'    Other statements can go here
End Sub
```

When Excel displays the dialog box, the ShowDialog macro halts until the user closes the dialog box. Then VBA executes any remaining statements in the procedure. Most of the time, you won't have any more code in the procedure. As you later see, you put your event-handler procedures in the Code window for the UserForm.

Using information from a UserForm

The VBE provides a name for each control you add to a UserForm. The control's name corresponds to its Name property. Use this name to refer to a particular control in your code. For example, if you add a CheckBox control to a UserForm named UserForm1, the CheckBox control is named CheckBox1 by default. The following statement makes this control appear with a check mark:

```
UserForm1.CheckBox1.Value = True
```

Most of the time, you write the code for a UserForm in the UserForm's code module. If that's the case, you can omit the UserForm object qualifier and write the statement like this:

```
CheckBox1.Value = True
```

Your VBA code can also check various properties of the controls and take appropriate actions. The following statement executes a macro named PrintReport if the check box (named CheckBox1) is checked:

```
If CheckBox1.Value = True Then Call PrintReport
```

I discuss this topic in detail in Chapter 17.

I recommend that you change the default name the VBE has given to your controls to something more meaningful. You might consider naming the check box described above "cbxPrintReport." Note that I precede the name with a three-letter prefix (for "checkbox"), indicating the type of control. It is a matter of taste whether you think doing so is a good practice.

A UserForm Example

This section's UserForm example is an enhanced version of the ChangeCase macro from the beginning of the chapter. Recall that the original version of this macro changes the text in the selected cells to uppercase. This modified version uses a UserForm to ask the user which type of change to make: uppercase, lowercase, or proper case.

This dialog box needs to obtain one piece of information from the user: the type of change to make to the text. Because the user has three choices, your best bet is a dialog box with three OptionButton controls. The dialog box also needs two more buttons: an OK button and a Cancel button. Clicking the OK button runs the code that does the work. Clicking the Cancel button causes the macro to finish without doing anything.

This workbook is available at the book's Web site. However, you get more out of this exercise if you follow the steps provided here and create it yourself.

Creating the UserForm

These steps create the UserForm. Start with an empty workbook.

1. **Press Alt+F11 to activate the VBE.**

2. **If multiple projects are in the Project window, select the project that corresponds to the workbook you're using.**

3. **Choose Insert⇨UserForm.**

 The VBE inserts a new UserForm object with an empty dialog box.

4. **Press F4 to display the Properties window.**

5. **In the Properties window, change the dialog box's Caption property to** Change Case.

6. **The dialog box is a bit too large, so you may want to click it and use the handles (on the right and bottom sides) to make it smaller.**

 Step 6 can also be done after you position all the controls in the dialog box.

Adding the CommandButtons

Ready to add two CommandButtons — OK and Cancel — to the dialog box?
Follow along:

1. **Make sure that the Toolbox is displayed. If it isn't, choose
 View⇨Toolbox.**

2. **If the Properties window isn't visible, press F4 to display it.**

3. **In the Toolbox, drag a CommandButton into the dialog box to create a
 button.**

 As you see in the Properties box, the button has a default name and cap-
 tion: CommandButton1.

4. **Make sure that the CommandButton is selected. Then activate the
 Properties window and change the following properties:**

Property	*Change To*
Name	**OKButton**
Caption	**OK**
Default	**True**

5. **Add a second CommandButton object to the UserForm and change the
 following properties:**

Property	*Change To*
Name	**CancelButton**
Caption	**Cancel**
Cancel	**True**

6. **Adjust the size and position of the controls so your dialog box looks
 something like Figure 16-4.**

Figure 16-4:
The
UserForm
with two
Command
Button
controls.

Adding the OptionButtons

In this section, you add three OptionButtons to the dialog box. Before adding the OptionButtons, you add a Frame object that contains the OptionButtons. The Frame isn't necessary, but it makes the dialog box look more professional.

1. **In the Toolbox, click the Frame tool and drag it into the dialog box.**

 This step creates a frame to hold the options buttons.

2. **Use the Properties window to change the frame's caption to** Options.

3. **In the Toolbox, click the OptionButton tool and drag it into the dialog box (within the Frame).**

 Doing this creates an OptionButton control.

4. **Select the OptionButton and use the Properties window to change the following properties:**

Property	*Change To*
Name	**OptionUpper**
Caption	**Upper Case**
Accelerator	**U**
Value	**True**

 Setting the Value property to True makes this OptionButton the default.

5. **Add another OptionButton and use the Properties window to change the following properties:**

Property	*Change To*
Name	**OptionLower**
Caption	**Lower Case**
Accelerator	**L**

6. **Add a third OptionButton and use the Properties window to change the following properties:**

Property	*Change To*
Name	**OptionProper**
Caption	**Proper Case**
Accelerator	**P**

7. **Adjust the size and position of the OptionButtons, Frame, and dialog box.**

 Your UserForm should look something like Figure 16-5.

If you'd like a sneak preview to see what the UserForm looks like when it's displayed, press F5. None of the controls are working yet, so you need to click the red "X" in the title bar to close the dialog box.

The Accelerator property determines which letter in the caption is underlined — more important, it determines what Alt-key combination selects that control. For example, you can select the Lower Case option by pressing Alt+L because the L is underlined. Accelerator keys are optional, but some users prefer to use the keyboard to navigate dialog boxes.

You may wonder why the OptionButtons have accelerator keys but the CommandButtons go without. Generally, OK and Cancel buttons never have accelerator keys because they can be accessed from the keyboard. Pressing Enter is equivalent to clicking OK because the control's Default property is True. Pressing Esc is equivalent to clicking Cancel because the control's Cancel property is True.

Adding event-handler procedures

Now it's time to make the UserForm actually do something. Here's how to add an event-handler procedure for the Cancel and OK buttons:

1. **Double-click the Cancel button.**

 VBE activates the Code window for the UserForm and inserts an empty procedure:

   ```
   Private Sub CancelButton_Click()
   ```

 The procedure named CancelButton_Click is executed when the Cancel button is clicked, but only when the dialog box is displayed. In other words, clicking the Cancel button when you're designing the dialog box

won't execute the procedure. Because the Cancel button's Cancel property is set to True, pressing Esc also triggers the CancelButton_Click procedure.

2. **Insert the following statement inside the procedure (before the End Sub statement):**

```
Unload UserForm1
```

This statement closes the UserForm (and removes it from memory) when the Cancel button is clicked.

3. **Press Shift+F7 to return to the UserForm.**

4. **Double-click the OK button.**

VBE activates the code window for the UserForm and inserts an empty Sub procedure called

```
Private Sub OKButton_Click()
```

When the UserForm is displayed, clicking OK executes this procedure. Because this button has its Default property set to True, pressing Enter also executes the OKButton_Click procedure.

5. **Enter the following code inside the procedure:**

```
Private Sub OKButton_Click()
    Dim WorkRange As Range

'   Process only text cells, no formulas
    On Error Resume Next
    Set WorkRange = Selection.SpecialCells _
        (xlCellTypeConstants, xlCellTypeConstants)

'   Upper case
    If OptionUpper Then
        For Each cell In WorkRange
            cell.Value = UCase(cell.Value)
        Next cell
    End If

'   Lower case
    If OptionLower Then
        For Each cell In WorkRange
            cell.Value = LCase(cell.Value)
        Next cell
    End If

'   Proper case
    If OptionProper Then
        For Each cell In WorkRange
            cell.Value = Application. _
            WorksheetFunction.Proper(cell.Value)
```

```
            Next cell
        End If
        Unload UserForm1
End Sub
```

The preceding code is an enhanced version of the original ChangeCase macro that I present at the beginning of the chapter. The macro consists of three separate blocks of code. This code uses three If-Then structures; each one has a For Each loop. Only one block is executed, determined by which OptionButton the user selects. The last statement *unloads* (closes) the dialog box after the work is finished.

Here's something kind of odd. Notice that VBA has a UCase function and an LCase function, but it doesn't have a function to convert text to proper case. Therefore, I use Excel's PROPER worksheet function (preceded by Application.WorksheetFunction) to do the proper case conversion. Another option is to use the VBA StrConv function. (See the Help system for details.) The StrConv function is not available in all Excel versions, so I use the PROPER worksheet function instead.

Creating a macro to display the dialog box

We're almost finished with this project. The only thing missing is a way to display the dialog box. Follow these steps to make the procedure that makes the dialog box appear:

1. **In the VBE window, choose Insert⇨Module.**

 The VBE adds an empty VBA module (named Module1) to the project.

2. **Enter the following code:**

```
Sub ChangeCase()
    If TypeName(Selection) = "Range" Then
        UserForm1.Show
    Else
        MsgBox "Select a range.", vbCritical
    End If
End Sub
```

This procedure is simple. It checks to make sure that a range is selected. If so, the dialog box is displayed (using the Show method). The user then interacts with the dialog box and the code stored in the UserForm's Code pane is executed. If a range is not selected, the user sees a MsgBox with the text, "Select a range."

Making the macro available

At this point, everything should be working properly. But you still need an easy way to execute the macro. Assign a shortcut key (Ctrl+Shift+C) that executes the ChangeCase macro:

1. **Activate the Excel window via Alt+F11.**

2. **Choose Developer➪Code➪Macros or press Alt+F8.**

3. **In the Macros dialog box, select the ChangeCase macro.**

4. **Click the Options button.**

 Excel displays its Macro Options dialog box.

5. **Enter an uppercase C for the Shortcut key.**

 See Figure 16-6.

6. **Enter a description of the macro in the Description field.**

7. **Click OK.**

8. **Click Cancel when you return to the Macro dialog box.**

Figure 16-6:
Assign a
shortcut key
to execute
the Change
Case macro.

After you perform this operation, pressing Ctrl+Shift+C executes the ChangeCase macro, which displays the UserForm if a range is selected.

You can also make this macro available from the Quick Access toolbar. Right-click the Quick Access toolbar and choose Customize Quick Access Toolbar. The Excel Options dialog box appears, and you'll find the ChangeCase macro listed under Macros (see Figure 16-7). Adding a macro to your Quick Access toolbar works much better in Excel 2010. If the workbook that contains the macro isn't open, Excel 2010 opens it and runs the macro. In Excel 2007, you get an error if the workbook isn't open.

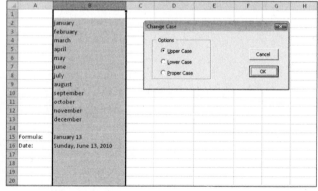

Figure 16-7: Adding the Change Chase macro to the Quick Access toolbar.

Testing the macro

Finally, you need to test the macro and dialog box to make sure they work properly:

1. **Activate a worksheet (any worksheet in any workbook).**

2. **Select some cells that contain text.**

3. **Press Ctrl+Shift+C.**

 The UserForm appears. Figure 16-8 shows how it should look.

4. **Make your choice and click OK.**

 If you did everything correctly, the macro makes the specified change to the text in the selected cells.

Figure 16-8: The UserForm is in action.

Figure 16-9 shows the worksheet after converting the text to uppercase. Notice that the formula in cell B15 and the date in cell B16 were not changed. The macro, as you recall, works only with cells that contain text.

	A	B	C
1			
2		JANUARY	
3		FEBRUARY	
4		MARCH	
5		APRIL	
6		MAY	
7		JUNE	
8		JULY	
9		AUGUST	
10		SEPTEMBER	
11		OCTOBER	
12		NOVEMBER	
13		DECEMBER	
14			
15	Formula:	January 13	
16	Date:	Sunday, June 13, 2010	
17			
18			

Figure 16-9:
The text has been converted to uppercase.

As long as the workbook is open, you can execute the macro from any other workbook. If you close the workbook that contains your macro, Ctrl+Shift+C no longer has any function.

If the macro doesn't work properly, double-check the preceding steps to locate and correct the error. Don't be alarmed; debugging is a normal part of developing macros. As a last resort, download the completed workbook from this book's Web site, and try to figure out where you went wrong.

Chapter 17

Using UserForm Controls

In This Chapter

▶ Understanding each type of dialog box control

▶ Changing each control's properties

▶ Working with dialog box controls

A user responds to a custom dialog box (also known as a *UserForm*) by using the various controls (buttons, edit boxes, option buttons, and so on) that the dialog box contains. Your VBA code then makes use of these responses to determine which actions to take. You have quite a few controls at your disposal, and this chapter tells you about them.

If you worked through the hands-on example in Chapter 16, you already have some experience with UserForm controls. This chapter fills in the gaps.

Getting Started with Dialog Box Controls

In this section, I tell you how to add controls to a UserForm, give them meaningful names, and adjust some of their properties.

Before you can do any of these things, you must have a UserForm, which you get by choosing Insert➪UserForm in the VBE. When you add a UserForm, make sure that the correct project is selected in the Project window (if more than one project is available).

Adding controls

Oddly enough, the VBE doesn't have menu commands that let you add controls to a dialog box. You must use the floating Toolbox, which I describe in Chapter 16, to add controls. Normally, the Toolbox pops up automatically when you activate a UserForm in the VBE. If it doesn't, you can display the Toolbox by choosing View➪Toolbox.

Follow along to add a control to the UserForm:

1. **Click the Toolbox tool that corresponds to the control you want to add.**

2. **Click in the UserForm and drag to size and position the control.**

 Alternatively, you can simply drag a control from the Toolbox to the UserForm to create a control with the default dimensions. Figure 17-1 shows a UserForm that contains a few controls.

Figure 17-1:
A UserForm
with a few
controls
added.

A UserForm may contain vertical and horizontal grid lines, which help align the controls you add. When you add or move a control, it *snaps* to the grid. If you don't like this feature, you can turn off the grids by following these steps:

1. **Choose Tools➪Options in the VBE.**

2. **In the Options dialog box, select the General tab.**

3. **Set your desired options in the Form Grid Settings section.**

Introducing control properties

Every control that you add to a UserForm has properties that determine how the control looks and behaves. You can change a control's properties at the following two times:

✔ At design time — when you're designing the UserForm. You do so manually, using the Properties window.

✔ At runtime — while your macro is running. You do so by writing VBA code. Changes made at runtime are always temporary; they are made to the copy of the dialog box you are showing, not to the actual UserForm object you designed.

When you add a control to a UserForm, you almost always need to make some design-time adjustments to its properties. You make these changes in the Properties window. (To display the Properties window, press F4.) Figure 17-2 shows the Properties window, which displays properties for the object selected in the UserForm — which happens to be a CheckBox control.

Figure 17-2: Use the Properties window to make design-time changes to a control's properties.

To change a control's properties at runtime, you must write VBA code. For example, you may want to hide a particular control when the user clicks a check box. In such a case, you write code to change the control's Visible property.

Each control has its own set of properties. All controls, however, share some common properties, such as Name, Width, and Height. Table 17-1 lists some of the common properties available for many controls.

Table 17-1	Common Control Properties
Property	**What It Is**
Accelerator	The letter underlined in the control's caption. The user presses this key in conjunction with the Alt key to select the control.
AutoSize	If True, the control resizes itself automatically based on the text in its caption.
BackColor	The control's background color.
BackStyle	The background style (transparent or opaque).

(continued)

Table 17-1 *(continued)*

Property	What It Is
Caption	The text that appears on the control.
Value	The control's value.
Left and Top	Values that determine the control's position.
Width and Height	Values that determine the control's width and height.
Visible	If False, the control is hidden.
Name	The control's name. By default, a control's name is based on the control type. You can change the name to any valid name, but each control's name must be unique within the dialog box.
Picture	A graphics image to display. The image can be from a graphics file, or you can select the Picture property and paste an image that you copied to the Clipboard.

When you select a control, that control's properties appear in the Properties window. To change a property, just select it in the Properties window and make the change. Some properties give you some help. For example, if you need to change the TextAlign property, the Properties window displays a drop-down list that contains all valid property values, as shown in Figure 17-3.

Figure 17-3:
Change
some
properties
by select-
ing from a
drop-down
list of valid
property
values.

Dialog Box Controls: The Details

In the following sections, I introduce you to each type of control you can use in custom dialog boxes and discuss some of the more useful properties. I don't discuss every property for every control because that would require a book that's about four times as thick (and it would be a very boring book).

The Help system for controls and properties is thorough. To find complete details for a particular property, select the property in the Properties window and press F1. Figure 17-4 shows the online help for the SpecialEffect property — useful for when you make your next blockbuster adventure UserForm.

All the sample files in this section are available at this book's Web site.

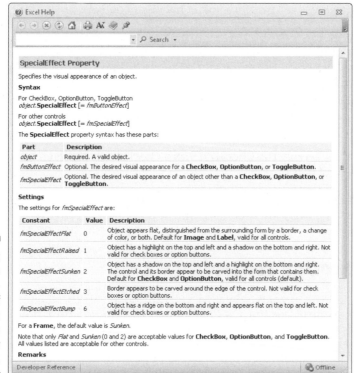

Figure 17-4:
The Help system provides lots of information for each property and control.

CheckBox control

A CheckBox control is useful for getting a binary choice: yes or no, true or false, on or off, and so on. Figure 17-5 shows some examples of CheckBox controls.

Figure 17-5:
CheckBox
controls.

The following is a description of a CheckBox control's most useful properties:

- ✔ **Accelerator:** A letter that lets the user change the value of the control by using the keyboard. For example, if the accelerator is A, pressing Alt+A changes the value of the CheckBox control (from checked to unchecked, or from unchecked to checked).

- ✔ **ControlSource:** The address of a worksheet cell that's linked to the CheckBox. The cell displays TRUE if the control is checked or FALSE if the control is not checked.

- ✔ **Value:** If True, the CheckBox has a check mark. If False, it does not have a check mark.

Don't confuse CheckBox controls with OptionButton controls. They look kind of similar, but they are used for different purposes.

ComboBox control

A ComboBox control is similar to a ListBox control (described later in the "ListBox control" section). A ComboBox, however, is a drop-down box and displays only one item at a time. Another difference is that the user may be allowed to enter a value that does not appear in the list of items. Figure 17-6 shows two ComboBox controls. The control on the right (for the year) is being used, so it displays its list of options.

Figure 17-6:
ComboBox
controls.

The following is a description of some useful ComboBox control properties:

- ✔ **BoundColumn:** If the list contains multiple columns, this property determines which column contains the returned value.
- ✔ **ColumnCount:** The number of columns in the list.
- ✔ **ControlSource:** A cell that stores the value selected in the ComboBox.
- ✔ **ListRows:** The number of items to display when the list drops down.
- ✔ **ListStyle:** The appearance of the list items.
- ✔ **RowSource:** A range address that contains the list of items displayed in the ComboBox.
- ✔ **Style:** Determines whether the control acts like a drop-down list or a combo box. A drop-down list doesn't allow the user to enter a new value.
- ✔ **Value:** The text of the item selected by the user and displayed in the ComboBox.

If your list of items is not in a worksheet, you can add items to a ComboBox control by using the AddItem method. More information on this method is in Chapter 18.

CommandButton control

CommandButton is just a common clickable button. It is of no use unless you provide an event-handler procedure to execute when the button is clicked. Figure 17-7 shows a dialog box with nine CommandButtons. Two of these buttons feature a clipart image (specified by copying the clipart and then pasting it into the Picture field in the Properties window).

Figure 17-7:
Command
Button
controls.

When a CommandButton is clicked, it executes an event-handler procedure with a name that consists of the CommandButton's name, an underscore, and the word *Click.* For example, if a command button is named MyButton, clicking it executes the macro named MyButton_Click. This macro is stored in the Code window for the UserForm.

The following is a description of some useful CommandButton control properties:

- ✔ **Cancel:** If True, pressing Esc executes the macro attached to the button. (Only one of the form's buttons should have this option set to True.)
- ✔ **Default:** If True, pressing Enter executes the macro attached to the button. (Again: Just one button should have this option set to True.)

Frame control

A Frame control encloses other controls. You do so either for aesthetic purposes or to logically group a set of controls. A frame is particularly useful when the dialog box contains more than one set of OptionButton controls. (See "OptionButton control," later in this chapter.)

The following list describes some useful Frame control properties:

- ✔ **BorderStyle:** The frame's appearance.
- ✔ **Caption:** The text displayed at the top of the frame. The caption can be an empty string if you don't want the control to display a caption.

Image control

An Image control displays an image. You may want to use an Image control to display your company's logo in a dialog box. Figure 17-8 shows a dialog box with an Image control that displays a photo of some guy who writes Excel books.

Figure 17-8: An Image control displays a photo.

The following list describes the most useful Image control properties:

- ✔ **Picture:** The graphics image that is displayed.
- ✔ **PictureSizeMode:** How the picture is displayed if the control size does not match the image size.

When you click the Picture property, you are prompted for a filename. However, the graphics image (once it's retrieved) is stored in the workbook. That way, if you distribute your workbook to someone else, you don't have to include a copy of the graphics file.

Excel's clipart collection is a great source of images. Use Insert➪Illustrations➪ Clipart and choose an image to place in your worksheet. Select the image and press Ctrl+C to copy it to the Clipboard. Then activate your UserForm, click the Image control, and select the Picture property in the Properties box. Press Ctrl+V to paste the copied image. You can then delete the clipart image in the worksheet.

Some graphics images are very large and can make your workbook size increase dramatically. For best results, use an image that's as small as possible.

Label control

A Label control simply displays text in your dialog box. Figure 17-9 shows a few Label controls. As you can see, you have a great deal of control over the formatting of a Label control.

Figure 17-9: Label controls are easily molded.

ListBox control

The ListBox control presents a list of items from which the user can choose one or more. Figure 17-10 shows a dialog box with two ListBox controls.

Figure 17-10:
ListBox
controls.

ListBox controls are very flexible. For example, you can specify a worksheet range that holds the ListBox items, and the range can consist of multiple columns. Or you can fill the ListBox with items by using VBA code. (Did I tell you I prefer that method?)

If a ListBox isn't tall enough to display all the items in the list, a scrollbar appears so the user can scroll down to see more items.

The following list is a description of the most useful ListBox control properties:

- ✔ **BoundColumn:** If the list contains multiple columns, this property determines which column contains the returned value.

- ✔ **ColumnCount:** The number of columns in the list.

- ✔ **ControlSource:** A cell that stores the value selected in the ListBox.

- ✔ **IntegralHeight:** This is True if the ListBox height adjusts automatically to display full lines of text when the list is scrolled vertically. If False, the ListBox may display partial lines of text when it is scrolled vertically. Note that when this property is True, the actual height of your ListBox may be slightly different, when your UserForm is shown, from what you had set it originally. Visual Basic may adjust the height to ensure that the last entry is entirely visible.

- ✔ **ListStyle:** The appearance of the list items.

- ✔ **MultiSelect:** Determines whether the user can select multiple items from the list.

- ✔ **RowSource:** A range address that contains the list of items displayed in the ListBox.

- ✔ **Value:** The text of the selected item in the ListBox.

If the ListBox has its MultiSelect property set to 1 or 2, then the user can select multiple items in the ListBox. In such a case, you cannot specify a ControlSource; you need to write a macro that determines which items are selected. Chapter 18 demonstrates how to do so.

MultiPage control

A MultiPage control lets you create tabbed dialog boxes, like the Format Cells dialog box (the one that appears when you press Ctrl+1 in Excel). Figure 17-11 shows an example of a custom dialog box that uses a MultiPage control. This particular control has three pages, or tabs.

Descriptions of the most useful MultiPage control properties follow:

- ✔ **Style:** Determines the appearance of the control. The tabs can appear normally (on the top), on the left, as buttons, or hidden (no tabs — your VBA code determines which page is displayed).

- ✔ **Value:** Determines which page or tab is displayed. A Value of 0 displays the first page, a Value of 1 displays the second page, and so on.

By default, a MultiPage control has two pages. To add pages, right-click a tab and select New Page from the resulting Context menu.

OptionButton control

OptionButtons are useful when the user needs to select from a small number of items. OptionButtons are always used in groups of at least two. Figure 17-12 shows two sets of OptionButtons, and each set is contained in a frame.

The following is a description of the most useful OptionButton control properties:

- **Accelerator:** A letter that lets the user select the option by using the keyboard. For example, if the accelerator for an option button is C, then pressing Alt+C selects the control.

- **GroupName:** A name that identifies an option button as being associated with other option buttons with the same GroupName property.

- **ControlSource:** The worksheet cell that's linked to the option button. The cell displays TRUE if the control is selected or FALSE if the control is not selected.

- **Value:** If True, the OptionButton is selected. If False, the OptionButton is not selected.

If your dialog box contains more than one set of OptionButtons, you *must* change the GroupName property for all OptionButtons in a particular set. Otherwise, all OptionButtons become part of the same set. Alternatively, you can enclose each set of OptionButtons in a Frame control, which automatically groups the OptionButtons in the frame.

RefEdit control

The RefEdit control is used when you need to let the user select a range in a worksheet. Figure 17-13 shows a UserForm with two RefEdit controls. Its Value property holds the address of the selected range (as a text string).

RefEdit Controls

Source Range: Sheet1!B1

Destination Range: Sheet2!B12

Cancel

OK

The RefEdit control sometimes causes trouble on more complex UserForms. For best results, do not place a RefEdit control inside a Frame or MultiPage control.

ScrollBar control

When you add a ScrollBar control, you can make it horizontal or vertical. The ScrollBar control is similar to a SpinButton control (described later). The difference is that the user can drag the ScrollBar's button to change the control's value in larger increments. Another difference is that when you click the up button on a vertical ScrollBar, the value decreases — which is a bit counter-intuitive. So, a ScrollBar is not always a good substitute for a SpinButton.

Figure 17-14 shows a ScrollBar control, with a horizontal orientation. Its Value property is displayed in a Label control, placed below the ScrollBar.

The following is a description of the most useful properties of a ScrollBar control:

- ✓ **Value:** The control's current value.
- ✓ **Min:** The control's minimum value.
- ✓ **Max:** The control's maximum value.
- ✓ **ControlSource:** The worksheet cell that displays the control's value.
- ✓ **SmallChange:** The amount that the control's value is changed by a click.
- ✓ **LargeChange:** The amount that the control's value is changed by click-ing either side of the button.

The ScrollBar control is most useful for specifying a value that extends across a wide range of possible values.

SpinButton control

The SpinButton control lets the user select a value by clicking the control, which has two arrows (one to increase the value and the other to decrease the value). As with a ScrollBar control, a SpinButton can be oriented either horizontally or vertically. Figure 17-15 shows a dialog box that uses two vertically oriented SpinButton controls. Each control is linked to the Label control on the right (by using VBA procedures).

Figure 17-15:
SpinButton
controls.

The following descriptions explain the most useful properties of a SpinButton control:

- ✔ **Value:** The control's current value.
- ✔ **Min:** The control's minimum value.
- ✔ **Max:** The control's maximum value.
- ✔ **ControlSource:** The worksheet cell that displays the control's value.
- ✔ **SmallChange:** The amount that the control's value is changed by a click. Usually this property is set to 1, but you can make it any value.

WARNING! If you use a ControlSource for a SpinButton, you should understand that the worksheet is recalculated every time the control's value is changed. Therefore, if the user changes the value from 0 to 12, the worksheet is calculated 12 times. If your worksheet takes a long time to calculate, you may want to avoid using a ControlSource to store the value.

TabStrip control

A TabStrip control is similar to a MultiPage control, but it's not as easy to use. In fact, I'm not sure why this control is even included. You can pretty much ignore it and use the MultiPage control instead.

TextBox control

A TextBox control lets the user enter text. Figure 17-16 shows a dialog box with two TextBox controls.

Figure 17-16:
TextBox
controls.

The following is a description of the most useful TextBox control properties:

- ✔ **AutoSize:** If True, the control adjusts its size automatically, depending on the amount of text.

- ✔ **ControlSource:** The address of a cell that contains the text in the TextBox.

- ✔ **IntegralHeight:** If True, the TextBox height adjusts automatically to display full lines of text when the list is scrolled vertically. If False, the TextBox may display partial lines of text when it is scrolled vertically.

- ✔ **MaxLength:** The maximum number of characters allowed in the TextBox. If 0, the number of characters is unlimited.

- ✔ **MultiLine:** If True, the TextBox can display more than one line of text.

- ✔ **TextAlign:** Determines how the text is aligned in the TextBox.

- ✔ **WordWrap:** Determines whether the control allows word wrap.

- ✔ **ScrollBars:** Determines the type of scroll bars for the control: horizontal, vertical, both, or none.

When you add a TextBox control, its WordWrap property is set to True, and its MultiLine property is set to False. The net effect? Word wrap doesn't work! So, if you want the words to wrap in a TextBox control, make sure that you set the MultiLine property to True.

ToggleButton control

A ToggleButton control has two states: on and off. Clicking the button toggles between these two states, and the button changes its appearance when clicked. Its value is either True (pressed) or False (not pressed). Figure 17-17 shows a dialog box with four ToggleButton controls. The top two are toggled.

I hardly ever use ToggleButton controls. I prefer to use CheckBox controls.

Figure 17-17:
Toggle
Button
controls.

Working with Dialog Box Controls

In this section, I discuss how to work with dialog box controls in a UserForm object.

Moving and resizing controls

After you place a control in a dialog box, you can move it and resize it by using standard mouse techniques. Or for precise control, you can use the Properties window to enter a value for the control's Height, Width, Left, or Top property.

You can select multiple controls by Ctrl+clicking the controls. Or you can click and drag to "lasso" a group of controls. When multiple controls are selected, the Properties window displays only the properties common to all selected controls. You can change those common properties, and the change will be made to all controls you selected, which is much quicker than doing them one at a time.

A control can hide another control; in other words, you can stack one control on top of another. Unless you have a good reason for doing so, make sure that you do not overlap controls.

Aligning and spacing controls

The Format menu in the VBE window provides several commands to help you precisely align and space the controls in a dialog box. Before you use these commands, select the controls you want to work with. These commands work just as you might expect, so I don't explain them here. Figure 17-18 shows a dialog box with several CheckBox controls about to be aligned.

Figure 17-18:
Use the
Format➪
Align com-
mand to
change the
alignment
of UserForm
controls.

When you select multiple controls, the last selected control appears with white handles rather than the normal black handles. The control with the white handles is the basis for aligning or resizing the other selected controls when you use the Format menu.

Accommodating keyboard users

Many users (including yours truly) prefer to navigate through a dialog box by using the keyboard: Pressing Tab or Shift+Tab cycles through the controls, while pressing a hot key instantly activates a particular control.

To make sure that your dialog box works properly for keyboard users, you must be mindful of two issues:

- ✔ Tab order
- ✔ Accelerator keys

Changing the tab order

The tab order determines the order in which the controls are activated when the user presses Tab or Shift+Tab. It also determines which control has the initial *focus* — that is, which control is the active control when the dialog box first appears. For example, if a user is entering text into a TextBox, the

TextBox has the focus. If the user clicks an OptionButton, the OptionButton has the focus. The first control in the tab order has the focus when Excel first displays a dialog box.

To set the control tab order, choose View➪Tab Order. You can also right-click the dialog box and choose Tab Order from the shortcut menu. In either case, Excel displays the Tab Order dialog box shown in Figure 17-19.

Figure 17-19:
The Tab
Order dialog
box.

The Tab Order dialog box lists all the controls in the UserForm. The tab order in the UserForm corresponds to the order of the items in the list. To change the tab order of a control, select it in the list and then click the arrow buttons up or down. You can choose more than one control (click while pressing Shift or Ctrl) and move them all at one time.

Rather than use the Tab Order dialog box, you can set a control's position in the tab order by using the Properties window. The first control in the tab order has a TabIndex property of 0. If you want to remove a control from the tab order, set its TabStop property to False.

Some controls (such as Frame or MultiPage controls) act as containers for other controls. The controls inside a container control have their own tab order. To set the tab order for a group of OptionButtons inside a Frame control, select the Frame control before you choose the View➪Tab Order command.

Setting hot keys

Normally, you want to assign an accelerator key, or *hot key,* to dialog box controls. You do so by entering a letter for the Accelerator property in the Properties window. If a control doesn't have an Accelerator property (a TextBox, for example), you can still allow direct keyboard access to it by using a Label control. That is, assign an accelerator key to the Label and put the Label directly before the TextBox in the tab order.

Figure 17-20 shows a UserForm with three TextBoxes. The Labels that describe the TextBoxes have accelerator keys, and each Label precedes its corresponding TextBox in the tab order. Pressing Alt+D, for example, activates the TextBox next to the Department Label.

Figure 17-20:
Use Labels
to provide
direct
access to
controls that
don't have
accelerator
keys.

Testing a UserForm

The VBE offers three ways to test a UserForm without calling it from a VBA procedure:

- ✔ Choose the Run⇨Run Sub/UserForm command.
- ✔ Press F5.
- ✔ Click the Run Sub/UserForm button on the Standard toolbar.

When a dialog box is displayed in this test mode, you can try out the tab order and the accelerator keys.

Dialog Box Aesthetics

Dialog boxes can look good, bad, or somewhere in between. A good-looking dialog box is easy on the eye, has nicely sized and aligned controls, and makes its function perfectly clear to the user. Bad-looking dialog boxes confuse the user, have misaligned controls, and give the impression that the developer didn't have a plan (or a clue).

Try to limit the number of controls on your form. If you do need many controls (a rule of thumb: more than 10 controls), consider using a MultiPage control to split the task the user has to do into logical (and smaller) steps.

A good rule to follow is to try to make your dialog boxes look like the Excel built-in dialog boxes. As you gain more experience with dialog box construction, you can duplicate almost all the features of the Excel dialog boxes.

Chapter 18

UserForm Techniques and Tricks

• •

• •

*T*he previous chapters show you how to insert a UserForm (which contains a custom dialog box), add controls to the UserForm, and adjust some of the control's properties. These skills, however, won't do you much good unless you understand how to make use of UserForms in your VBA code. This chapter provides these missing details and presents some useful techniques and tricks in the process.

Using Dialog Boxes

When you use a custom dialog box in your application, you normally write VBA code that does the following:

✔ Initializes the UserForm controls. For example, you may write code that sets the default values for the controls.

✔ Displays the dialog box by using the UserForm object's Show method.

✔ Responds to the events that occur for the various controls.

✔ Validates the information provided by the user (if the user did not cancel the dialog box). This step is not always necessary.

✔ Takes some action with the information provided by the user (if the information is valid).

A UserForm Example

This example demonstrates the five points I describe in the preceding section. In this example, you use a dialog box to get two pieces of information: a person's name and sex. The dialog box uses a TextBox control to get the

name, and it uses three OptionButtons to get the sex (Male, Female, or Unknown). The information collected in the dialog box is then sent to the next blank row in a worksheet.

Creating the dialog box

Figure 18-1 shows the finished UserForm for this example. For best results, start with a new workbook with only one worksheet in it. Then follow these steps:

1. **Press Alt+F11 to activate the VBE.**

2. **In the Project window, select the empty workbook and choose Insert⇨UserForm.**

 An empty UserForm is added to the project.

3. **Change the UserForm's Caption property to** Get Name and Sex.

 If the Properties window isn't visible, press F4.

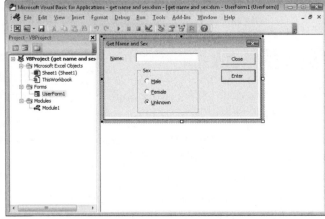

Figure 18-1:
This dialog box asks the user to enter a Name and choose a Sex.

This dialog box has eight controls:

 ✔ **A Label.** I modified the following properties for this control:

Property	Value
Accelerator	N
Caption	Name
TabIndex	0

✔ **A TextBox.** I modified the following properties for this control:

Property	Value
Name	TextName
TabIndex	1

✔ **A Frame object.** I modified the following properties for this control:

Property	Value
Caption	Sex
TabIndex	2

✔ **An OptionButton.** I modified the following properties for this control:

Property	Value
Accelerator	M
Caption	Male
Name	OptionMale
TabIndex	0

✔ **Another OptionButton.** I modified the following properties for this control:

Property	Value
Accelerator	F
Caption	Female
Name	OptionFemale
TabIndex	1

✔ **Another OptionButton.** I modified the following properties for this control:

Property	Value
Accelerator	U
Caption	Unknown
Name	OptionUnknown
TabIndex	2
Value	True

✔ **A CommandButton.** I modified the following properties for this control:

Property	Value
Caption	Enter
Default	True
Name	EnterButton
TabIndex	3

✔ **Another CommandButton.** I modified the following properties for this control:

Property	Value
Caption	**Close**
Cancel	**True**
Name	**CloseButton**
TabIndex	**4**

If you're following along on your computer (and you should be), take a few minutes to create this UserForm by using the preceding information. Make sure to create the Frame object before adding the OptionButtons to it.

In some cases, you may find copying an existing control easier than creating a new one. To copy a control, press Ctrl while you drag the control.

If you prefer to cut to the chase, you can download the example from this book's Web site.

Writing code to display the dialog box

After you've added the controls to the UserForm, your next step is to develop some VBA code to display this dialog box:

1. **In the VBE window, choose Insert⇨Module to insert a VBA module.**

2. **Enter the following macro:**

```
Sub GetData()
    UserForm1.Show
End Sub
```

This short procedure uses the UserForm object's Show method to display the dialog box.

Making the macro available

The next set of steps gives the user an easy way to execute the procedure:

1. **Activate Excel.**

2. **Choose Developer⇨Controls⇨Insert and click the Button icon in the Forms section.**

3. **Drag in the worksheet to create the button.**

 The Assign Macro dialog box appears.

4. **Assign the GetData macro to the button.**

5. **Edit the button's caption so that it reads** Data Entry.

If you want to get really fancy, you can add an icon to your Quick Access toolbar. Then clicking the icon runs the GetData macro. To set this up, right-click your Quick Access toolbar and choose Customize Quick Access Toolbar, which displays the Quick Access Toolbar tab of the Excel Options dialog box. In the Choose Commands From drop-down menu, select Macros. Then select the GetData macro and click Add. If you like, you can click the Modify button and change the icon. If you use Excel 2010, you make the Quick Access Toolbar icon visible only when the appropriate workbook is activated. Before you add the macro, use the drop-down control at the top-right of the Excel Options dialog box to specify the workbook name, rather than For All Documents (Default).

Trying out your dialog box

Follow these steps to test your dialog box:

1. **Click the Data Entry button on the worksheet. Or click the Quick Access toolbar icon if you set one up.**

 The dialog box appears, as shown in Figure 18-2.

Figure 18-2: Executing the GetData procedure displays the dialog box.

2. **Enter some text into the edit box.**

3. **Click Enter or Close.**

 Nothing happens — which is understandable because you haven't created any procedures yet.

4. **Click the "X" button in the dialog box's title bar to get rid of the dialog box.**

Adding event-handler procedures

In this section, I explain how to write the procedures that handle the events that occur when the dialog box is displayed.

1. **Press Alt+F11 to activate the VBE, and then make sure that the UserForm is displayed.**

2. **Double-click the Close button on the UserForm.**

 The VBE activates the Code window for the UserForm and provides an empty procedure named CloseButton_Click.

3. **Modify the procedure as follows:**

```
Private Sub CloseButton_Click()
    Unload UserForm1
End Sub
```

 This procedure, which is executed when the user clicks the Close button, simply unloads the dialog box from memory.

4. **Press Shift+F7 to redisplay UserForm1.**

5. **Double-click the Enter button and enter the following procedure:**

```
Private Sub EnterButton_Click()
    Dim NextRow As Long

    '   Make sure Sheet1 is active
    Sheets("Sheet1").Activate

    '   Determine the next empty row
    NextRow = Application.WorksheetFunction. _
        CountA(Range("A:A")) + 1

    '   Transfer the name
    Cells(NextRow, 1) = TextName.Text

    '   Transfer the sex
    If OptionMale Then Cells(NextRow, 2) = "Male"
    If OptionFemale Then Cells(NextRow, 2) = "Female"
    If OptionUnknown Then Cells(NextRow, 2) = _
        "Unknown"

    '   Clear the controls for the next entry
    TextName.Text = ""
    OptionUnknown = True
    TextName.SetFocus
End Sub
```

6. **Now activate Excel and run the procedure again by clicking the Data Entry button.**

 The dialog box works just fine. Figure 18-3 shows how this looks in action.

Figure 18-3:
Use the
custom
dialog box
for data
entry.

Here's how the EnterButton_Click procedure works:

✔ First, the code makes sure that the proper worksheet (Sheet1) is active.

✔ It then uses the Excel COUNTA function to count the number of entries in column A and to determine the next blank cell in the column.

✔ Next, the procedure transfers the text from the TextBox to Column A.

✔ It then uses a series of If statements to determine which OptionButton was selected and writes the appropriate text (Male, Female, or Unknown) to column B.

✔ Finally, the dialog box is reset to make it ready for the next entry. Notice that clicking the Enter button doesn't close the dialog box, because the user will probably want to enter more data. To end data entry, click the Close button.

Validating the data

Play around with this routine some more and you find that the macro has a small problem: It doesn't ensure that the user actually enters a name into the TextBox. The following code — which is inserted in the EnterButton_Click procedure before the text is transferred to the worksheet — ensures that the user enters some text in the TextBox. If the TextBox is empty, a message appears and the routine stops.

```
'  Make sure a name is entered
   If TextName.Text = "" Then
       MsgBox "You must enter a name."
       Exit Sub
   End If
```

Now the dialog box works

After making these modifications, you find that the dialog box works flaw-lessly. In real life, you'd probably need to collect more information than just name and sex. However, the same basic principles apply. You just have to deal with more UserForm controls.

One more thing to remember: If the data doesn't begin in row 1 or if the data area contains any blank rows, the counting for the NextRow variable will be wrong. The COUNTA function is counting the number of cells in A1, and the assumption is that the data begins in cell A1 and there are no blank cells above the last name in the column. Here's another way of determining the next empty row:

```
NextRow = Cells(Rows.Count, 1).End(xlUp).Row + 1
```

The statement simulates activating the last cell in column A, pressing End, pressing Up Arrow, and then moving down one row. If you do that manually, the cell pointer will be in the next empty cell in column A — even if the data area doesn't begin in row 1 and contains blank rows.

More UserForm Examples

I could probably fill an entire book with interesting and useful tips for work-ing with custom dialog boxes. Unfortunately, this book has a limited number of pages, so I wrap it up with a few more examples.

A ListBox example

ListBoxes are useful controls, but working with them can be a bit tricky. Before displaying a dialog box that uses a ListBox, fill the ListBox with items. Then when the dialog box is closed, you need to determine which item(s) the user selected.

When dealing with ListBoxes, you need to know about the following properties and methods:

- **AddItem:** You use this method to add an item to a ListBox.

- **ListCount:** This property returns the number of items in the ListBox.

- **ListIndex:** This property returns the index number of the selected item or sets the item that's selected (single selections only). The first item has a ListIndex of 0 (not 1).

✔ **MultiSelect:** This property determines whether the user can select more than one item from the ListBox.

✔ **RemoveAllItems:** Use this method to remove all items from a ListBox.

✔ **Selected:** This property returns an array indicating selected items (applicable only when multiple selections are allowed).

✔ **Value:** This property returns the selected item in a ListBox.

Most of the methods and properties that work with ListBoxes also work with ComboBoxes. Thus, after you have figured out how to handle ListBoxes, you can transfer that knowledge to your work with ComboBoxes.

Filling a ListBox

For best results, start with an empty workbook. The example in this section assumes the following:

✔ You've added a UserForm.

✔ The UserForm contains a ListBox control named ListBox1.

✔ The UserForm has a CommandButton named OKButton.

✔ The UserForm has a CommandButton named CancelButton, which has the following event-handler procedure:

```
Private Sub CancelButton_Click()
    Unload UserForm1
End Sub
```

The following procedure is stored in the Initialize procedure for the UserForm:

1. **Select your UserForm and press F7 to activate its Code window.**

 The VBE displays the Code window for your form and is ready for you to input the code for the Initialize event.

2. **Using the Procedure drop-down list at the top of the Code window, choose Initialize.**

3. **Add the initialization code for the form:**

```
Sub UserForm_Initialize()
'   Fill the list box
    With ListBox1
        .AddItem "January"
        .AddItem "February"
        .AddItem "March"
        .AddItem "April"
        .AddItem "May"
        .AddItem "June"
```

```
            .AddItem "July"
            .AddItem "August"
            .AddItem "September"
            .AddItem "October"
            .AddItem "November"
            .AddItem "December"
        End With

'     Select the first list item
        ListBox1.ListIndex = 0
    End Sub
```

This initialization routine runs automatically whenever your UserForm is loaded. So when you use the Show method for the UserForm, the code is executed and your ListBox is populated with 12 items, each added via the AddItem method.

4. **Insert a VBA module and type a short Sub procedure to display the dialog box:**

```
Sub ShowList()
    UserForm1.Show
End Sub
```

 It is not mandatory to use the Initialize event procedure to populate your lists. You could do so in a regular VBA procedure. Using an Initialize event procedure just seems like a natural place to take care of such a mundane (though important) step. If you hide the UserForm by using UserForm1.Hide and later on show the form again (UserForm1.Show), the Initialize event does not fire again.

Determining the selected item

The preceding code merely displays a dialog box with a ListBox filled with month names. What's missing is a procedure to determine which item in the ListBox is selected.

Add the following to the OKButton_Click procedure:

```
Private Sub OKButton_Click()
    Dim Msg As String
    Msg = "You selected item # "
    Msg = Msg & ListBox1.ListIndex
    Msg = Msg & vbNewLine
    Msg = Msg & ListBox1.Value
    MsgBox Msg
    Unload UserForm1
End Sub
```

This procedure displays a message box with the selected item number and the selected item.

If no item in the ListBox is selected, the ListIndex property returns –1. However, this will never be the case for this particular ListBox, because code in the UserForm_Initialize procedure selected the first item. So, there will *always* be a selected item, if the user doesn't actually select a month.

Figure 18-4 shows how this looks.

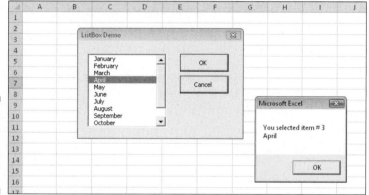

Figure 18-4:
Determining
which item
in a ListBox
is selected.

The first item in a ListBox has a ListIndex of 0, not 1 (as you might expect). This is always the case, even if you use an Option Base 1 statement to change the default lower bound for arrays.

This example is available at this book's Web site.

Determining multiple selections

If your ListBox is set up so the user can select more than one item, you find that the ListIndex property returns only the *last* item selected. To determine all selected items, you need to use the Selected property, which contains an array.

To allow multiple selections in a ListBox, set the MultiSelect property to either 1 or 2. You can do so at design time by using the Properties window or at run-time by using a VBA statement such as this:

```
UserForm1.ListBox1.MultiSelect = 1
```

The MultiSelect property has three possible settings. The meaning of each is shown in Table 18-1.

Table 18-1	Settings for the MultiSelect property	
Value	*VBA Constant*	*Meaning*
0	fmMultiSelectSingle	Only a single item can be selected.
1	fmMultiSelectMulti	Clicking an item or pressing the space bar selects or deselects an item in the list.
2	fmMultiSelect Extended	Items are added to or removed from the selection set by holding down the Shift or Ctrl key as you click items.

The following procedure displays a message box that lists all selected items in a ListBox. Figure 18-5 shows an example.

Figure 18-5: Determining the selected items in a ListBox allows multiple selections.

```
Private Sub OKButton_Click()
    Dim Msg As String
    Dim i As Integer
    Dim Counter As Integer
    Msg = "You selected:" & vbNewLine
    For i = 0 To ListBox1.ListCount - 1
        If ListBox1.Selected(i) Then
            Counter = Counter + 1
            Msg = Msg & ListBox1.List(i) & vbNewLine
        End If
    Next i
    If Counter = 0 Then Msg = Msg & "(nothing)"
    MsgBox Msg
    Unload UserForm1
End Sub
```

This routine uses a For-Next loop to cycle though each item in the ListBox. Notice that the loop starts with item 0 (the first item) and ends with the last item (determined by the value of the ListCount property minus 1). If an item's Selected property is True, it means that the list item was selected. The code also uses a variable (Counter) to keep track of how many items are selected. An If-Then statement modifies the message if nothing is selected.

This example is available at this book's Web site.

Selecting a range

In some cases, you may want the user to select a range while a dialog box is displayed. An example of this choice occurs in the Create Table dialog box, which is displayed when you choose Home⇨Insert⇨Tables⇨Table. The dialog box has a range selector control that contains Excel's guess regarding the range to be converted — but you can use this control to change the range by selecting cells in the worksheet.

To allow a range selection in your dialog box, add a RefEdit control. The following example displays a dialog box with the current region's range address displayed in a RefEdit control, as shown in Figure 18-6. The current region is the block of nonempty cells that contains the active cell. The user can accept or change this range. When the user clicks OK, the procedure makes the range bold.

	A	B	C	D	E	F	G	H	I	J	K
1	17	8	10	75	11	64					
2	63	8	22	27	11	54					
3	5	45	70	13	6	48					
4	30	22	15	1	3	15					
5	73	56	87	70	24	87					
6	86	93	69	95	49	92					
7	31	37	30	70	26	93					
8	31	68	1	62	63	87					
9	72	97	58	21	42	61					
10	22	28	92	32	76	58					
11	15	90	55	72	22	1					
12	75	14	21	98	18	9					
13	82	79	43	96	50	15					
14	89	38	92	69	32	33					
15	1	38	93	78	58	45					
16	37	42	11	63	0	60					
17	40	59	14	57	2	37					
18	12	1	14	67	74	46					
19	15	10	25	27	70	36					
20	61	41	84	47	29	71					
21	51	78	21	89	16	95					
22	74	5	31	11	7	55					
23											
24											

RefEdit Demo

Range to make bold:

A1:F22

Cancel OK

Figure 18-6:
This dialog box lets the user select a range.

This example assumes the following:

- ✔ You have a UserForm named UserForm1.
- ✔ The UserForm contains a CommandButton control named OKButton.
- ✔ The UserForm contains a CommandButton control named CancelButton.
- ✔ The UserForm contains a RefEdit control named RefEdit1.

The code is stored in a VBA module and shown here. This code does two things: initializes the dialog box by assigning the current region's address to the RefEdit control and displays the UserForm.

```
Sub BoldCells()
'    Exit if worksheet is not active
     If TypeName(ActiveSheet) <> "Worksheet" Then Exit Sub

'    Select the current region
     ActiveCell.CurrentRegion.Select

'    Initialize RefEdit control
     UserForm1.RefEdit1.Text = Selection.Address

'    Show dialog
     UserForm1.Show
End Sub
```

The following procedure is executed when the OK button is clicked. This procedure does some simple error checking to make sure that the range specified in the RefEdit control is valid.

```
Private Sub OKButton_Click()
     On Error GoTo BadRange
     Range(RefEdit1.Text).Font.Bold = True
     Unload UserForm1
     Exit Sub
BadRange:
     MsgBox "The specified range is not valid."
End Sub
```

If an error occurs (most likely an invalid range specification in the RefEdit control), the code jumps to the BadRange label, and a message box is displayed. The dialog box remains open so the user can select another range.

Using multiple sets of OptionButtons

Figure 18-7 shows a custom dialog box with three sets of OptionButtons. If your UserForm contains more than one set of OptionButtons, make sure that each set of OptionButtons works as a group. You can do so in either of two ways:

✔ Enclose each set of OptionButtons in a Frame control. This approach is the easiest, and also makes the dialog box look more organized. It's easier to add the Frame before adding the OptionButtons. You can, however, also drag existing OptionButtons into a Frame.

✔ Make sure that each set of OptionButtons has a unique GroupName property (which you specify in the Properties box). If the OptionButtons are in a Frame, you don't have to be concerned with the GroupName property.

Figure 18-7:
This dialog box contains three sets of Option Button controls.

Only one OptionButton in a group can have a value of True. To specify a default option for a set of OptionButtons, just set the Value property for the default item to True. You can do this directly in the Properties box or by using VBA code:

```
UserForm1.OptionButton1.Value = True
```

This example is available at this book's Web site. It also has code that displays the selected options when the user clicks OK.

Using a SpinButton and a TextBox

A SpinButton control lets the user specify a number by clicking arrows. This control consists only of arrows (no text), so you usually want a method to display the selected number. One option is to use a Label control, but this has a disadvantage: The user can't type text in a Label. A better choice is to use a TextBox.

A SpinButton control and TextBox control form a natural pair, and Excel uses them frequently. For example, check out Excel's Page Setup dialog box for a few examples. Ideally, the SpinButton and its TextBox are always in sync: If the user clicks the SpinButton, the SpinButton's value should appear

in the TextBox. And if the user enters a value directly into the TextBox, the SpinButton should take on that value. Figure 18-8 shows a custom dialog box with a SpinButton and a TextBox.

This UserForm contains the following controls:

- A SpinButton named SpinButton1, with its Min property set to 1 and its Max property set to 100
- A TextBox named TextBox1
- A CommandButton named OKButton

The event-handler procedure for the SpinButton follows. This procedure handles the Change event, which is triggered whenever the SpinButton value is changed. When the SpinButton's value changes (when it's clicked), this procedure assigns the SpinButton's value to the TextBox. To create this procedure, double-click the SpinButton to activate the Code window for the UserForm. Then enter this code:

```
Private Sub SpinButton1_Change()
    TextBox1.Text = SpinButton1.Value
End Sub
```

The event-handler for the TextBox, which is listed next, is a bit more complicated. To create this procedure, double-click the TextBox to activate the Code window for the UserForm. This procedure is executed whenever the user changes the text in the TextBox.

```
Private Sub TextBox1_Change()
    Dim NewVal As Integer

    NewVal = Val(TextBox1.Text)
    If NewVal >= SpinButton1.Min And _
        NewVal <= SpinButton1.Max Then _
        SpinButton1.Value = NewVal
End Sub
```

This procedure uses a variable, which stores the text in the TextBox (converted to a value with the Val function). It then checks to ensure that the value is within the proper range. If so, the SpinButton is set to the value in the TextBox. The net effect is that the SpinButton's value is always equal to the value in the TextBox (assuming that the SpinButton's value is in the proper range).

If you use F8 to single-step through the code in debugging mode, you will notice that when the line SpinButton1.Value = NewVal is executed, the change event of the SpinButton immediately fires. In turn, the SpinButton1_Change event sets the value of TextBox1. Luckily, this in turn does not fire the TextBox1_Change event, because its value is not actually changed by the SpinButton1_Change event. But you can imagine this effect can cause surprising results in your UserForm. Confused? Just remember that if your code changes the Value of a control, the Change event of that control will fire.

This example is available at this book's Web site. It also has a few other bells and whistles that you may find useful.

Using a UserForm as a progress indicator

One of the most common Excel programming questions I hear is, "How can I display the progress of a lengthy macro?"

Answer: Use a UserForm to create an attractive progress indicator, as shown in Figure 18-9. Such a use of dialog boxes does, however, require a few tricks — which I'm about to show you.

Figure 18-9: This UserForm functions as a progress indicator for a lengthy macro.

	A	B	C	D	E	F	G	H	I	J	K
1	705	533	579	289	301	774	14	760	814	709	45
2	793	857	93	541	415	73	451	698	499	406	945
3	894	866	Progress					779	308	78	879
4	885	486	Entering random numbers...					205	443	685	281
5	781	245	66%					584	893	815	691
6	116	93						631	332	18	778
7	593	489						117	250	379	601
8	969	722	820	888	290	208	268	80	353	344	127
9	198	495	374	858	730	84	297	271	199	806	997
10	820	748	509	30	740	726	611	860	87	426	537
11	604	738	760	853	786	291	50	390	201	213	32
12	435	371	732	584	910	223	596	980	1	355	231
13	460	772	353	492	112	79	887	776	859	294	123
14	472	121	401	316	997	611	985	655	956	54	947
15	555	727	259	959	661	88	389	180	416	821	456
16	976	357	941	448	837	881	305	800	702	769	439
17	321	814	350	137	278	286	155	303	254	143	480
18	888	764	796	155	406	603	350	536	380	579	978
19	327	819	762	115	197	466	299	318	397	689	411
20	534	858	921	64	323	422	680	685	22	887	850
21	786	609	399	685	544	754	950	322	11	465	728
22	134	478	291	755	346	564	118	272	51	926	855

Creating the progress indicator dialog box

The first step is to create your UserForm. In this example, the dialog box displays the progress while a macro inserts random numbers into 100 columns and 1,000 rows of the active worksheet. To create the dialog box, follow these steps:

1. **Activate the VBE and insert a new UserForm.**

2. **Change the UserForm's caption to** Progress.

3. **Add a Frame object and set the following properties:**

Property	Value
Caption	0%
Name	**FrameProgress**
SpecialEffect	**2 — fmSpecialEffectSunken**
Width	204
Height	28

4. **Add a Label object inside the Frame and set the following properties:**

Property	Value
Name	**LabelProgress**
BackColor	**&H000000FF& (red)**
Caption	(no caption)
SpecialEffect	**1 — fmSpecialEffectRaised**
Width	20
Height	13
Top	5
Left	2

5. **Add another Label above the frame and change its caption to** Entering random numbers. . .

The UserForm should resemble Figure 18-10.

Figure 18-10:
The
progress
indicator
UserForm.

The procedures

This example uses two procedures and a module level variable.

- ✔ **The module level variable.** Located in a VBA module. This variable holds the copy of the userform:

```
Dim ProgressIndicator as UserForm1
```

- ✔ **EnterRandomNumbers.** It does all the work and is executed when the UserForm is shown. Notice that it calls the UpdateProgress procedure, which updates the progress indicator in the dialog box:

```
Sub EnterRandomNumbers ()
'     Inserts random numbers on the active worksheet
      Dim Counter As Long
      Dim RowMax As Long, ColMax As Long
      Dim r As Long, c As Long
      Dim PctDone As Single

'     Create a copy of the form in a variable
      Set ProgressIndicator = New UserForm1

'     Show ProgressIndicator in modeless state
      ProgressIndicator.Show vbModeless
      If TypeName(ActiveSheet) <> "Worksheet" Then
          Unload ProgressIndicator
          Exit Sub
      End If

'     Enter the random numbers
      Cells.Clear
      Counter = 1
      RowMax = 200
      ColMax = 50
      For r = 1 To RowMax
          For c = 1 To ColMax
              Cells(r, c) = Int(Rnd * 1000)
              Counter = Counter + 1
          Next c
          PctDone = Counter / (RowMax * ColMax)
          Call UpdateProgress(PctDone)
      Next r
      Unload ProgressIndicator
      Set ProgressIndicator = Nothing
End Sub
```

- ✔ **UpdateProgress.** This procedure accepts one argument and updates the progress indicator in the dialog box:

```
Sub UpdateProgress(pct)
      With ProgressIndicator
          .FrameProgress.Caption = Format(pct, "0%")
          .LabelProgress.Width = pct * (.FrameProgress _
```

```
                .Width - 10)
        End With
    '   The DoEvents statement makes the form update
        DoEvents
    End Sub
```

How this example works

When the EnterRandomNumbers procedure is executed, it loads a copy of UserForm1 into the module variable named ProgressIndicator. Then it sets the width of the LabelProgress label to 0 and displays the UserForm in modeless state (so the code will continue to run).

The EnterRandomNumber procedure checks the active sheet. If it's not a worksheet, the UserForm (ProgressIndicator) is closed, and the procedure ends with no action. If the active sheet is a worksheet, the procedure does the following:

1. Erases all cells on the active worksheet.

2. Loops through the rows and columns (specified by the RowMax and ColMax variables) and inserts a random number.

3. Increments the Counter variable and calculates the percentage completed (which is stored in the PctDone variable).

4. Calls the UpdateProgress procedure, which displays the percentage completed by changing the width of the LabelProgress label and updating the caption of the frame control.

5. Last, the UserForm is unloaded.

Using a progress indicator will, of course, make your macro run a bit slower because the code is doing additional work updating the UserForm. If speed is absolutely critical, think twice about using a progress indicator.

If you adapt this technique for your own use, you need to figure out how to determine the macro's progress, which varies depending on your macro. Then call the UpdateProgress procedure at periodic intervals while your macro is executing.

This example is available at this book's Web site.

Creating a tabbed dialog box

Tabbed dialog boxes are useful because they let you present information in small, organized chunks. Excel's Format Cells dialog box (which is displayed

when you right-click a cell and choose Format Cells) is a good example. The dialog box in this example uses three tabs to help organize some of Excel's display options.

Creating your own tabbed dialog boxes is relatively easy, thanks to the MultiPage control. Figure 18-11 shows a custom dialog box that uses a MultiPage control with three *pages,* or *tabs*. When the user clicks a tab, a new page is activated, and only the controls on that page are displayed.

Notice that this is a modeless dialog box. In other words, the user can keep it displayed while working. Each of the controls has an immediate effect, so there is no need to have an OK button.

Figure 18-11:
The three tabs of a MultiPage control.

Keep the following points in mind when using the MultiPage control to create a tabbed dialog box:

✔ Use only one MultiPage control per dialog box.

✔ Make sure to use the MultiPage control, not the TabStrip control. The TabStrip control is more difficult to use.

✔ To make some controls (such as OK, Cancel, or Close buttons) visible at all times, place these controls outside the MultiPage control.

✔ Right-click a tab on the MultiPage control to display a shortcut menu that lets you add, remove, rename, or move a tab.

✔ At design time, click a tab to activate the page. After it is activated, add other controls to the page by using normal procedures.

✔ To select the MultiPage control itself (rather than a page on the control), click the border of the MultiPage control. Keep your eye on the Properties window, which displays the name and type of the selected control. You can also select the MultiPage control by selecting its name from the drop-down list in the Properties window.

✔ You can change the look of the MultiPage control by changing the Style and TabOrientation properties.

✔ The Value property of a MultiPage control determines which page is displayed. For example, if you write code to set the Value property to 0, the first page of the MultiPage control is displayed.

This example is available at this book's Web site.

Displaying a chart in a UserForm

If you need to display a chart in a UserForm, you find that Excel doesn't provide any direct way to do so. Therefore, you need to get creative. This section describes a technique that lets you display one or more charts in a UserForm.

Figure 18-12 shows an example, which displays three charts. The UserForm has an Image control. The trick is to use VBA code to save the chart as a GIF file and then specify that file as the Image control's Picture property (which loads the image from your disk). The Previous and Next buttons switch the displayed chart.

Figure 18-12:
Displaying
a chart in a
UserForm.

In this example, which is also available on this book's Web site, the three charts are on a sheet named Charts. The Previous and Next buttons determine which chart to display, and this chart number is stored as a Public variable named ChartNum, which is accessible to all procedures. A procedure named UpdateChart, which is listed here, does the actual work.

```
Private Sub UpdateChart()
    Dim CurrentChart As Chart
    Dim Fname As String

    Set CurrentChart = _
      Sheets("Charts").ChartObjects(ChartNum).Chart
    CurrentChart.Parent.Width = 300
    CurrentChart.Parent.Height = 150

'   Save chart as GIF
    Fname = ThisWorkbook.Path & "\temp.gif"
    CurrentChart.Export FileName:=Fname, FilterName:="GIF"

'   Show the chart
    Image1.Picture = LoadPicture(Fname)
End Sub
```

This procedure determines a name for the saved chart and then uses the Export method to export the GIF file. Finally, it uses the VBA LoadPicture function to specify the Picture property of the Image object.

A Dialog Box Checklist

I wrap up this chapter with a checklist for use when creating dialog boxes:

❏ Are the controls aligned with each other?

❏ Are similar controls the same size?

❏ Are controls evenly spaced?

❏ Does the dialog box have an appropriate caption?

❏ Is the dialog box overwhelming? If so, you may want to use a series of dialog boxes or divide them over a MultiPage control.

❏ Can the user access every control with an accelerator key?

❏ Are any accelerator keys duplicated?

❏ Are the controls grouped logically, by function?

❑ Is the tab order set correctly? The user should be able to tab through the dialog box and access the controls sequentially.

❑ If you plan to store the dialog box in an add-in, did you test it thoroughly after creating the add-in?

❑ Will your VBA code take appropriate action if the user cancels the dialog box or presses Esc or uses the close button?

❑ Does the text contain any misspellings? Unfortunately, the Excel spell checker doesn't work with UserForms, so you're on your own when it comes to spelling.

❑ Will your dialog box fit on the screen in the lowest resolution to be used (usually 800×600 mode)? In other words, if you develop your dialog box by using a high-resolution video mode, your dialog box may be too big to fit on a screen in lower resolution.

❑ Do all TextBox controls have the appropriate validation setting? If you intend to use the WordWrap property, is the MultiLine property also set to True?

❑ Do all ScrollBars and SpinButtons allow valid values only?

❑ Do all ListBoxes have their MultiSelect property set properly?

The best way to master custom dialog boxes is by creating dialog boxes — lots of them. Start simply and experiment with the controls and their properties. And don't forget about the Help system; it's your best source for details about every control and property.

Chapter 19

Accessing Your Macros through the User Interface

• •

In This Chapter

▶ A sneak peek into customizing the Ribbon using XML

▶ Adding items to a right-click menu

▶ Adding a button to the Quick Access toolbar (manually)

▶ Customizing the Ribbon (manually)

• •

*B*efore Excel 2007, users had access to dozens of built-in toolbars, and creating new toolbars was a snap. But, as Bob Dylan wrote, "The Times They Are A-Changin." This chapter describes what has changed, beginning with Excel 2007, and shows you a little bit of what you can do to show your macros in the user interface.

What Happened to CommandBars?

When programming in Excel 2003 and before, you wrote code to create a toolbar (called a CommandBar in VBA). The toolbar contained buttons to allow the user (or yourself) to access your macros. In addition, you could use the CommandBar object to add new commands to Excel's menus. Beginning with Excel 2007, it's the new Ribbon user interface that changes the picture drastically. There is good news and bad news.

The good news is that most of the old CommandBar code written in VBA will still work.

The bad news is that your finely crafted VBA code that tries to create a toolbar or add a command to a menu is intercepted by Excel. Instead of displaying your well-thought-out interface enhancement, Excel 2007 (and Excel 2010) simply dumps your customized menus and toolbars into a catchall Ribbon tab named Add-Ins.

Ribbon Customization

Just about everything I've written in this book applies to both Excel 2007 and Excel 2010. I'm about to point out a significant difference between these two versions, and it involves customizing the Ribbon.

If you use Excel 2007, you have one way to customize the Ribbon: Learn to write RibbonX code and add the modification to a workbook. This is not a simple task, as you'll see later. But if you use Excel 2010, you can also modify the Ribbon manually, using the Customize Ribbon tab of the Excel Options dialog box.

You cannot make changes to the Ribbon by using VBA. Sad, but true. For example, if you write an application and you'd like to add a few new buttons to the Ribbon, you need to program those changes outside of Excel, using something called RibbonX.

Customizing the Ribbon manually

It's very easy to make changes to the Ribbon manually, but you must be using Excel 2010. If you use Excel 2007, you should just skip this section because it doesn't apply to you.

You can customize the Ribbon in these ways:

- ✔ Tabs
 - Add a new custom tab.
 - Delete custom tabs.
 - Add a new group to tab.
 - Change the order of the tabs.
 - Change the name of a tab.
 - Hide built-in tabs.
- ✔ Groups
 - Add new custom groups.
 - Add commands to a custom group.
 - Remove commands from custom groups.
 - Remove groups from a tab.

- Move a group to a different tab.
- Change the order of the groups within a tab.
- Change the name of a group.

That's a fairly comprehensive list of customization options, but there are some actions that you *cannot* do (no matter how hard you try):

✔ You cannot remove built-in tabs — but you *can* hide them.

✔ You cannot remove commands from built-in groups.

✔ You cannot change the order of commands in a built-in group.

You make manual changes to the Ribbon in the Customize Ribbon panel of the Excel Options dialog box (see Figure 19-1). The quickest way to display this dialog box is to right-click anywhere in the Ribbon and choose Customize The Ribbon.

Figure 19-1:
The Customize Ribbon tab of the Excel Options dialog box.

The process of customizing the Ribbon is very similar to customizing the Quick Access toolbar, which is described later in this chapter. The only difference is that you need to decide where to put the command within the Ribbon. The general procedure is:

1. Use the drop-down list on the left (labeled Choose Command From) to display various groups of commands.

2. Locate the command in the list box on the left, and select it.

3. Use the drop-down list on the left (labeled Customize The Ribbon) to choose a group of tabs. Main Tabs refer to the tabs that are always visible; Tool Tabs refer to the context tabs that appear when a particular object is selected.

4. In the list box on the right, select the tab and the group where you would like to put the command. You'll need to click the "plus sign" controls to expand the hierarchical lists.

5. Click the Add button to add the selected command from the left to the group on the right.

Keep in mind that you can use the New Tab button to create a new tab, and the New Group button to create a new group within a tab. New tabs and groups are given generic names, so you'll probably want to give them more meaningful names. Use the Rename button to rename the selected tab or group. You can also rename built-in tabs and groups.

Although you cannot remove a built-in tab, you can hide the tab by unchecking the check box next to its name.

Fortunately, you can also add macros to the Ribbon. Choose Macros from the drop-down list on the left, and all of the currently available macros are listed, ready to be added to the Ribbon.

If you customize the Ribbon to include a macro, the macro command in the Ribbon is visible even when the workbook that contains the macro is not open. Clicking the command will open the workbook that contains the macro.

Customizing the Ribbon with XML

In some situations, you may want to modify the ribbon automatically, when a workbook or add-in is opened. Doing so makes it easy for the user to access your macro. It also eliminates the need for the user to modify the Ribbon manually by using the Excel Options dialog box.

Making automatic changes to the Ribbon can be done with Excel 2007 and Excel 2010, but it's not easy. Modifying the Ribbon involves writing XML code in a text editor, copying that XML file into the workbook file, editing a bunch of XML files (which also are stashed away inside the new Excel file format, which in reality is nothing more than a zipped container of individual — but related — files), and then writing VBA procedures to handle the clicking of the controls you put in the XML file.

Get the software

If you'd like to follow along with the Ribbon customization example, you need to download a small program called Custom UI Editor for Microsoft Office. This is a free program that greatly simplifies the process of customizing the Ribbon in Microsoft Office applications. Using this software still requires a lot of work, but it's a lot easier than doing it manually.

As I was writing this, the software was available here:

```
http://openxmldeveloper.org/articles/customuieditor.aspx
```

If that URL doesn't work, search the Web for "Custom UI Editor for Microsoft Office" and you'll find the software. It's a small download, and it's free.

Fortunately, software is available to assist you with customizing the Ribbon — but you still need to be on familiar terms with XML.

Explaining all the intricate details involved in customizing the Ribbon is well beyond the scope of this book. However, I walk you through a quick example that demonstrates the steps required to add a new Ribbon group to the Home tab. The new Ribbon group is named Excel VBA For Dummies, and it contains one button, labeled Click Me. Clicking that button runs a VBA macro named ShowMessage.

You can download a sample file from this book's Web site, which contains this customization. If you'd like to create it yourself, follow these steps exactly:

1. **Create a new Excel workbook.**

2. **Save the workbook, and name it ribbon modification.xlsm.**

3. **Close the workbook. This step is very important.**

4. **Launch the Custom UI Editor for Microsoft Office. If you don't have this software, you need to find it and install it. Refer to the sidebar, "Get the software," earlier in this chapter.**

5. **In the Custom UI Editor, choose File⇨Open, and find the workbook you saved in Step 2.**

6. **Choose Insert⇨Office 2007 Custom UI Part. Choose this command even if you're using Excel 2010.**

7. **Type the following code into the code panel (named customUI.xml) displayed in the Custom UI Editor (see Figure 19-2):**

```
<customUI xmlns='http://schemas.microsoft.com/
        office/2006/01/customui'>
<ribbon>
<tabs>
<tab idMso='TabHome'>
  <group  id='Group1' label='Excel VBA For Dummies'>
    <button id='Button1'
        label='Click Me'
        size='large'
        onAction='ShowMessage'
        imageMso='FileStartWorkflow' />
  </group>
</tab>
</tabs>
</ribbon>
</customUI>
```

8. **Click the Validate button in the toolbar. If the code has any syntax errors, you will get a message that describes the problem. If any errors are identified, you must correct them.**

9. **Click the Generate Callback button.**

 The Custom UI Editor creates a VBA Sub procedure that is executed when the button is clicked (see Figure 19-3). This procedure is not actually inserted into the workbook, so you need to copy it for later use (or memorize it if you have a good memory).

10. **Go back to the customUI.xml module and choose File⇨Save (or click the Save icon in the toolbar).**

11. **Close the file by using the File⇨Close command.**

12. **Open the workbook in Excel. Click the Home tab, and you should see the new Ribbon group and Ribbon button. But it doesn't work yet.**

13. **Press Alt+F11 to activate the VBE.**

14. **Insert a new VBA module and paste (or type) the callback procedure that was generated in Step 9. Add a MsgBox statement, so you'll know if the procedure is actually being executed. The procedure is:**

```
Sub ShowMessage(control As IRibbonControl)
    MsgBox "Congrats. You found the new ribbon
        command."
End Sub
```

15. **Press Alt+F11 to jump back to Excel. Click the new button on the Ribbon. If all went well, you'll see the MsgBox shown in Figure 19-4.**

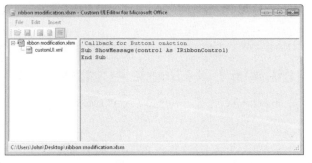

Figure 19-2:
RibbonX code displayed in the Custom UI Editor.

```
ribbon modification.xlsm - Custom UI Editor for Microsoft Office

File   Edit   Insert

ribbon modification.xlsm
    customUI.xml

<customUI xmlns='http://schemas.microsoft.com/office/2006/01/customui'>
<ribbon>
<tabs>
<tab idMso='TabHome'>
  <group  id='Group1' label='Excel VBA For Dummies'>
     <button id='Button1'
         label='Click Me'
         size='large'
         onAction='ShowMessage'
         imageMso='FileStartWorkflow' />
  </group>
</tab>
</tabs>
</ribbon>
</customUI>

C:\Users\John\Desktop\ribbon modification.xlsm
```

Figure 19-3:
The VBA callback procedure that is executed by clicking the Ribbon button.

```
ribbon modification.xlsm - Custom UI Editor for Microsoft Office

File   Edit   Insert

ribbon modification.xlsm
    customUI.xml

'Callback for Button1 onAction
Sub ShowMessage(control As IRibbonControl)
End Sub

C:\Users\John\Desktop\ribbon modification.xlsm
```

Figure 19-4:
Proof that adding a new Ribbon command using XML is actually possible.

Microsoft Excel

Congrats. You found the new ribbon command.

OK

In the Custom UI Editor, when you choose Insert⇨Office 2007 Custom UI Part, you insert a UI part for Excel 2007. The Custom UI Editor also has an option to insert a UI part for Excel 2010. If you choose that option, the Ribbon modification will not work in Excel 2007. In addition, you need to specify a different Namespace in the first XML statement:

```
<customUI xmlns='http://schemas.microsoft.com/
          office/2009/07/customui'>
```

You only need to insert a UI part for Excel 2010 if you use features that are unique to Excel 2010. You can also have a UI part for each version, but that's rarely necessary.

You probably realize that making Ribbon modification using XML is not exactly intuitive. Even with a good tool to help (such as the Custom UI Editor), you still need to understand XML. If that sounds appealing to you, check the bookstores. You'll find books devoted exclusively to customizing the Ribbon interface in Microsoft Office. This isn't one of them.

Adding a button to the Quick Access toolbar

If you create a macro that you use frequently, you may want to add a new button to the Quick Access toolbar. Doing so is easy, but you must do it manually. The Quick Access toolbar is intended to be customized by end users only — not programmers. Here's how to do it:

1. **Right-click the Quick Access toolbar and select Customize Quick Access toolbar to display the Quick Access toolbar tab of the Excel Options dialog box. In Excel 2007, this tab is labeled Customize.**

2. **In the drop-down box labeled Choose Commands From, select Macros.**

3. **Select your macro from the list.**

4. **Click the Add button, and the macro is added to the Quick Access toolbar list on the right.**

5. **If you like, click the Modify button to change the icon and (optionally) the display name.**

If you use Excel 2007, the Quick Access toolbar button works only when the workbook that contains the macro is open. Even worse, the macro works only when that workbook is the active workbook. But these problems were fixed in Excel 2010. When you click a macro button on the Quick Access toolbar, the workbook that contains the macro is opened (if it's not already open). And the macro can be executed when any workbook is open.

Excel 2010 also has an option to display the Quick Access toolbar button only when a particular workbook is open. Before you add the macro, use the drop-down control at the top-right of the Excel Options dialog box, and specify the workbook name, rather than For All Documents (Default).

If you have macros that are useful for many different workbooks, storing them in your Personal Macro Workbook is a good idea.

Because this XML stuff is way too complex for the beginner VBA programmer, the remainder of this chapter focuses on UI customization that uses the *old* method (VBA only). It's not as slick as the Ribbon, but it's a lot easier, and it still provides quick access to your macros.

Customizing Shortcut Menus

Before Excel 2007, VBA programmers used the CommandBar object for creating custom menus, custom toolbars, and custom shortcut (right-click) menus.

Beginning with Excel 2007, the CommandBar object is in a rather odd position. If you write code to customize a menu or a toolbar, Excel intercepts that code and ignores many of your commands. As I noted earlier in this chapter, menu and toolbar customizations end up in the Add-Ins⇨Menu Commands or the Add-Ins⇨Custom Toolbars group. So, for all practical purposes, you're limited to the shortcut menus. And that's what I cover in the sections that follow.

Commanding the CommandBars collection

Excel supports three types of CommandBars, differentiated by their Type property. For shortcut menus, you're nterested in type 2, also known by its built-in constant name, msoBarTypePopup.

Listing all shortcut menus

The procedure listed here uses the CommandBars collection. It displays, in a worksheet, the names of all shortcut menus — CommandBars that have a Type property of 2 (msoBarTypePopup). For each CommandBar, the procedure lists its Index and Name.

```
Sub ShowShortcutMenusName()
    Dim Row As Long
    Dim cbar As CommandBar
    Row = 1
    For Each cbar In Application.CommandBars
        If cbar.Type = msoBarTypePopup Then
            Cells(Row, 1) = cbar.Index
            Cells(Row, 2) = cbar.Name
            Row = Row + 1
        End If
    Next cbar
End Sub
```

ON THE WEB

Figure 19-5 shows a portion of the result of running this procedure, which is available at this book's Web site. For example, you see that the shortcut menu named Workbook Tabs has an index of 34. That's the shortcut menu that appears when you right-click a sheet tab.

	A	B	C
1	21	PivotChart Menu	
2	34	Workbook tabs	
3	35	Cell	
4	36	Column	
5	37	Row	
6	38	Cell	
7	39	Column	
8	40	Row	
9	41	Ply	
10	42	XLM Cell	
11	43	Document	
12	44	Desktop	
13	45	Nondefault Drag and Drop	
14	46	AutoFill	
15	47	Button	
16	48	Dialog	
17	49	Series	
18	50	Plot Area	
19	51	Floor and Walls	
20	52	Trendline	
21	53	Chart	
22	54	Format Data Series	
23	55	Format Axis	
24	56	Format Legend Entry	
25	57	Formula Bar	

Figure 19-5: A VBA macro produced this list of all short-cut menu names.

Referring to CommandBars

You can refer to a particular CommandBar by its Index or by its Name. If you refer to Figure 19-5, you see that the Cell right-click menu has an Index of 35 or 38. This is because the content of the cell right-click menu differs when Excel is in a different state. Number 35 is the one you get when Excel is in Normal view mode, number 38 shows when you are in Page Break Preview mode. You can refer to the shortcut menu in either of two ways:

```
Application.CommandBars(35)
```

or

```
Application.CommandBars("Cell")
```

WARNING!

Even though there are two Cell CommandBars, the second line of code above always addresses the one with index 35. For some reason, Microsoft isn't consistent in naming the CommandBars. You would expect each separate CommandBar to have its own unique name, but they obviously don't. Right-click menus that differ in content — depending on the state Excel is

in — appear more than once in the list of available CommandBars. You might think that referring to CommandBars by using their Index property is better. Wrong! But even that can cause problems because the Index numbers have not always remained constant across the different Excel versions. In fact, the Index property can even vary within a single version of Excel.

Referring to controls in a CommandBar

A CommandBar object contains Control objects, which are buttons, menus, or menu items. The following procedure displays the Caption property for the first Control in the cell's right-click menu:

```
Sub ShowCaption()
    MsgBox Application.CommandBars("Cell"). _
        Controls(1).Caption
End Sub
```

When you execute this procedure, you see the message box shown in Figure 19-6. The ampersand is used to indicate the underlined letter in the text — the keystroke that will execute the menu item.

Figure 19-6:
Displaying
the Caption
property for
a control.

In some cases, Control objects on a shortcut menu contain other Control objects. For example, the Sort control on the Cell right-click menu contains other controls.

Each control has a Name and an Id property. You can access a control by using either of these properties (locating a control by its Id is slightly more complex though):

```
Sub AccessControlByName()
    MsgBox CommandBars("Cell").Controls("Copy").Caption
End Sub

Sub AccessControlById()
    MsgBox CommandBars("Cell").FindControl(ID:=19).Caption
End Sub
```

Don't use the Caption property to access a control if you are writing code that may be used by users with a different language version of Excel. The Caption is language specific, so your code will fail on those users' systems. Instead, use the FindControl method in conjunction with the Id of the control (which is language independent). Luckily, the CommandBar names are not internationalized.

Properties of CommandBar controls

CommandBar controls have a number of properties that determine how the controls look and work. This list contains some of the more useful properties for CommandBar controls:

- ✔ **Caption:** The text displayed for the control. If the control shows only an image, the Caption appears when you move the mouse over the control.

- ✔ **FaceID:** A number that represents a graphics image displayed next to the control's text.

- ✔ **BeginGroup:** True if a separator bar appears before the control.

- ✔ **OnAction:** The name of a VBA macro that executes when the user clicks the control.

- ✔ **BuiltIn:** True if the control is an Excel built-in control.

- ✔ **Enabled:** True if the control can be clicked.

- ✔ **Visible:** True if the control is visible. Many of the shortcut menus contain hidden controls.

- ✔ **ToolTipText:** Text that appears when the user moves the mouse pointer over the control.

The ShowShortcutMenuItems procedure lists all the first-level controls on every shortcut menu. In addition, it identifies hidden controls by placing their Captions in angle brackets.

```
Sub ShowShortcutMenuItems()
  Dim Row As Long, Col As Long
  Dim Cbar As CommandBar
  Dim Ctl As CommandBarControl
  Row = 1
  Application.ScreenUpdating = False
  For Each Cbar In Application.CommandBars
    If Cbar.Type = msoBarTypePopup Then
      Cells(Row, 1) = Cbar.Index
      Cells(Row, 2) = Cbar.Name
      Col = 3
      For Each Ctl In Cbar.Controls
```

```
            If Ctl.Visible Then
                Cells(Row, Col) = Ctl.Caption
            Else
                Cells(Row, Col) = "<" & Ctl.Caption & ">"
            End If
            Col = Col + 1
        Next Ctl
        Row = Row + 1
      End If
    Next Cbar
End Sub
```

Figure 19-7 shows a portion of the output.

The ShowShortcutMenuItems procedure is available at this book's Web site. If you run the macro, you can see that many of the shortcut menus contain hidden controls.

	A	B	C	D	E	F	G
1	21	PivotChart Menu	Field Setti&ngs	&Options...	&Refresh Data	&Hide PivotChart Field Buttons	For&mulas
2	34	Workbook tabs	Sheet1	<&Sheet List>	<&Sheet List>	<&Sheet List>	<&Sheet List>
3	35	Cell	Cu&t	&Copy	&Paste		&Paste Table
4	36	Column	Cu&t	&Copy	&Paste		&Paste Table
5	37	Row	Cu&t	&Copy	&Paste		&Paste Table
6	38	Cell	Cu&t	&Copy	&Paste		&Paste Table
7	39	Column	Cu&t	&Copy	&Paste		&Paste Table
8	40	Row	Cu&t	&Copy	&Paste		&Paste Table
9	41	Ply	&Insert...	&Delete	&Rename	&Move or Copy...	&View Code
10	42	XLM Cell	Cu&t	&Copy	&Paste	Paste &Special...	&Paste Table
11	43	Document	&Save	Save &As...	&Print...	Page Set&up...	&Spelling...
12	44	Desktop	&New...	&Open...	Save &Workspace...	&Calculate Now	<F&ull Screen>
13	45	Nondefault Drag and Drop	&Move Here	&Copy Here	Copy Here as &Values Only	Copy Here as &Formats Only	&Link Here
14	46	AutoFill	&Copy Cells	Fill &Series	Fill &Formatting Only	Fill With&out Formatting	Fill &Days
15	47	Button	Cu&t	&Copy	Copy Ink As &Text	&Paste	Clear
16	48	Dialog	&Paste	Ta&b Order...	&Run Dialog	<F&ull Screen>	
17	49	Series	&Selected Object	Chart T&ype...	S&elect Data...	Add T&rendline...	Cle&ar
18	50	Plot Area	&Selected Object	Chart T&ype...	S&elect Data...	Chart Opt&ions...	&Move Chart...
19	51	Floor and Walls	&Selected Object	3-D &View...	Cle&ar		
20	52	Trendline	&Selected Object	Cle&ar			
21	53	Chart	&Selected Object	Cle&ar			
22	54	Format Data Series	&Selected Object	Chart T&ype...	S&elect Data...	Add T&rendline...	&Hide Detail
23	55	Format Axis	&Selected Object	Cle&ar	&Hide Detail	&Show Detail	
24	56	Format Legend Entry	&Selected Object	&Hide Detail	&Show Detail	Cle&ar	
25	57	Formula Bar	Cu&t	&Copy	&Paste	&Format Cells...	Pic&k From Drop
26	58	PivotTable Context Menu	&Copy	&Format Cells...	<Number Forma&t...>	&Refresh	<&Sort>

Figure 19-7: Listing all top-level controls in all shortcut menus.

This has been a quick and dirty overview of CommandBars. There's a lot more to CommandBars, of course, but this is as far as I take it in this book. The next section provides some examples that may help clear up any confusion you have.

With the introduction of the new Ribbon user interface, a lot has changed. Some of the changes are for the better, and some for the worse. The possibilities for gaining control over the user interface by using just VBA are now very limited.

VBA Shortcut Menu Examples

This section contains a few examples of using VBA to manipulate the Excel right-click menus — commonly known as shortcut menus. These examples give you an idea of the types of things you can do, and they can all be modified to suit your needs.

Resetting all built-in right-click menusThe following procedure resets all built-in toolbars to their original state:

```
Sub ResetAll()
    Dim cbar As CommandBar
    For Each cbar In Application.CommandBars
        If cbar.Type = msoBarTypePopup Then
            cbar.Reset
            cbar.Enabled = True
        End If
    Next cbar
End Sub
```

This procedure will have no effect unless someone has executed some VBA code that adds items, removes items, or disables shortcut menus.

Adding a new item to the Cell shortcut menu

In Chapter 16 I describe the Change Case utility. You can enhance that utility a bit by making it available from the Cell shortcut menu.

This example is available at this book's Web site.

The AddToShortcut procedure adds a new menu item to the Cell shortcut menu. Recall that Excel has two Cell shortcut menus. This procedure modifies the normal right-click menu, but not the right-click menu that appears in Page Break Preview mode.

```
Sub AddToShortCut()
    Dim Bar As CommandBar
    Dim NewControl As CommandBarButton
    DeleteFromShortcut
    Set Bar = Application.CommandBars("Cell")
    Set NewControl = Bar.Controls.Add _
        (Type:=msoControlButton, ID:=1, _
        temporary:=True)
    With NewControl
        .Caption = "&Change Case"
```

```
        .OnAction = "ChangeCase"
        .Style = msoButtonIconAndCaption
    End With
End Sub
```

When you modify a shortcut menu, that modification remains in effect until you restart Excel. In other words, modified shortcut menus don't reset themselves when you close the workbook that contains the VBA code. Therefore, if you write code to modify a shortcut menu, you almost always write code to reverse the effect of your modification.

The DeleteFromShortcut procedure removes the new menu item from the Cell shortcut menu.

```
Sub DeleteFromShortcut()
    On Error Resume Next
    Application.CommandBars("Cell").Controls _
        ("&Change Case").Delete
End Sub
```

Figure 19-8 shows the new menu item displayed after right-clicking a cell.

Figure 19-8:
The Cell
shortcut
menu
showing
a custom
menu item.

The first actual command after the declaration of a couple of variables calls the DeleteFromShortcut procedure. This statement ensures that only one Change Case menu item appears on the shortcut Cell menu. Try commenting out that line (put an apostrophe at the start of the line) and running the

procedure a few times — now don't get carried away! Right-click a cell, and you can see multiple instances of the Change Case menu item. Get rid of all the entries by running DeleteFromShortcut multiple times (once for each extra menu item).

Finally, you need a way to add the shortcut menu item when the workbook is opened and to delete the menu item when the workbook is closed. Doing this is easy . . . if you've read Chapter 11. Just add these two event procedures to the ThisWorkbook code module:

```
Private Sub Workbook_Open()
    Call AddToShortCut
End Sub

Private Sub Workbook_BeforeClose(Cancel As Boolean)
    Call DeleteFromShortcut
End Sub
```

The Workbook_Open procedure is executed when the workbook is opened, and the Workbook_BeforeClose procedure is executed before the workbook is closed. Just what the doctor ordered.

Disabling a shortcut menu

If you're so inclined, you can disable an entire shortcut menu. For example, you can make it so that right-clicking a cell does not display the normal shortcut menu. The following procedure, which is executed automatically when the workbook is opened, disables the Cell shortcut menu:

```
Private Sub Workbook_Open()
    Application.CommandBars("Cell").Enabled = False
End Sub
```

And here's its companion procedure that enables the shortcut menu when the workbook is closed.

```
Private Sub Workbook_BeforeClose(Cancel As Boolean)
    Application.CommandBars("Cell").Enabled = True
End Sub
```

Keep in mind that changes to CommandBars are permanent. If you don't execute the procedure to enable the disabled shortcut menu, that shortcut menu will not be available until you restart Excel. The ResetAll procedure mentioned earlier in this chapter shows you how to get all your CommandBars back to their bare-bones state again.

Creating a Custom Toolbar

If you check out all the CommandBars available, you may have noticed one
called Built-in Menus. This CommandBar contains all the old Excel 2003 menu
commands. Figure 19-9 shows part of this giant pop-up menu. All the old com-
mands are there, but they aren't arranged very well.

Figure 19-9:
Displaying
the Built-in
Menus
shortcut
menu.

In this example, I present a VBA procedure that (kind of) re-creates the old
Excel 2003 menu bar. It creates a new CommandBar and then copies the con-
trols from the Built-in Menus CommandBar.

```
Sub MakeOldMenus()
    Dim cb As CommandBar
    Dim cbc As CommandBarControl
    Dim OldMenu As CommandBar

'   Delete it, if it exists
    On Error Resume Next
    Application.CommandBars("Old Menus").Delete
    On Error GoTo 0

'   Create an old-style toolbar
'   Set the last argument to False for a more compact menu
    Set OldMenu = Application.CommandBars.Add
      _("Old Menus", , True)

'   Copy the controls from Excel's "Built-in Menus"
            shortcut menu
    With CommandBars("Built-in Menus")
```

```
          .Controls("&File").Copy OldMenu
          .Controls("&Edit").Copy OldMenu
          .Controls("&View").Copy OldMenu
          .Controls("&Insert").Copy OldMenu
          .Controls("F&ormat").Copy OldMenu
          .Controls("&Tools").Copy OldMenu
          .Controls("&Data").Copy OldMenu
          .Controls("&Window").Copy OldMenu
          .Controls("&Help").Copy OldMenu
     End With

'    Make it visible. It appears in the Add-Ins tab
     Application.CommandBars("Old Menus").Visible = True
End Sub
```

Figure 19-10 shows the result of running the MakeOldMenus procedure. Notice that it appears in the Custom Toolbars group of the Add-Ins tab. This menu is, after all, a toolbar. It just looks like a menu.

Figure 19-10:
A toolbar, pretending to be the Excel 2003 menu system.

The new CommandBar is named Old Menus. The procedure starts by deleting that toolbar, if it already exists. Then code copies the "top level" controls from the CommandBar named Built-in Menus to the Old Menus CommandBar. A new CommandBar is hidden by default, so the final statement makes it visible.

The new "menu" system isn't perfect. A few of the commands don't work. You'll also notice that the recent files on the File menu show only placeholders. To get rid of the toolbar, right-click it and choose Delete Custom Toolbar.

This example is available on the book's Web site.

Part V
Putting It All Together

OVER-SPREADSHEETING

"According to your current physical symptoms, you'll be bald well before you're fat."

In this part . . .

The preceding 19 chapters cover quite a bit of material. At this point, you may still feel a bit disjointed about all the VBA stuff. The chapters in this part fill in the gaps and tie everything together. You learn how to include your own custom buttons in the Excel user interface. I discuss custom worksheet functions (a very useful feature), describe add-ins, provide more programming examples, and wrap up with a discussion of user-oriented applications.

Chapter 20

Creating Worksheet Functions — and Living to Tell about It

..

..

*F*or many people, VBA's main attraction is the capability to create custom worksheet functions — functions that look, work, and feel just like those that Microsoft built into Excel. A *custom function* offers the added advantage of working exactly how you want it to (because *you* wrote it). I introduce custom functions in Chapter 5. In this chapter, I get down to the nitty-gritty and describe some tricks of the trade.

Why Create Custom Functions?

You are undoubtedly familiar with Excel's worksheet functions — even Excel novices know how to use common worksheet functions, such as SUM, AVERAGE, and IF. By my count, Excel 2007 contains more than 350 predefined worksheet functions, and Excel 2010 adds about 50 more. And if that's not enough, you can create functions by using VBA.

With all the functions available in Excel and VBA, you may wonder why you would ever need to create functions. The answer: to simplify your work. With a bit of planning, custom functions are very useful in worksheet formulas and VBA procedures. Often, for example, you can significantly shorten a formula by creating a custom function. After all, shorter formulas are more readable and easier to work with.

What custom worksheet functions can't do

As you develop custom functions for use in your worksheet formulas, it's important that you understand a key point. VBA worksheet Function procedures are essentially *passive*. For example, code within a Function procedure cannot manipulate ranges, change formatting, or do many of the other things that are possible with a Sub procedure. An example may help.

It might be useful to create a function that changes the color of text in a cell based on the cell's value. Try as you might, however, you can't write such a function. It always returns an error value.

Just remember this: A function used in a worksheet formula returns a value — it does not perform actions with objects.

That said, there are a few exceptions to this rule. For example, here's a Function procedure that changes the text in a cell comment:

```
Function ChangeComment(cell, NewText)
    cell.Comment.Text NewText
End Function
```

And here's a formula that uses the function. It assumes that cell A1 already has a comment. When the formula is calculated, the comment is changed.

```
=ChangeComment(A1,"I changed the comment!")
```

I'm not sure if this is an oversight or a feature. But it's a rare example of a VBA function that changes something in a worksheet.

Understanding VBA Function Basics

Time for a quick review. A VBA *function* is a procedure that's stored in a VBA module. You can use these functions in other VBA procedures or in your worksheet formulas.

A *module* can contain any number of functions. You can use a custom function in a formula just as if it were a built-in function. If the function is defined in a different workbook, however, you must precede the function name with the workbook name. For example, assume you developed a function called DiscountPrice (which takes one argument), and the function is stored in a workbook named pricing.xlsm.

To use this function in the pricing.xlsm workbook, enter a formula such as this:

```
=DiscountPrice(A1)
```

If you want to use this function in a *different* workbook, enter a formula such as this:

```
=pricing.xlsm!discountprice(A1)
```

If the custom function is stored in an add-in, you don't need to precede the function name with the workbook name. I discuss add-ins in Chapter 21.

Custom functions appear in the Insert Function dialog box, in the User Defined category. Pressing Shift+F3 is one way to display the Insert Function dialog box.

Writing Functions

Remember that a function's name acts like a variable. The final value of this variable is the value returned by the function. To demonstrate, examine the following function, which returns the user's first name:

```
Function FirstName()
    Dim FullName As String
    Dim FirstSpace As Integer
    FullName = Application.UserName
    FirstSpace = InStr(FullName, " ")
    If FirstSpace = 0 Then
        FirstName = FullName
    Else
        FirstName = Left(FullName, FirstSpace - 1)
    End If
End Function
```

This function starts by assigning the UserName property of the Application object to a variable named FullName. Next, it uses the VBA InStr function to locate the first space in the name. If there is no space, FirstSpace is equal to 0, and FirstName is equal to the entire name. If FullName *does* have a space, the Left function extracts the text to the left of the space and assigns it to FirstName.

Notice that FirstName is the name of the function and is also used as a variable name *in* the function. The final value of FirstName is the value that's returned by the function. Several intermediate calculations may be going on in the function, but the function always returns the last value assigned to the variable that is the same as the function's name.

All the examples in this chapter are available at this book's Web site.

Working with Function Arguments

To work with functions, you need to understand how to work with arguments. The following points apply to the arguments for Excel worksheet functions and custom VBA functions:

- ✔ *Arguments* can be cell references, variables (including arrays), constants, literal values, or expressions.
- ✔ Some functions have no arguments.
- ✔ Some functions have a fixed number of required arguments (from 1 to 60).
- ✔ Some functions have a combination of required and optional arguments.

Function Examples

The examples in this section demonstrate how to work with various types of arguments.

A function with no argument

Like Sub procedures, Function procedures need not have arguments. For example, Excel has a few built-in worksheet functions that don't use arguments, including RAND, TODAY, and NOW.

Here's an example of a function with no arguments. The following function returns the UserName property of the Application object. This name appears in the General tab of the Excel Options dialog box (In Excel 2007, it's called the Popular tab). This simple but useful example shows the only way you can get the user's name to appear in a worksheet cell:

```
Function User()
'    Returns the name of the current user
     User = Application.UserName
End Function
```

When you enter the following formula into a worksheet cell, the cell displays the current user's name:

```
=User()
```

As with the Excel built-in functions, you must include a set of empty parentheses when using a function with no arguments. Otherwise, Excel tries to interpret the function as a named range.

A function with one argument

The single-argument function in this section is designed for sales managers who need to calculate the commissions earned by their salespeople. The commission rate depends on the monthly sales volume; those who sell more earn

a higher commission rate. The function returns the commission amount based on the monthly sales (which is the function's only argument — a required argument). The calculations in this example are based on Table 20-1.

Table 20-1	Commission Rates by Sales
Monthly Sales	*Commission Rate*
$0–$9,999	8.0%
$10,000–$19,999	10.5%
$20,000–$39,999	12.0%
$40,000+	14.0%

You can use several approaches to calculate commissions for sales amounts entered into a worksheet. You *could* write a lengthy worksheet formula such as this:

```
=IF(AND(A1>=0,A1<=9999.99),A1*0.08,IF(AND(A1>=10000,
A1<=19999.99),A1*0.105,IF(AND(A1>=20000,A1<=39999.99),
A1*0.12,IF(A1>=40000,A1*0.14,0))))
```

A couple reasons make this a bad approach. First, the formula is overly complex. Second, the values are hard-coded into the formula, making the formula difficult to modify if the commission structure changes.

A better approach is to create a table of commission values and use a LOOKUP table function to compute the commissions:

```
=VLOOKUP(A1,Table,2)*A1
```

Another approach, which doesn't require a table of commissions, is to create a custom function:

```
Function Commission(Sales)
'    Calculates sales commissions
     Const Tier1 As Double = 0.08
     Const Tier2 As Double = 0.105
     Const Tier3 As Double = 0.12
     Const Tier4 As Double = 0.14
     Select Case Sales
          Case 0 To 9999.99: Commission = Sales * Tier1
          Case 10000 To 19999.99: Commission = Sales * Tier2
          Case 20000 To 39999.99: Commission = Sales * Tier3
          Case Is >= 40000: Commission = Sales * Tier4
     End Select

     Commission = Round(Commission, 2)
End Function
```

Notice that the four commission rates are declared as constants, rather than hard-coded. This makes it very easy to modify the function if the commission rates change.

After you define this function in a VBA module, you can use it in a worksheet formula. Entering the following formula into a cell produces a result of 3,000. The amount of 25000 qualifies for a commission rate of 12 percent:

```
=Commission(25000)
```

Figure 20-1 shows a worksheet that uses the Commission function in formulas in column C.

	A	B	C	D
1	Name	Sales	Commission	
2	Adams	$61,983.00	$8,677.62	
3	Baker	$3,506.00	$280.48	
4	Douglas	$38,973.00	$4,676.76	
5	Emmett	$32,092.00	$3,851.04	
6	Franklin	$27,354.00	$3,282.48	
7	Johnson	$17,833.00	$1,872.46	
8	Kent	$41,598.00	$5,823.72	
9	Mays	$32,000.00	$3,840.00	
10	Quincy	$5,000.00	$400.00	
11	Randall	$68,793.00	$9,631.02	
12	Smith	$31,093.00	$3,731.16	
13	Walker	$24,509.00	$2,941.08	
14	Zeller	$41,544.00	$5,816.16	
15				

Figure 20-1: Using the Commission function in a worksheet.

A function with two arguments

The next example builds on the preceding one. Imagine that the sales manager implements a new policy to reward long-term employees: The total commission paid increases by 1 percent for every year the salesperson has been with the company.

I modified the custom Commission function (defined in the preceding section) so that it takes two arguments, both of which are required arguments. Call this new function *Commission2:*

```
Function Commission2(Sales, Years)
'    Calculates sales commissions based on years in service
     Const Tier1 As Double = 0.08
     Const Tier2 As Double = 0.105
     Const Tier3 As Double = 0.12
     Const Tier4 As Double = 0.14
```

```
    Select Case Sales
        Case 0 To 9999.99: Commission2=Sales*Tier1
        Case 10000 To 19999.99: Commission2=Sales*Tier2
        Case 20000 To 39999.99: Commission2=Sales*Tier3
        Case Is>=40000: Commission2=Sales*Tier4
    End Select
    Commission2=Commission2+(Commission2*Years/100)
    Commission2=Round(Commission2, 2)
End Function
```

I simply added the second argument (Years) to the Function statement and included an additional computation that adjusts the commission before exiting the function. This additional computation multiplies the original commission by the number of years in services, divides by 100, and then adds the result to the original computation.

Here's an example of how you can write a formula by using this function. (It assumes that the sales amount is in cell A1; cell B1 specifies the number of years the salesperson has worked.)

```
=Commission2(A1,B1)
```

A function with a range argument

Using a worksheet range as an argument is not at all tricky; Excel takes care of the behind-the-scenes details.

Assume that you want to calculate the average of the five largest values in a range named Data. Excel doesn't have a function that can do this, so you would probably write a formula:

```
=(LARGE(Data,1)+LARGE(Data,2)+LARGE(Data,3)+
LARGE(Data,4)+LARGE(Data,5))/5
```

This formula uses Excel's LARGE function, which returns the *n*th largest value in a range. The formula adds the five largest values in the range named Data and then divides the result by 5. The formula works fine, but it's rather unwieldy. And what if you decide that you need to compute the average of the top six values? You would need to rewrite the formula — and make sure that you update all copies of the formula.

Wouldn't this be easier if Excel had a function named TopAvg? Then you could compute the average by using the following (nonexistent) function:

```
=TopAvg(Data,5)
```

This example shows a case in which a custom function can make things much easier for you. The following custom VBA function, named TopAvg, returns the average of the *N* largest values in a range:

```
Function TopAvg(InRange, N)
'    Returns the average of the highest N values in InRange
    Dim Sum As Double
    Dim I As Long
    Sum = 0
    For i = 1 To N
        Sum = Sum + WorksheetFunction.Large(InRange, i)
    Next i
    TopAvg = Sum / N
End Function
```

This function takes two arguments: InRange (which is a worksheet range) and N (the number of values to average). It starts by initializing the Sum variable to 0. It then uses a For-Next loop to calculate the sum of the *N* largest values in the range. Note that I use the Excel LARGE function within the loop. Finally, TopAvg is assigned the value of Sum divided by N.

You can use all Excel worksheet functions in your VBA procedures *except* those that have equivalents in VBA. For example, VBA has a Rnd function that returns a random number. Therefore, you can't use the Excel RAND function in a VBA procedure.

A function with an optional argument

Many Excel built-in worksheet functions use optional arguments. An example is the LEFT function, which returns characters from the left side of a string. Its official syntax follows:

```
LEFT(text[,num_chars])
```

The first argument is required, but the second (in square brackets) is optional. If you omit the optional argument, Excel assumes a value of 1. Therefore, the following formulas return the same result:

```
=LEFT(A1,1)
=LEFT(A1)
```

The custom functions you develop in VBA also can have optional arguments. You specify an optional argument by preceding the argument's name with

the keyword Optional, followed by an equal sign and the default value. If the optional argument is missing, the code uses the default value.

The following example shows a custom function that uses an optional argument:

```
Function DrawOne(InRange, Optional Recalc = 0)
'    Chooses one cell at random from a range

    Randomize
'    Make function volatile if Recalc is 1
    If Recalc = 1 Then Application.Volatile True

'    Determine a random cell
    DrawOne = InRange(Int((InRange.Count) * Rnd + 1))
End Function
```

This function randomly chooses one cell from an input range. The range passed as an argument is actually an array (I explain arrays in Chapter 7), and the function selects one item from the array at random. If the second argument is 1, the selected value changes whenever the worksheet is recalculated. (The function is made *volatile*.) If the second argument is 0 (or is omitted), the function is not recalculated unless one of the cells in the input range is modified.

Debugging custom functions

Debugging a Function procedure can be a bit more challenging than debugging a Sub procedure. If you develop a function for use in worksheet formulas, you find that an error in the Function procedure simply results in an error display in the formula cell (usually #VALUE!). In other words, you don't receive the normal runtime error message that helps you locate the offending statement.

You can choose among three methods for debugging custom functions:

✔ Place MsgBox functions at strategic locations to monitor the value of specific variables. Fortunately, message boxes in Function procedures pop up when you execute the procedure. Make sure that only one formula in the worksheet uses your function, or the message boxes appear for each formula that's evaluated — which could get very annoying.

✔ Test the procedure by calling it from a Sub procedure. Run-time errors appear normally in a pop-up window, and you can either correct the problem (if you know it) or jump right into the debugger.

✔ Set a breakpoint in the function and then use the Excel debugger to step through the function. You can then access all the usual debugging tools. Refer to Chapter 13 to find out about the debugger.

I use the Randomize statement to ensure that a different random number "seed" is chosen each time the workbook is opened. Without this statement, the same random numbers are generated each time the workbook is opened.

You can use this function for choosing lottery numbers, selecting a winner from a list of names, and so on.

A function with an indefinite number of arguments

Some Excel worksheet functions take an indefinite number of arguments. A familiar example is the SUM function, which has the following syntax:

```
SUM(number1,number2...)
```

The first argument is required, but you can have as many as 254 additional arguments. Here's an example of a SUM function with four range arguments:

```
=SUM(A1:A5,C1:C5,E1:E5,G1:G5)
```

Here's a VBA function that can have any number of single-value arguments. This function doesn't work with multi-cell range arguments.

```
Function Concat(string1, ParamArray string2())
'    Demonstrates indefinite number of function arguments
    Dim Args As Variant

'    Process the first argument
    Concat = string1

'    Process additional arguments (if any)
    If UBound(string2) <> -1 Then
        For Args = LBound(string2) To UBound(string2)
            Concat = Concat & " " & string2(Args)
        Next Args
    End If
End Function
```

This function is similar to the Excel CONCATENATE function, which combines text arguments into a single string. The difference is that this custom function inserts a space between each pair of concatenated strings.

The second argument, string2(), is an array preceded by the ParamArray keyword. If the second argument is empty, the UBound function returns –1 and the function ends. If the second argument is not empty, the procedure loops through the elements of the string2 array and processes each additional

argument. The LBound and UBound functions determine the beginning and ending elements of the array. The beginning element is normally 0 unless you either declare it as something else or use an Option Base 1 statement at the beginning of your module.

ParamArray can apply to only the *last* argument in the procedure. It is always a Variant data type, and it is always an optional argument (although you don't use the Optional keyword). Figure 20-2 shows this function in use. Examine the figure to see how the results differ from those produced by the Excel CONCATENATE function, which doesn't insert a space between the concatenated items.

Figure 20-2:
Using the
Concat
function in
worksheet
formulas.

	A	B	C	D
1	Title	First	Last	Concat
2	Mr.	Jim	Smith	Mr. Jim Smith
3	Dr.	Tina	Peterson	Dr. Tina Peterson
4	Ms.	Jane	Doe	Ms. Jane Doe
5		Frank	Franklin	Frank Franklin
6	Mr.	Willie	Nielson	Mr. Willie Nielson
7	Mrs.	Steve	Marks	Mrs. Steve Marks
8		Hank	Walker	Hank Walker
9	Mr.	Bill		Mr. Bill
10				

Functions That Return an Array

Array formulas are one of Excel's most powerful features. If you're familiar with array formulas, you'll be happy to know that you can create VBA functions that return an array.

Returning an array of month names

I'll start out with a simple example. The MonthNames function returns a 12-element array of — you guessed it — month names.

```
Function MonthNames()
    MonthNames = Array("January", "February", "March", _
        "April", "May", "June", "July", "August", _
        "September", "October", "November", "December")
End Function
```

To use the MonthNames function in a worksheet, you must enter it as a 12-cell array formula. For example, select range A1:L1 and enter **=MonthNames()**. Then use Ctrl+Shift+Enter to enter the array formula in all 12 selected cells. Figure 20-3 shows the result.

Figure 20-3:
Using the
Month
Names
function
to return a
12-element
array.

If you want the month names to display in a column, select 12 cells in
a column and use this array formula (don't forget to enter it by using
Ctrl+Shift+Enter):

```
=TRANSPOSE(MonthNames())
```

Returning a sorted list

Suppose that you have a list of names you want to show in sorted order in
another range of cells. Wouldn't it be nice to have a worksheet function do
that for you?

The custom function in this section does just that: It takes a single-column
range of cells as its argument and then returns an array of those cells sorted.
Figure 20-4 shows how it works. Range A2:A13 contains some names. Range
C2:C13 contains this multi-cell array formula. (Remember, the formula must
be entered by pressing Ctrl+Shift+Enter.)

```
=Sorted(A2:A13)
```

Here's the code for the Sorted function:

```
Function Sorted(Rng As Range)
    Dim SortedData() As Variant
    Dim Cell As Range
    Dim Temp As Variant, i As Long, j As Long
    Dim NonEmpty As Long

'    Transfer data to SortedData
    For Each Cell In Rng
        If Not IsEmpty(Cell) Then
            NonEmpty = NonEmpty + 1
            ReDim Preserve SortedData(1 To NonEmpty)
            SortedData(NonEmpty) = Cell.Value
        End If
    Next Cell
```

```
'    Sort the array
    For i = 1 To NonEmpty
        For j = i + 1 To NonEmpty
            If SortedData(i) > SortedData(j) Then
                Temp = SortedData(j)
                SortedData(j) = SortedData(i)
                SortedData(i) = Temp
            End If
        Next j
    Next i

'    Transpose the array and return it
    Sorted = Application.Transpose(SortedData)
End Function
```

Figure 20-4:
Using a
custom
function
to return
a sorted
range.

	A	B	C	D
1	**Unsorted**		**Sorted**	
2	Keith		Abigail	
3	Frank		Ann	
4	Jackie		Darren	
5	Tim		Frank	
6	Ann		Jackie	
7	Louise		Keith	
8	Zola		Louise	
9	Opie		Mary	
10	Ralph		Opie	
11	Mary		Ralph	
12	Abigail		Tim	
13	Darren		Zola	

The Sorted function starts by creating an array named SortedData. This array contains all the nonblank values in the argument range. Next, the SortedData array is sorted, using a bubble sort algorithm. Because the array is a horizontal array, it must be transposed before it is returned by the function.

The Sorted Function works with a range of any size, as long as it's in a single column or row. If the unsorted data is in a row, your formula needs to use Excel's TRANSPOSE function to display the sorted data horizontally. For example:

```
=TRANSPOSE(Sorted(A16:L16))
```

Using the Insert Function Dialog Box

The Excel Insert Function dialog box is a handy tool that lets you choose a worksheet function from a list and prompts you for the function's arguments. And, as I note earlier in this chapter, your custom worksheet functions also

appear in the Insert Function dialog box. Custom functions appear in the User Defined category.

TIP

Function procedures defined with the Private keyword do not appear in the Insert Function dialog box. Therefore, if you write a Function procedure that's designed to be used only by other VBA procedures (but not in formulas), you should declare the function as Private.

Displaying the function's description

The Insert Function dialog box displays a description of each built-in function. But, as you can see in Figure 20-5, a custom function displays the following text as its description: No help available.

Figure 20-5:
By default, the Insert Function dialog box does not provide a description for custom functions.

To display a meaningful description of your custom function in the Insert Function dialog box, perform a few additional (nonintuitive) steps:

1. **Activate a worksheet in the workbook that contains the custom function.**

2. **Choose Developer➪Code➪Macros (or press Alt+F8).**

 The Macro dialog box appears.

3. **In the Macro Name field, type the function's name.**

 Note that the function does not appear in the list of macros; you must type the name in.

4. **Click the Options button.**

 The Macro Options dialog box appears.

5. **In the Description field, type a description of the function.**

6. **Click OK.**

7. **Click Cancel.**

Now the Insert Function dialog box displays the description for your function; see Figure 20-6.

Figure 20-6:
The custom function now displays a description.

Custom functions, by default, are listed in the User Defined category. To add a function to a different category, you need to use VBA. This statement, when executed, adds the TopAvg function to the Math & Trig category (which is category #3):

```
Application.MacroOptions Macro:="TopAvg", Category:=3
```

Check the Help system for other category numbers. And remember, you need to execute this statement only one time. After you execute it (and save the workbook), the category number is permanently assigned to the function.

Argument descriptions

When you access a built-in function from the Insert Function dialog box, the Function Arguments dialog box displays a description of each argument. (See Figure 20-7.) If you use Excel 2007, there is no direct way to provide such descriptions for custom functions.

But if you use Excel 2010, a new feature lets you specify descriptions for your custom functions. You do this by using the MacroOptions method. Here's an example that adds descriptions for the arguments used by the TopAvg function:

```
Sub AddArgumentDescriptions()
    Application.MacroOptions Macro:="TopAvg", _
        ArgumentDescriptions:= _
            Array("Range that contains the values", _
        "Number of values to average")
End Sub
```

You need to execute this procedure only one time. After you execute it, the argument descriptions are stored in the workbook and are associated with the function.

Notice that the argument descriptions appear as arguments for the Array function. You must use the Array function even if you're assigning a description for a function that has only one argument.

Figure 20-7: By default, the Function Arguments dialog box displays function argument descriptions for built-in functions only.

This chapter provides lots of information about creating custom worksheet functions. Use these examples as models when you create functions for your own work. As usual, the online help provides additional details. Turn to Chapter 21 if you want to find out how to make your custom functions more accessible by storing them in an add-in.

Chapter 21

Creating Excel Add-Ins

..

..

*O*ne of the slickest features of Excel — at least in *my* mind — is the capability to create add-ins. In this chapter, I explain why I like this feature and show you how to create add-ins by using only the tools built into Excel.

Okay . . . So What's an Add-In?

What's an add-in? Glad you asked. An Excel *add-in* is something you add to enhance Excel's functionality. Some add-ins provide new worksheet functions you can use in formulas; other add-ins provide new commands or utilities. If the add-in is designed properly, the new features blend in well with the original interface so they appear to be part of the program.

Excel ships with several add-ins, including the Analysis ToolPak and Solver. You can also get Excel add-ins from third-party suppliers or as shareware. My Power Utility Pak is an example of an add-in (it adds about 70 new features to Excel, plus a slew of new worksheet functions).

Any knowledgeable user can create add-ins, but VBA programming skills are required. An Excel add-in is basically a different form of an XLSM workbook file. More specifically, an add-in is a normal XLSM workbook with the following differences:

 ✔ The IsAddin property of the Workbook object is True.

 ✔ The workbook window is hidden and can't be unhidden by using the View➪Window➪Unhide command.

 ✔ The workbook is not a member of the Workbooks collection. Rather, it's in the AddIns collection.

You can convert any workbook file into an add-in, but not all workbooks are good candidates. Because add-ins are always hidden, you can't display worksheets or chart sheets contained in an add-in. However, you can access an add-in's VBA Sub and Function procedures and display dialog boxes contained on UserForms.

Excel add-ins usually have an XLAM file extension to distinguish them from XLSM worksheet files. Earlier versions of Excel created add-ins with an XLA extension.

Why Create Add-Ins?

You might decide to convert your Excel application into an add-in for any of the following reasons:

- **Make it more difficult to access your code:** When you distribute an application as an add-in (and you protect its VBA project), casual users can't view the sheets in the workbook. If you use proprietary techniques in your VBA code, you can make it more difficult for others to copy the code. Excel's protection features aren't perfect though, and password-cracking utilities are available.

- **Avoid confusion:** If a user loads your application as an add-in, the file is invisible and therefore less likely to confuse novice users or get in the way. Unlike a hidden workbook, the contents of an add-in can't be revealed.

- **Simplify access to worksheet functions:** Custom worksheet functions that you store in an add-in don't require the workbook name qualifier. For example, if you store a custom function named MOVAVG in a workbook named NEWFUNC.XLSM, you must use syntax like the following to use this function in a different workbook:

```
=NEWFUNC.XLSM!MOVAVG(A1:A50)
```

But if this function is stored in an add-in file that's open, you can use much simpler syntax because you don't need to include the file reference:

```
=MOVAVG(A1:A50)
```

- **Provide easier access for users:** After you identify the location of your add-in, it appears in the Add-Ins dialog box, with a friendly name and a description of what it does. The user can easily enable or disable your add-in.

✔ **Gain better control over loading:** Add-ins can be opened automatically when Excel starts, regardless of the directory in which they are stored.

✔ **Avoid displaying prompts when unloading:** When an add-in is closed, the user never sees the dialog box prompt asking if you want to save changes in the file.

Working with Add-Ins

You load and unload add-ins by using the Add-Ins dialog box. To display this dialog box, choose File⇨Options⇨Add-Ins. Then select Excel Add-Ins from the drop-down list at the bottom of this dialog screen and click Go. If you're using Excel 2010, getting to this dialog box is a bit easier: Choose Developer⇨Add-Ins⇨Add-Ins. But the easiest method is to just press Alt+TI (the old Excel 2003 keyboard shortcut).

Any of these methods displays the Add-Ins dialog box shown in Figure 21-1. The list box contains the names of all add-ins that Excel knows about. In this list, check marks identify any currently open add-ins. You can open and close add-ins from the Add-Ins dialog box by selecting or deselecting the check boxes.

Figure 21-1:
The Add-Ins dialog box lists all the add-ins known to Excel.

You can also open most add-in files (as if they were workbook files) by choosing the File⇨Open command. An add-in opened in this manner does not appear in the Add-Ins dialog box. In addition, if the add-in was opened by using the Open command, you can't close it by choosing File⇨Close. You can remove the add-in only by exiting and restarting Excel or by writing a macro to close the add-in.

When you open an add-in, you may or may not notice anything different. In many cases, however, the Ribbon changes in some way — Excel displays either a new tab or one or more new groups on an existing tab. For example, opening the Analysis ToolPak add-in gives you a new item on the Data tab: Analysis⇨Data Analysis. If the add-in contains only custom worksheet functions, the new functions appear in the Insert Function dialog box, and you'll see no change to Excel's user interface.

Add-In Basics

Although you can convert any workbook to an add-in, not all workbooks benefit from this conversion. A workbook with no macros makes a completely useless add-in. In fact, the only types of workbooks that benefit from being converted to an add-in are those with macros. For example, a workbook that consists of general-purpose macros (Sub and Function procedures) makes an ideal add-in.

Creating an add-in isn't difficult, but it does require a bit of extra work. Use the following steps to create an add-in from a normal workbook file:

1. **Develop your application and make sure that everything works properly.**

 Don't forget to include a method for executing the macro or macros. You might want to define a shortcut key or customize the user interface in some way (see Chapter 19). If the add-in consists only of functions, there's no need to include a method to execute them because they will appear in the Insert Function dialog box.

2. **Test the application by executing it when a *different* workbook is active.**

 Doing so simulates the application's behavior when it's used as an add-in because an add-in is never the active workbook.

3. **Activate the VBE and select the workbook in the Project window; choose Tools⇨*VBAProject* Properties and click the Protection tab; select the Lock Project for Viewing check box and enter a password (twice); click OK.**

 This step is necessary only if you want to prevent others from viewing or modifying your macros or UserForms.

4. **In Excel 2010, choose Developer⇨Document Panel. In Excel 2007, choose Office⇨Prepare⇨Properties.**

 Excel displays its Document Properties pane below the Ribbon.

5. **In the Document Properties pane, enter a brief descriptive title in the Title field and a longer description in the Comments field.**

 Steps 4 and 5 are not required but make the add-in easier to use, because the descriptions you enter appear in the Add-Ins dialog box when your add-in is selected.

6. **Choose File⇨Save As.**

7. **In the Save As dialog box, select Excel add-in (*.xlam) from the Save as Type drop-down list.**

8. **Specify the folder that will store the add-in.**

 Excel proposes a folder named AddIns, but you can save the file in any folder you like.

9. **Click Save.**

A copy of your workbook is converted to an add-in and saved with an XLAM extension. Your original workbook remains open.

An Add-In Example

In this section, I discuss the basic steps involved in creating a useful add-in. The example is based on the Change Case text conversion utility that I describe in Chapter 16.

The XLSM version of this example is available at this book's Web site. You can create an add-in from this workbook.

Setting up the workbook

The workbook consists of one blank worksheet, a VBA module, and a UserForm. In Chapter 19, I already added code to the workbook that creates a new menu item on the Cell right-click shortcut menu.

The original version of the utility included options for uppercase, lowercase, and proper case. For the add-in version, I added two new options to the UserForm, so it has the same options as the built-in tool in Microsoft Word:

- ✔ **Sentence Case:** Makes the first letter uppercase, and all other letters lowercase.

- ✔ **Toggle Case:** All uppercase characters are converted to lowercase, and vice versa.

Figure 21-2 shows UserForm1. The five OptionButton controls are inside a Frame control. In addition, the UserForm has a Cancel button (named CancelButton) and an OK button (named OKButton).

The code executed when the Cancel button is clicked is very simple. This procedure unloads the UserForm with no action:

```
Private Sub CancelButton_Click()
    Unload UserForm1
End Sub
```

The code that's executed when the OK button is clicked follows. This code does all the work:

```
Private Sub OKButton_Click()
    Dim TextCells As Range
    Dim cell As Range
    Dim Text As String
    Dim i As Long

'   Create an object with just text constants
    On Error Resume Next
    Set TextCells = Selection.SpecialCells(xlConstants, _
        xlTextValues)

'   Turn off screen updating
    Application.ScreenUpdating = False

'   Loop through the cells
    For Each cell In TextCells
        Text = cell.Value
        Select Case True
        Case OptionLower 'lowercase
            cell.Value = LCase(cell.Value)
        Case OptionUpper 'UPPERCASE
            cell.Value = UCase(cell.Value)
        Case OptionProper 'Proper Case
            cell.Value = _
                WorksheetFunction.Proper(cell.Value)
```

```
        Case OptionSentence 'Sentence case
            Text = UCase(Left(cell.Value, 1))
            Text = Text & LCase(Mid(cell.Value, 2,
        Len(cell.Value)))
            cell.Value = Text
        Case OptionToggle 'tOGGLE CASE
            For i = 1 To Len(Text)
                If Mid(Text, i, 1) Like "[A-Z]" Then
                    Mid(Text, i, 1) = LCase(Mid(Text, i, 1))
                Else
                    Mid(Text, i, 1) = UCase(Mid(Text, i, 1))
                End If
            Next i
            cell.Value = Text
        End Select
    Next

'   Unload the dialog box
    Unload UserForm1
End Sub
```

In addition to the two new options, this version of the Change Case utility differs from the version in Chapter 16 in two other ways:

✔ I use the SpecialCells method to create an object variable that consists of the cells in the selection that contain a text constant (not a formula). This technique makes the routine run a bit faster if the selection contains many formula cells. See Chapter 14 for more information on this technique.

✔ I added the Change Case menu item to the Row and the Column shortcut menus. So now, you can execute the utility by right-clicking a range selection, a complete row selection, or a complete column selection.

Testing the workbook

Test the add-in before converting this workbook. To simulate what happens when the workbook is an add-in, you should test the workbook when a different workbook is active. Remember, an add-in is never the active sheet or workbook, so testing it when a different workbook is open may help you identify some potential errors.

1. **Open a new workbook and enter information into some cells.**

 For testing purposes, enter various types of information, including text, values, and formulas. Or just open an existing workbook and use it for your tests — remember that any changes to the workbook cannot be undone, so you may want to use a copy.

2. **Select one or more cells (or entire rows and columns).**

3. **Execute the ChangeCase macro by choosing the new Change Case command from your Cell (or Row or Column) right-click menu.**

If the Change Case command doesn't appear on your right-click menu, the most likely reason is that you did not enable macros when you opened the change case.xlsm workbook. Close the workbook and then reopen it — and make sure that you enable macros.

Adding descriptive information

I recommend entering a description of your add-in, but this isn't required.

1. **Activate the change case.xlsm workbook.**

2. **In Excel 2010, choose Developer➪Document Panel. In Excel 2007, choose Office➪Prepare➪Properties.**

 Excel displays the Document Properties panel above the Formula bar. See Figure 21-3.

3. **Enter a title for the add-in in the Title field.**

 This text appears in the list of add-ins in the Add-Ins dialog box. For this example, enter **Change Case.**

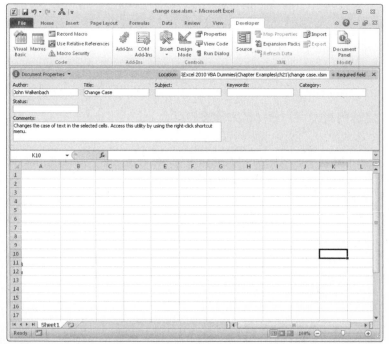

Figure 21-3: Use the Document Properties panel to enter descriptive information about your add-in.

4. **In the Comments field, enter a description.**

This information appears at the bottom of the Add-Ins dialog box when the add-in is selected. For this example, enter **Changes the case of text in selected cells. Access this utility by using the right-click shortcut menu.**

Protecting the VBA code

If you want to add a password to prevent others from viewing the VBA code, follow these steps:

1. **Activate the VBE and select the change case.xlsm workbook in the Project window.**

2. **Choose Tools⇨*VBAProject* Properties and click the Protection tab on the dialog box that appears.**

3. **Select the Lock Project for Viewing check box and enter a password (twice).**

4. **Click OK.**

5. **Save the workbook by choosing File⇨Save from the VBE's menu or by going back to the Excel window and choosing File⇨Save.**

Creating the add-in

At this point, you've tested the change case.xlsm file, and it's working correctly. The next step is to create the add-in:

1. **If needed, reactivate Excel.**

2. **Activate the change case.xlsm workbook and choose File⇨Save As.**

Excel displays its Save As dialog box.

3. **In the Save as Type drop-down menu, select Add-In (*.xlam).**

4. **Specify the location and click Save.**

A new add-in file (with an XLAM extension) is created, and the original XLSM version remains open.

Opening the add-in

To avoid confusion, close the XLSM workbook before opening the add-in that you created from that workbook.

Open the add-in with these steps:

1. **Press Alt+TI.**

 Excel displays the Add-Ins dialog box.

2. **Click the Browse button.**

3. **Locate and select the add-in you just created.**

4. **Click OK to close the Browse dialog box.**

 After you find your new add-in, the Add-Ins dialog box lists the add-in. As shown in Figure 21-4, the Add-Ins dialog box also displays the descriptive information you provided in the Document Properties panel.

5. **Make sure that the Add-Ins dialog box has a check mark for your new add-in.**

6. **Click OK to close the dialog box.**

 Excel opens the add-in, and you can now use it with all your workbooks.

Figure 21-4:
The Add-Ins dialog box has the new add-in selected.

Distributing the add-in

If you're in a generous mood, you can distribute this add-in to other Excel users simply by giving them a copy of the XLAM file (they don't need the XLSM version). When they open the add-in, the new Change Case command appears on the shortcut menu when they select a range, one or more rows, or one or more columns. If you locked the VBA project with a password, others cannot view your macro code (unless they know the password).

Modifying the add-in

If you ever need to modify the add-in (and you protected the VBA project with a password), you need to unlock it:

1. **Open your XLAM file if it's not already open.**

2. **Activate the VBE.**

3. **Double-click the project's name in the Project window.**

 You are prompted for the password.

4. **Enter your password and click OK.**

5. **Make your changes to the code.**

6. **Save the file from the VBE by choosing File⇨Save.**

If you create an add-in that stores information in a worksheet, you must set the workbook's IsAddIn property to False to view the workbook. You do this in the Property window when the ThisWorkbook object is selected (see Figure 21-5). After you've made your changes to the workbook, make sure that you set the IsAddIn property back to True before you save the file.

You now know how to work with add-ins and why you might want to create your own add-ins.

Figure 21-5:
Making an
add-in not
an add-in.

Part VI
The Part of Tens

In this part . . .

For reasons that are historical — as well as useful — all the books in the *For Dummies* series have chapters with lists in them. The next two chapters contain my own "ten" lists, which deal with frequently asked questions and other resources.

Chapter 22

Ten VBA Questions (And Answers)

*T*he following ten questions (and answers) address some of the most common issues asked by VBA newcomers.

I created a custom VBA function. When I try to use it in a formula, the formula displays #NAME?. What's wrong?

You probably put your function code in the wrong location. VBA code for worksheet functions must be in a standard VBA module — not in a module for a sheet or in ThisWorkbook. In the VBE, use Insert⇨Module to insert a standard module. Then cut and paste your code to the new VBA module.

This is a very common mistake, because a Sheet module looks exactly like a standard VBA module. Resist the temptation to put your code there. Spend four seconds and choose Insert⇨Module.

Can I use the VBA macro recorder to record all my macros?

Only if your macros are very simple. Normally, you use it only to record simple macros or as a starting point for a more complex macro. The macro recorder can't record macros that use variables, looping, or any other type of program flow constructs. In addition, you cannot record a Function procedure in the VBA macro recorder. Unfortunately, Excel 2007 refuses to record many actions that are related to charts and shapes. This oversight was corrected in Excel 2010.

How can I prevent others from viewing my VBA code?

1. **Activate your project in the VBE, and choose Tools⇨xxxxx Properties. The xxxxx corresponds to the name of your VBA project.**

2. **In the dialog box that appears, click the Protection tab and select Lock Project for Viewing.**

3. **Enter a password (twice) and click OK.**

4. **Save your workbook.**

Doing so prevents casual users from viewing your code, but password protection is certainly not 100 percent secure. Password-cracking utilities exist.

What's the VBA code for increasing or decreasing the number of rows and columns in a worksheet?

No such code exists. The number of rows and columns is fixed and cannot be changed. However, if you open a workbook that has been created by using an earlier Excel version (before Excel 2007), the text Compatibility Mode appears in the title bar. This notice indicates that this workbook is limited to the old 256-x-65536 cell grid. You can get out of this mode (and thus get the new, bigger cell grid) by saving the file as a normal (XLSX or XLSM) workbook and then closing and reopening this new file.

When I refer to a worksheet in my VBA code, I get a "subscript out of range" error. I'm not using any subscripts. What gives?

This error occurs if you attempt to access an element in a collection that doesn't exist. For example, this statement generates the error if the active workbook doesn't contain a sheet named MySheet:

```
Set X = ActiveWorkbook.Sheets("MySheet")
```

In your case, the workbook that you *think* is open is probably not open (so it's not in the Workbooks collection). Or, maybe you misspelled the workbook name.

Is there a VBA command that selects a range from the active cell to the last entry in a column or a row? (In other words, how can a macro accomplish the same thing as Ctrl+Shift+↓ or Ctrl+Shift+→?)

Here's the VBA equivalent for Ctrl+Shift+↓:

```
Range(ActiveCell, ActiveCell.End(xlDown)).Select
```

For the other directions, use the constants xlToLeft, xlToRight, or xlUp rather than xlDown.

How can I make my VBA code run as fast as possible?

Here are a few tips:

- ✔ Be sure to declare all your variables as a specific data type. (Use Option Explicit in each module's Declarations section to force yourself to declare all variables.)
- ✔ If you reference an object (such as a range) more than once, create an object variable using the Set keyword.
- ✔ Use the With-End With construct whenever possible.
- ✔ If your macro writes data to a worksheet and you have lots of complex formulas, set the calculation mode to Manual while the macro runs (but make sure you do a calculation when you need to use the results!).
- ✔ If your macro writes information to a worksheet, turn off screen updating by using Application.ScreenUpdating = False.

Don't forget to reinstate these last two settings to their starting value when your macro is finished.

How can I display multiline messages in a message box?

The easiest way is to build your message in a string variable, using the vbNewLine constant to indicate where you want your line breaks to occur. The following is a quick example:

```
Msg = "You selected the following:" & vbNewLine
Msg = Msg & UserAns
MsgBox Msg
```

I wrote some code that deletes worksheets. How can I avoid showing Excel's warning prompt?

Insert this statement before the code that deletes the worksheets:

```
Application.DisplayAlerts = False
```

Why can't I get the VBA line-continuation character (underscore) to work?

The line continuation sequence is actually two characters: a space followed by an underscore. Be sure to use both characters and press Enter after the underscore.

Chapter 23

(Almost) Ten Excel Resources

*T*his book is only an introduction to Excel VBA programming. If you hunger for more information, feel free to feed on the list of additional resources I've compiled here. You can discover new techniques, communicate with other Excel users, download useful files, ask questions, access the extensive Microsoft Knowledge Base, and lots more.

 Several of these resources are online services or Internet resources, which tend to change frequently. The descriptions are accurate at the time I'm writing this, but I can't guarantee that this information will remain current. That's how the Internet works.

The VBA Help System

I hope you've already discovered VBA's Help system. I find this reference source particularly useful for identifying objects, properties, and methods. It's readily available, it's free, and (for the most part) it's accurate. So use it.

Microsoft Product Support

Microsoft offers a wide variety of technical support options (some for free, others for a fee). To access Microsoft's support services (including the useful Knowledge Base), go here:

```
http://support.microsoft.com
```

And don't forget about Microsoft's Office site, which has lots of material related to Excel:

```
http://office.microsoft.com
```

Another great resource is the Microsoft Developer Network site (MSDN). It has lots and lots of information aimed at the developer (yes, that is you!). Here is a link to the main site, where you can search for Excel-related information:

```
http://msdn.microsoft.com
```

Internet Newsgroups

Microsoft's newsgroups are perhaps the best place to go if you have a question. You can find hundreds of newsgroups devoted to Microsoft products — including a dozen or so newsgroups just for Excel. The best way to access these newsgroups is by using special newsreader software. Or, use the e-mail client that comes with Windows. Depending on your version of Windows, it's called Outlook Express, Windows Mail, or Windows Live Mail. All these programs let you connect to newsgroups. Set your newsreader software to access the news server at msnews.microsoft.com.

The more popular English-language, Excel-related newsgroups are listed here:

```
microsoft.public.excel.charting

microsoft.public.excel.misc

microsoft.public.excel.printing

microsoft.public.excel.programming

microsoft.public.excel.setup

microsoft.public.excel.worksheet.functions
```

If you prefer to access the newsgroups by using your Web browser, you have two choices:

```
http://microsoft.com/communities/
```
```
http://groups.google.com
```

Without even knowing what your question is, I'm willing to bet that it has already been answered. To search old newsgroup messages by keyword, point your Web browser to:

```
http://groups.google.com
```

Internet Web Sites

Several Web sites contain Excel-related material. A good place to start your Web surfing is my very own site, which is named The Spreadsheet Page. After you get there, you can check out my material and then visit my Resources section, which leads you to dozens of other Excel-related sites. The URL for my site is:

```
http://spreadsheetpage.com
```

Excel Blogs

You can find literally millions of blogs (short for *weblogs*) on the Web. A *blog* is basically a frequently updated diary about a particular topic. Quite a few blogs are devoted exclusively to Excel. I maintain a list of Excel blogs at my site:

```
http://spreadsheetpage.com/index.php/excelfeeds
```

Google

When I have a question about any topic (including Excel programming), my first line of attack is Google — currently the world's most popular search site.

```
http://google.com
```

Enter a few key search terms and see what Google finds. I get an answer about 90 percent of the time. If that fails, then I search the newsgroups (described earlier) by using this URL:

```
http://groups.google.com
```

Bing

Bing is Microsoft's answer to the Google search site. Some people prefer it over Google; others don't. If you haven't tried it, the URL is:

```
http://bing.com
```

Local User Groups

Many larger communities and universities have an Excel user group that meets periodically. If you can find a user group in your area, check it out. These groups are often an excellent source for contacts and sharing ideas.

My Other Books

Sorry, but I couldn't resist the opportunity for a blatant plug. To take VBA programming to the next level, check out my *Excel 2007 Power Programming with VBA* or *Excel 2010 Power Programming with VBA* (both published by Wiley).

Index

Note: BC (Bonus Chapter) in a page number denotes content located on this book's companion Web site (www.dummies.com/go/excelvbaprogrammingfd2e).

Business/Accounting & Bookkeeping

Bookkeeping For Dummies
978-0-7645-9848-7

eBay Business
All-in-One For Dummies,
2nd Edition
978-0-470-38536-4

Job Interviews
For Dummies,
3rd Edition
978-0-470-17748-8

Resumes For Dummies,
5th Edition
978-0-470-08037-5

Stock Investing
For Dummies,
3rd Edition
978-0-470-40114-9

Successful Time
Management
For Dummies
978-0-470-29034-7

Computer Hardware

BlackBerry For Dummies,
3rd Edition
978-0-470-45762-7

Computers For Seniors
For Dummies
978-0-470-24055-7

iPhone For Dummies,
2nd Edition
978-0-470-42342-4

Laptops For Dummies,
3rd Edition
978-0-470-27759-1

Macs For Dummies,
10th Edition
978-0-470-27817-8

Cooking & Entertaining

Cooking Basics
For Dummies,
3rd Edition
978-0-7645-7206-7

Wine For Dummies,
4th Edition
978-0-470-04579-4

Diet & Nutrition

Dieting For Dummies,
2nd Edition
978-0-7645-4149-0

Nutrition For Dummies,
4th Edition
978-0-471-79868-2

Weight Training
For Dummies,
3rd Edition
978-0-471-76845-6

Digital Photography

Digital Photography
For Dummies,
6th Edition
978-0-470-25074-7

Photoshop Elements 7
For Dummies
978-0-470-39700-8

Gardening

Gardening Basics
For Dummies
978-0-470-03749-2

Organic Gardening
For Dummies,
2nd Edition
978-0-470-43067-5

Green/Sustainable

Green Building
& Remodeling
For Dummies
978-0-470-17559-0

Green Cleaning
For Dummies
978-0-470-39106-8

Green IT For Dummies
978-0-470-38688-0

Health

Diabetes For Dummies,
3rd Edition
978-0-470-27086-8

Food Allergies
For Dummies
978-0-470-09584-3

Living Gluten-Free
For Dummies
978-0-471-77383-2

Hobbies/General

Chess For Dummies,
2nd Edition
978-0-7645-8404-6

Drawing For Dummies
978-0-7645-5476-6

Knitting For Dummies,
2nd Edition
978-0-470-28747-7

Organizing For Dummies
978-0-7645-5300-4

SuDoku For Dummies
978-0-470-01892-7

Home Improvement

Energy Efficient Homes
For Dummies
978-0-470-37602-7

Home Theater
For Dummies,
3rd Edition
978-0-470-41189-6

Living the Country Lifestyle
All-in-One For Dummies
978-0-470-43061-3

Solar Power Your Home
For Dummies
978-0-470-17569-9

Internet

Blogging For Dummies,
2nd Edition
978-0-470-23017-6

eBay For Dummies,
6th Edition
978-0-470-49741-8

Facebook For Dummies
978-0-470-26273-3

Google Blogger
For Dummies
978-0-470-40742-4

Web Marketing
For Dummies,
2nd Edition
978-0-470-37181-7

WordPress For Dummies,
2nd Edition
978-0-470-40296-2

Language & Foreign Language

French For Dummies
978-0-7645-5193-2

Italian Phrases
For Dummies
978-0-7645-7203-6

Spanish For Dummies
978-0-7645-5194-9

Spanish For Dummies,
Audio Set
978-0-470-09585-0

Macintosh

Mac OS X Snow Leopard
For Dummies
978-0-470-43543-4

Math & Science

Algebra I For Dummies,
2nd Edition
978-0-470-55964-2

Biology For Dummies
978-0-7645-5326-4

Calculus For Dummies
978-0-7645-2498-1

Chemistry For Dummies
978-0-7645-5430-8

Microsoft Office

Excel 2007 For Dummies
978-0-470-03737-9

Office 2007 All-in-One
Desk Reference
For Dummies
978-0-471-78279-7

Music

Guitar For Dummies,
2nd Edition
978-0-7645-9904-0

iPod & iTunes
For Dummies,
6th Edition
978-0-470-39062-7

Piano Exercises
For Dummies
978-0-470-38765-8

Parenting & Education

Parenting For Dummies,
2nd Edition
978-0-7645-5418-6

Type 1 Diabetes
For Dummies
978-0-470-17811-9

Pets

Cats For Dummies,
2nd Edition
978-0-7645-5275-5

Dog Training For Dummies,
2nd Edition
978-0-7645-8418-3

Puppies For Dummies,
2nd Edition
978-0-470-03717-1

Religion & Inspiration

The Bible For Dummies
978-0-7645-5296-0

Catholicism For Dummies
978-0-7645-5391-2

Women in the Bible
For Dummies
978-0-7645-8475-6

Self-Help & Relationship

Anger Management
For Dummies
978-0-470-03715-7

Overcoming Anxiety
For Dummies
978-0-7645-5447-6

Sports

Baseball For Dummies,
3rd Edition
978-0-7645-7537-2

Basketball For Dummies,
2nd Edition
978-0-7645-5248-9

Golf For Dummies,
3rd Edition
978-0-471-76871-5

Web Development

Web Design All-in-One
For Dummies
978-0-470-41796-6

Windows Vista

Windows Vista
For Dummies
978-0-471-75421-3